INTERNATIONAL HARVESTER
TRACTORS

Randy Leffingwell

8-16

MBI Publishing Company

DEDICATION

I owe tremendous gratitude to the authors and historians who wrote about International Harvester before me. My task was made easier because of research and thought invested in IHC by Charles H. Wendel, Robert Pripps, Lee Klancher, Guy Fay, Ken Updike, Ralph Baumheckel, and Kent Borghoff, and also by Tom Stonehouse and Eldon Brumbaugh. Beyond these popularly published authors there are LeRoy Baumgardner, Dave Boomgarden, Lorry Dunning, and Doug Strawser, to name a few, who have sifted through documents and have come to understand this interesting story. To you historians, I dedicate this next effort at recording and reporting the history of the tractors and the company we admire so much.

First published in 1999 by MBI Publishing Company, 729 Prospect Avenue, PO Box 1, Osceola, WI 54020-0001 USA

© Randy Leffingwell, 1999

The information in this book is true and complete to the best of our knowledge. All recommendations are made without any guarantee on the part of the author or Publisher, who also disclaim any liability incurred in connection with the use of this data or specific details.

We recognize that some words, model names and designations, for example, mentioned herein are the property of the trademark holder. We use them for identification purposes only. This is not an official publication.

MBI Publishing Company books are also available at discounts in bulk quantity for industrial or sales-promotional use. For details write to Special Sales Manager at Motorbooks International Wholesalers & Distributors, 729 Prospect Avenue, PO Box 1, Osceola, WI 54020-0001 USA.

Library of Congress Cataloging-in-Publication Data Available
ISBN 0-7603-0423-8

On the front cover: The Farmall Letter Series represents International Harvester at it's very best. The features were industry standard, the look was timeless, and the reliability was legendary. This flawless restoration of a 1948 Farmall HV represents the high-crop version of one of the most popular single models of farm tractors ever built.

On the front flap: By the time this 1920 Titan 10-20 was sold, it was old technology that IH was using to wage war against Henry Ford's price cuts on the Fordson. Even at bottom dollar, the Titan was still approximately twice the cost of the Fordson.

On the frontispiece: This 1961 International 460 is outfitted for orchard use. Low-slung and outfitted with full coverage orchard fenders and a low-mounted exhaust, the 460 could slide under branches with ease.

On the title page: The follow-up to the Titan 10-20 was the International 8-16. With the look of an Indy car and more modern technology, the 8-16 should have been IH's next big thing. Manufacturing difficulties and a myriad of engine and drivetrain problems kept the 8-16 from succeeding.

On the back flap: This 1958 Farmall 450 met the demand for diesel power with an aftermarket Cummins engine. Such conversions became commercially available beginning with the Letter Series, and remained so until IH's own diesel line took over.

On the back cover: This 1936 F-12 represented the last year of F-series tractors to wear gray paint. In November of that year, IH made the switch for the staid gray to the flashier red paint scheme.

Edited by: Lee Klancher

Designed by: Bruce Leckie

Printed in Hong Kong

CONTENTS

ACKNOWLEDGMENTS

Foremost, I wish to thank Guy Fay, my friend and extraordinary researcher, for his enormous help with this book. His knowledge of the company, its history, and its products never failed to amaze and educate me. His intuition and insights are reflected throughout this book.

At the State Historical Society of Wisconsin, Madison, a number of people were extremely helpful, encouraging and generous with their time and resources, including Nicollette Bromberg, curator, Visual Materials Archive, Society headquarters, Madison, WI; and Judy Meyerdierks, curator, Stonefield Village Historic Site, Cassville, WI. I am also grateful to Lisa Hinzman, business manager, and Sheri Dolfen, photo lab technician, for their work with historical photographs.

At Navistar International Transportation Corporation, Chicago, IL, my sincere thanks goes to Greg Lennes, corporate secretary; Julia Brunni, records analyst; and Jim Clark, librarian.

Further thanks go to Larry N. Jones, museum specialist, Division of Agriculture and Natural Resources, National Museum of American History, Smithsonian Institution, Washington, D.C., for his generous cooperation and friendship.

I am grateful for the continuing support and encouragement of John Skarstad, Department of Special Collections, University of California, Davis, Library. These thanks extend to my friend, Lorry Dunning, Historical Consultant, Davis, California, who is steadily earning the title of "keeper of all knowledge."

Collector owners have played a huge role in making this book look good and read well. I offer many thanks to the following individuals who opened their barns, sheds, memories, and records to me:

John and Jane Alling, Valley Center, CA; Arden and Joan Baeseman, Edgar, WI; LeRoy and Gail Baumgardner Jr., Spring Grove, PA; Ralph and Priscilla Baumheckel, Indianapolis, IN; Dave and Anita Boomgarden, Chatsworth, IL; Vercel and Marilyn Bovee, Lowell, MI; Paul Brecheisen, Helena, OH; Loren and Eric Brunius, Sierra Rock, Placerville, CA; Jerry Clark, Ceres, CA; David and Gail Fay, Greenville, PA; Keith and Cheri Feldman, Alto, MI; Lyman Feldman, Alto, MI; Hilton Fiedler, Prescott, WI; Bob and Michelle Findling, Gladwin, Michigan; Allen and Joan Fredrickson, Lakewood, CA; Kent and Judy Freeman, Owosso, MI; David and Carol Garber, Goshen, IN; Jack, Tammy, and Kelsey Gaston, Athens, OH; Wilson and Portia Gatewood, Noblesville, IN; Jay Graber, Parker, SD; David and Linda Grandy, Waconia, MN; William Grohoski, the Shop Mule Registry, New Hampton, NY; Edith Heidrick and the late Joseph Heidrick collection, and Joe Heidrick Jr., Woodland, CA; Joan Hollenitsch, Garden Grove, CA; Ken Holmstrom, Harris, MN; Wayne and Betty Hutton, Clarence, MO; Dean Iverson, Lake Park, MN; Vernon Iverson, Lamberton, MN; Kenny and Charlene Kass, Dunkerton, IA; Hajime Kayano, Garden Grove, CA; Wendell and Mary Kelch, Bethel, OH; Perry Kelley Jr., Harlan, IA; Don and Jane Kleven, Deerfield, WI; Bob Koski, Owosso, MI; Ira and Pat Matheny, Ceres, CA; Harold McTaggart, Port Hope, MI; Jerry and Joyce Mez, Avoca, IA; Jerry Miguel, University Farm, California State University, Chico, CA; Lee and Charlotte Miller, Clinton, PA; Bill Milligan, Somis, CA; George and Barbara Morrison, Gladwin, MI; Joe Nehl, Komatsu America International Company, Vernon Hills, IL; Scott Parsons, Oceanside, CA; Olin Pash, Harlan, IA; Loren and Elaine Peterson, Sparta, MI; Albert and Eleanor Pollock, Vail, IA; Bob and Mary Pollock, Denison, IA; Al and Eleanor Sapak, and Tom and Patty Sapak, Saginaw, MI; Fred and Janet Schenkel, Dryden, MI; Denis and Pat Schrank, Batesvlle, IN; Pete and Chris Smith, Fairfield, CA; Randy and Bonnie Sottong, Kempton, IN; Eric Stokstad, Stoughton, WI; Neal and Shirley Stone, Wisconsin Dells, WI; Joe, Jennifer and Wesley Swindel, Swindel Farm Equipment, Wilkinson, IN; Lawrence Terhune, Princeton, NJ; Martin and Marsha Thieme, Noblesville, IN; John Tysse, Crosby, ND; Ken and Char Updike, Brooklyn, WI; Denis and Linda Van De Maele, Isleton, CA; Mike and Paul Van Wormer, Frankenmuth, MI; John and Barbara Wagner, White Pigeon, MI; Robert and Doris Wasmiller, Burt, MI; Louis, Linda, and Tim Wehrman, Reese, MI; Lloyd Westerlind, Mercer, ND; and Bob, Kathy, and Randy Zarse, Reynolds, IN.

To you all, I offer my most heartfelt thanks,

—*Randy Leffingwell,*
Ojai, California

PROLOGUE

Consolidated Power, 1870–1905

John Fletcher Steward could not be objective. To him, Cyrus McCormick's family was rewriting history to bolster its name and the company's reputation. Steward worked for McCormick's biggest competitor, Deering Harvester Company, as superintendent for William Deering himself. Deering had been in business in Chicago since 1870 with partner E. H. Gammon (where Deering met Steward). Gammon & Deering marketed C. W. Marsh's grain harvester and J. Appleby's twine binder.

Cyrus Hall McCormick had come to Chicago in 1847, a year after his father died, to be nearer the great plains west of the Mississippi River than he had been at home in Virginia. Cyrus chose Chicago for himself, partially because of new producers there, Charles Grey and Seth Warner, but also because the city had escaped an influenza epidemic that swept throughout the Midwest. Leander, his youngest brother, joined him in 1848, resuming his role as production supervisor. Middle brother William, the family business manager, arrived in 1849. Years later, Leander, by then vice president of production, became jealous of Cyrus' fame. He claimed that their father, Robert, was the reaper's true inventor, he was its builder and Cyrus had been merely a salesman. Leander (and his son, Robert Hall McCormick, known just by his middle name) rarely came to the factory. Hall marketed a McCormick steam traction engine and a threshing machine, produced for him by an outside manufacturer, by 1875. When he and Leander did show up, they actually slowed production.

Cyrus fired Hall and Leander in April 1880, as the factory sped up for harvest season manufacture.

Cyrus hired Lewis Wilkinson, who had managed production at the Colt firearms armory in Hartford, Connecticut. Wilkinson quickly established a night shift to meet equipment orders. Cyrus McCormick Jr., graduating from Princeton University, arrived home to find his father excited by the factory for the first time in years. Cyrus Jr. watched Wilkinson introduce precise manufacturing techniques and the concept of interchangeable parts.

Deering's John Steward had listened to and read the claims and boasts of the McCormicks for years.

Ed Johnston and Bert Benjamin collaborated on this most ingenious invention, the McCormick Auto-Mower. The operator steered it by the tiller bar, and raised or lowered the cutter with the long vertical handle. The shorter handle engaged the cutter drive.

McCormick's inclusion in the Paris Exposition World's Fair did not come cheap. Deering filled the official Salon d'Agriculture with 17 showcases and 202 exhibits, so McCormick offered to construct its own building. Signs identified its French distributors as R. Wallut & Co. Ed Johnston posed on his twin-cylinder Auto-Mower.

Ed Johnston built single- and a twin-cylinder air-cooled engines and installed one of each in frame surrounding a cutter that fellow McCormick engineer Bert Benjamin had strengthened to handle the internal combustion engine. This single-cylinder engine's chain drove a kind of differential. The shaft forward powered the cutter bar, while the opposite bevel gear drove the pinion gear propelling the machine forward or back.

Deering, McCormick and others had nearly merged in 1891, but terms seemed unequal among all the companies involved. Competition resumed, intensifying into the "harvester wars" that cut prices and strained every maker. In 1897, Deering, retiring after a lifetime of business success, happily agreed to sell his company to McCormick, but they couldn't agree on the value of their holdings. Worse, Cyrus Jr. and his brother Harold couldn't convince financiers of any benefit to consolidation. The two companies, controlling nearly two-thirds of the harvesting machinery production and sales in the United States, resumed their rivalry.

One year later, in 1898, Ferdinand W. Peck, American commissioner general to the Paris Exposition World's Fair of 1900, nominated Deering Harvester Company alone among all American makers "as the proper one to make the retrospective and historical exhibition" of harvesting machinery. Deering asked Steward, his patent expert, to prepare the exhibit. Steward's display consisted of 17 showcases containing 96 working scale models of mowers, reapers and automatic binders. Viewers made each machine operate by tugging a cord threaded through the showcase. Steward included 106 photographs, portraits of inventors, illustrations of harvesting scenes, paintings of earlier techniques and drawings of tools. The 202 elaborate, detailed exhibits included 10 models attributed to Cyrus McCormick as inventor.

Steward's contribution to the World's Fair didn't end there. George H. Ellis, a Deering Harvester engineer, had produced an Automobile Mower in 1894. Deering hired the 23-year-old Canadian in 1889, because Ellis' experience in manufacturing twine was something Deering needed for his twine-making operations. In the spring of 1891, Ellis began experiments with gasoline engines at his home near Chicago's Lincoln Park, where he completed a small six-horsepower vertical two-cylinder engine. After watching it run for a solid hour, Deering was impressed. However he needed to keep it secret—from his sons, Charles and James, who doubted the value of internal combustion, and espe-

cially from McCormick, who knew anything Deering did had value. He moved it from Ellis' basement to John Steward's in Ravenswood, Illinois, now part of Chicago. They mounted it onto a Deering New Ideal mower, and demonstrated it for Deering and B. A. Kennedy, Deering's plant superintendent, in October 1891.

"The demonstration was modestly successful," Ellis recalled in a letter nearly 40 years later, "but it was plainly evident that there was not sufficient power." He began at once to develop a 16-horsepower two-cylinder opposed-twin engine. As work progressed on the new twin, he and Steward put his first engine on a chain-drive, planetary transmission-equipped "horseless carriage" that Ellis also built in Steward's basement. It first ran February 28, 1892. He gave Deering his first ride in mid-March. A day later Deering's daughter, Abbie, insisted on her first run as well.

Over the next several months, Ellis completed the opposed-twin. He and Steward's assistant, a Mr. Pitkin, mounted it on a horse-drawn corn binder in place of the ground-power bull-wheel. When they tested it in December 1892, it frightened the draft horses, which ran away with it. Ellis continued working, and in 1894, he placed the same engine on a mower. He ran that extensively before Deering produced a few of these "Auto-Mowers," which they tested widely and publicly. From 1894 through 1896, the opposed-twin engine operated a shredder; then Ellis mounted it on a wagon frame to use as a portable power source. Deering then let Ellis create a stronger single-cylinder engine for heavier farm uses. Ellis placed both intake and exhaust valves in the cylinder head to improve combustion.

Organizers of the 1900 Paris Exposition invited Deering, Steward, and Ellis to bring the Auto-Mower to show new technology with Deering's historical displays. McCormick, sensing a promotional opportunity not to be missed, set his staff to work creating a two-showcase exhibition with five scale models. Their own newly built Auto-Mower appeared with 12 production harvesters, binders, pickers and cutters in their own building.

"Not to be outdone," Steward wrote, "the McCormick Company, inspired by the fact that the Deering Company [had sent] an Auto-Mower, 'got a move on,' to quote a street phrase, and between February and June one was received at Paris. It failed

to operate before the Jury of Awards; however another arrived and tested in mowing with the Deering machine in August . . . It was a quick move, late to begin, however."

Cyrus H. McCormick Jr. had his version of the story. From his point of view, it was essential to be among the 1,600 exhibitors from around the world in all fields of manufacture. His company's recitation of harvesting history

Johnston's first version, the single-cylinder model, was not strong enough, and it failed in its first tests in Paris. In August, his two-cylinder model, with two-speed forward, one-speed reverse transmission and completely independent power take-off drive to the cutter, won a competition against the Deering.

The first patented collaboration between John Steward and his young protégé, George Ellis, was this "Moto-Cycle," powered by a small, parallel, two-cylinder horizontal engine. This was one of the first applications of Ellis' six-horsepower engine, which he designed as a vertical power plant. He and Steward laid it flat to power this early utility vehicle.

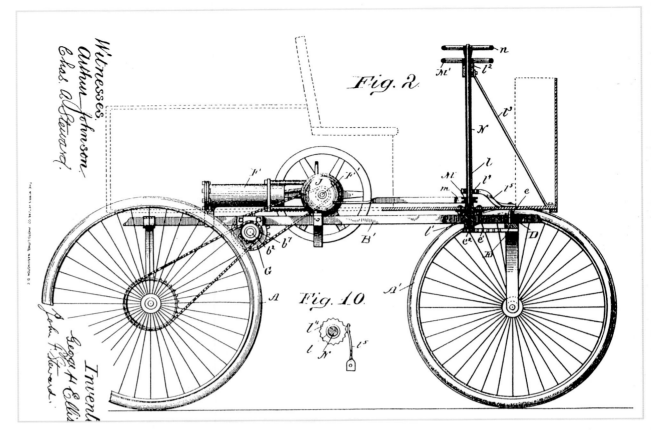

placed it no less than equal to Deering (and sometimes far beyond) in significance. To have Deering at a World's Fair without McCormick was unacceptable.

Quickly, Cyrus set Edward A. Johnston to work. Another youngster raised in his parents' implement business, Johnston had joined McCormick's Experimental Department in 1893 at age 15. (That was a good year for finding talent; McCormick also hired a 23-year-old, farm-bred Iowa State College engineering graduate named Bert Benjamin to work with implement design.) Johnston made his first air-cooled gas engine in 1897. He installed his second one with a two-speed forward, one-speed reverse transmission in a carriage in 1898. McCormick, just as Deering's company did, produced a full line of harvesting machinery and Johnston mounted one of his two-cylinder engines on a Bert Benjamin-strengthened cutter that McCormick also named the Auto-Mower.

Both Johnston's machine and Ellis/Steward's version were innovative. Each solved the problem of using one power source to propel the mower as well as power the cutters. The Ellis/Steward patent, granted in 1903, addressed the technology of transmitting engine power through gears and shafts to the functional portions of the implement. This was power taken off the engine and put to work on the tool, an early form of power-take-off, or PTO. Their system was not independent of the transmission, however. It could not be disconnected. Under heavy mowing conditions, the load on the cutter bogged the engine. Worse, the transmission had no reverse gear; the engine was designed to run forward or backward. To get the mower out of tall grass required stopping the engine and restarting it rotating the other way. The cutter blade depended on the engine and running gear for its power. During the test, its blade jammed with a heavy growth of alfalfa. The operator could not restart the engine.

Johnston's PTO worked from his two-speed transmission and could be disengaged from forward or reverse motion. In tall or heavy grass, its operator stopped the drive wheels while the tough cutter bar

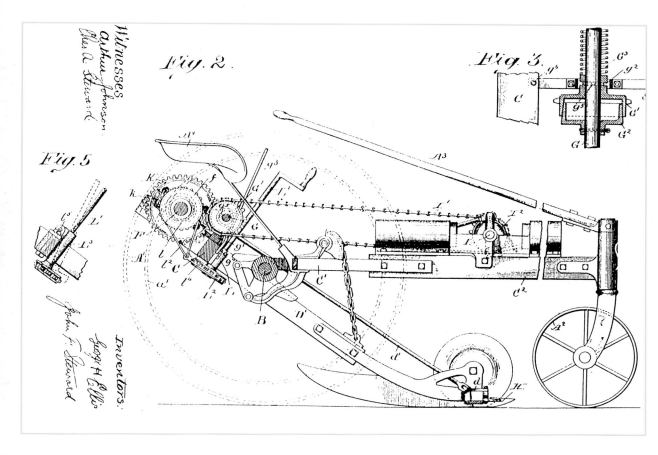

Fig. 2.

Fig. 3.

Fig. 5.

Witnesses
Arthur Johnson
Chas. A. Steward

Inventors.
George H. Ellis
John F. Steward

In 1897, Ellis and Steward devised their first motorized harvester. Ellis revised his engine layout for this machine, creating a two-cylinder flat-opposed version. An extremely simple machine, the reciprocating shaft, a1, operates the cutter bar. Viewed from the top, it is easy to see how the cutter bar might have been replaced with cultivating blades. This predates Ed Johnston's Motor Cultivator by nearly 20 years.

chopped through the thicker crop. The McCormick Auto-Mower out-performed all competition. Johnston applied for a patent for the machine in 1902 to protect both the reverse gear transmission and his "independent," or "live," PTO. It was granted in 1904. Johnston made a second Auto-Mower for the 1903 St. Louis Exposition, using a single-cylinder engine.

Neither Deering nor McCormick put an Auto-Mower into production. Even in 1902 or 1903, it may have been, as Steward surmised earlier, that the time was not yet ripe for them. On top of that, the money that might be used to further develop Auto-Mowers was targeted instead for manufacture of stationary engines and other products. McCormick, despite his competitiveness, admired Deering's corporation and its organization. While McCormick and his staff were skilled at sales, they held huge accounts receivable. Deering's people were efficient at collection, and they controlled all the elements of manufacture. Only Deering Harvester matched McCormick in industrial investment, and it stood alone in owning steel mills.

McCormick needed its own ore fields, steel mills, coal mines and forests as Deering had. Cyrus Jr. and Deering's sons tried again in late 1901 to get together, after William retired. They accepted that each company had what the other needed, but again, mutual distrust kept them apart.

Then in February 1902, Judge Elbert H. Gary telephoned McCormick. Judge Gary, the chairman of United States Steel, sold his products to McCormick. According to John Garraty in his book, Right Hand Man: The Life of George W. Perkins, Gary knew Deering's mills and foundries cut their costs so Deering could compete against McCormick. The judge feared that Cyrus Jr. wanted the same economies. Gary not only wanted to retain McCormick's business, he also meant to limit steel-making capacity in America. Gary suggested that consolidating operations with Deering might be a less expensive way to cut costs.

Cyrus Jr. accepted this. He needed steel-making facilities. Depending on who's telling it, there are various authors of the 1902 merger; like any great invention, this one had many fathers. One

Five years brought much greater complexity to the machinery of grain cutting. Ellis and Steward's Automobile Mowing Machine, the Deering Auto Mower, was a busy, whirring collection of bevel gears. Ellis' engine would run forward or backward, eliminating need for a reverse gear. The main advantage this machine offered over his 1897 version was that this kept all the wheels out of uncut crops.

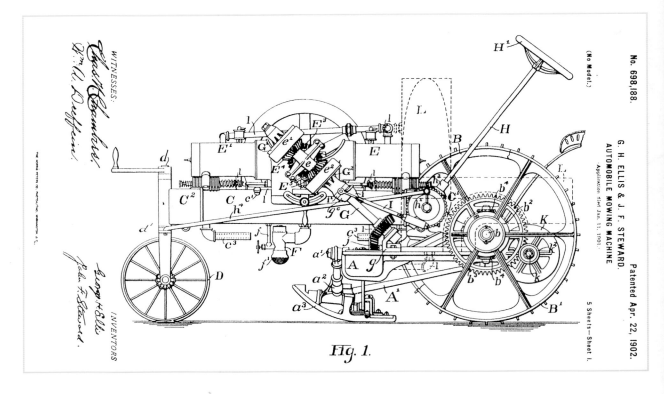

version suggests that Cyrus Jr. asked John D. Rockefeller to buy out Deering. Cyrus' brother Harold had married John D.'s daughter, Edith, in 1895. Rockefeller offered to loan them the money instead, recognizing that owning Deering neither increased McCormick's market share nor gave them enough foundry and milling capacity. Cyrus knew the only way to get the Deerings' cooperation was through outside intervention. John D. suggested going to J. P. Morgan's lawyer, Francis Lynde Stetson, and in June 1902, he contacted George W. Perkins, a partner at Morgan and Company, to arrange a meeting. Perkins and the House of Morgan had a client with vested interests, U.S. Steel's Elbert Gary, whose merger Perkins not only had directed but Morgan also had partially financed. Cyrus and his brother Stanley invited Perkins in to engineer a merger, recognizing that they and Deering each would want to control the resulting company. For the next three months Perkins orchestrated Gary's grand scheme (and in the process, protected Morgan's investment in U.S. Steel). Perkins con-

vinced the two harvester manufacturers that through consolidation there was self-preservation. He avoided the matter of control by simply postponing it, creating a voting trust where he was the tie-breaker.

On August 12, 1902, McCormick, Deering and three other significant harvesting equipment makers came together, consolidated in business under the name International Harvester Company, IHC. Together with Warder, Bushnell & Glessner Company, makers of Champion harvesting machines from Springfield, Ohio, the Milwaukee Harvester Company of Milwaukee, Wisconsin, and the Plano Manufacturing Company in West Pullman, Illinois, Deering and McCormick now controlled nearly 90 percent of grain binder production and about 80 percent of the mowers in the United States. (For their facilities and cash investment, the McCormicks received 42.6 percent and the Deerings 34.4 percent of the IHC stock.) McCormick's growing sales force throughout Europe and beyond prompted J. P. Morgan to add the word "Interna-

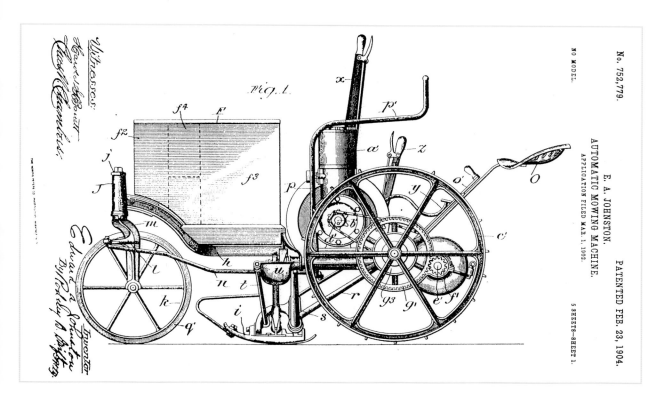

Where the Ellis/Stewart Auto Mower was a marvel of complexity, Ed Johnston's Auto-Mower was much simpler, while providing the additional benefit of independent, or "live" power take-off. Its weakest link was its steering and the strength of the gooseneck casting supporting the front wheel. The large fuel tank and its contents placed about 100 pounds on the wheel, adding to the mower's approximately 500-pound weight.

tional" to the group's new name, a way, he hoped, of suggesting the conglomerate's goal was not a domestic monopoly but worldwide opportunity. IHC named Cyrus McCormick Jr. its president and appointed Charles Deering, William's son, as chairman of its ruling organization, which held the company stock in trust for 10 years. The U.S. Bureau of Corporations set value of International Harvester Corporation at $100 million. Morgan and Perkins capitalized the new company higher, at $120 million, based on $60 million in assets of the five companies, $50 million in accounts receivable and an additional $10 million in new IHC stock sold to Morgan in exchange for operating cash. Perkins took a $3 million fee and effectively ran the organization, keeping the former rivals at peace.

In the last years of his life, Cyrus Hall McCormick often was accused, mostly by his brother Leander, of stealing the title of inventor of the reaper. If not the machine itself, Cyrus did invent the means of selling it and of protecting its technology. He probably created the sales

techniques of free trials, time payments and satisfaction-or-money-back guarantees. His son championed some of these accomplishments during and after the Paris Exposition in 1900. For the show Cyrus Jr. commissioned his own catalog as well as dozens of magazine and newspaper stories that appeared to ignore the entire Deering exhibit in the main agriculture hall while overstating the significance of his company's two display cases in a separate building that McCormick constructed for the Exposition.

Perhaps Cyrus Jr. didn't yet understand the significance of Johnston's machine. It certainly was worth little compared to the control of IHC. McCormick (and IHC) insisted their engineers and inventors assign patent rights to the company, one reason Johnston left in 1902. Curious then, that while Cyrus McCormick Jr., had legitimate claim to his employee's idea, he didn't boast about the independent power-take-off—an invention whose impact has lasted longer than International Harvester Corporation itself.

1902–1913

One

COMPLICATION, CONFUSION AND DUPLICATION

*C*harles Deering, Cyrus McCormick Jr., and George Perkins had plenty on their minds following the creation of IHC. In its first year, the company acquired D. M. Osborne & Co., Minneapolis Harvester Co., and the factories of Aultman Miller Co. Charles Deering proposed buying every harvester maker in North America, putting the entire industry under IHC control. Perkins and McCormick resisted; such efforts raised federal government scrutiny, and some makers weren't worth having. Still, IHC picked up other competitors, adding Keystone Company, makers of grain and hay harvesters, in 1904.

1908 15-horsepower Friction Drive
By the time this 1908 model appeared, Ohio Manufacturing had produced "gas traction engines" for IHC for almost two years, in 10-, 12-, and 15-horsepower models with a 20-horsepower model coming later in the year.

During the late 1890s, William Deering had pulled together industries necessary to manufacture everything he could conceive. By owning companies that provided each element or component used to make his own products, Deering efficiently created large quantities of machinery, which benefited farmers and was pivotal to farming in North America. When Deering merged its resources into IHC, the conglomerate relocated some of this top-to-bottom capability among various plants, to centralize manufacturing nearer to major distribution and shipping facilities.

The variety of its holdings made more harvesters available; every farmer who needed one could get one. Farmers could reap everything they could sow. With harvesters in every barn, farmers began wondering about new machines to work the soil, to open untouched lands. But a binder on every farm meant that demand slowed, so IHC cut production to accommodate diminished sales. (IHC also reined in sales, insisting

This photo appears in sales catalogs without the word "International" on the radiator. This 1908 15-horsepower Friction Drive, No. 1230, was shipped to W. J. Roberts at Marine City, Michigan. The engine number, CB120, indicates this was the 20th 15-horsepower tractor engine produced. *State Historical Society of Wisconsin*

sales representatives make sure a customer could pay for the machine before they accepted the order.) This freed shop space to develop and manufacture new implements and machines.

William Deering wanted George Ellis to continue his gas engine projects. In 1898, Ellis bolted his eight-horsepower single-cylinder horizontal engines onto a sliding framework mounted on a chassis he fabricated at Deering Works. Moving the engine forward or backward made contact with friction wheels with chains to drive the rear axle. "The tractor was quite heavy," Ellis explained, "but it was used for plowing, harrowing, and hauling throughout the summer of 1898. It failed because the friction wheels wore out too fast, and they tended to slip in wet weather," hinting at machines and problems to come. After 1902, Ellis continued to work for William, although he did so secretly. Deering pushed him hard, and Ellis devised a cotton picker with T. H. Price, who had patented one earlier.

One stated goal of the IHC consolidation was unification. Yet developments still were guarded jealously. No one shared secrets. Sales created competition that developed similar products from former Deering staff and those who worked for McCormick. Perkins attempted to enforce order by

naming Clarence S. Funk as IHC general manager. Funk had managed the Champion firm and carried no loyalty to either McCormick or Deering. Funk's independence, however, couldn't discourage the them-against-us mentality between divisions.

Cyrus McCormick Jr. approved acquisition of a Morton Traction Truck in early 1905, setting a 15-horsepower Famous one-cylinder stationary engine on a framework that moved forward or back on casters, like George Ellis' invention. Samuel S. Morton of York, Pennsylvania, had received patents on August 5, 1902, and April 21, 1903, for his vehicle, which first ran in May 1899. Buyers provided engines to propel the vehicle. The engine-driven friction pulley made contact with the other friction pulley geared to rear drive wheels (while Ellis' drove by chains). Morton's friction pulley wheels functioned as a clutch. Several engine manufacturers experimented with him. In 1903, Ohio Manufacturing Company acquired his patents and Morton himself, and set up a factory in Upper Sandusky, Ohio, to build his vehicles.

It took work to revise IHC's stationaries to propel Morton's traction-trucks. Three changes were necessary: the full-height base had to be lowered; they extended the crankshaft to fit the fiber pulley that did the driving; and they also went to smaller-diameter flywheels. Moses W. Kouns, as part owner-engineer at Ohio's plant, was critical to that process. After it tested the first one, IHC contracted with Ohio to produce 14 in 1906.

Sometime in 1905, IHC's Executive Council created a product planning and review group informally called the New Work Committee; on April 20, 1906, that name became official. Maurice Kane, a McCormick employee and office general manager of IHC's new Experimental Department, was a member. Ohio's Moses Kouns asked IHC to go to smaller friction drive wheels for the 15-horsepower Famous engines. "This change," Kane reported to the busy committee's 23rd meeting on November 5, 1906, reduced "the speed of the tractor traveling on the road. The tractor would stand this speed, but a threshing machine towed behind it would not long stand pulling at the present speed over rough roads."

IHC shifted Milwaukee Harvester Company's binder and harvester manufacture down to Chicago and relocated gas engine production from the Deering and McCormick Works in Chicago to the now-vacant Milwaukee plant. It established separate Engineering and Experimental Departments there and named Harold A. Waterman plant superintendent. IHC's first 14 buyers loved Morton's Traction Trucks, so it increased its order to 100 for 1907. The Manufacturing Department bought another 100, "knocked down," or unassembled, for manufacture in Milwaukee. IHC sold 153 that year.

Acquiring Keystone Co. in 1904 brought to IHC not only its Rock Falls, Illinois, plant but it also returned Ed Johnston to International Harvester. He resumed gas engine development in 1905 at Keystone Works. McCormick believed Johnston's Auto Buggy could meet farmers' hauling needs. Johnston revised it to run 20 miles per hour, carry a ton of cargo and climb a 25 percent grade. Then he began work on a tricycle-configuration gas traction engine. A year later, in November 1906, because "Mr. Johnston had all his time taken up with the Auto Buggy . . ., it is now sitting at Keystone Works practically complete" but without an engine. McCormick Experimental Department engineer William Cavanaugh suggested shipping it to Harry Waterman's staff in Milwaukee for completion. It never ran, nor was it the last time a Johnston project languished.

When IHC began to manufacture Auto Buggies in February 1907, the Executive Council moved Johnston and his experimental projects to larger space at McCormick Works in Chicago. The sales department sold out his first run of 100 buggies as he completed his second attempt at a traction engine from scratch. Then in October 1907, IHC interrupted Johnston's work again, moving him to Akron Works. There he mated his new three-cylinder 40-horsepower- gas engine to an improved version of his two-speed-forward, one-speed reverse transmission, which he had used on the Auto-Mower. He installed this into his three-wheel frame.

Expecting to repeat its Paris success in 1900, IHC entered Johnston's tricycle (and two other Morton-type friction-drive four-wheelers) in the Winnipeg Industrial Exhibition's First Agricultural Motor Contest in Manitoba, Canada, July 11–17, 1908. (The word "tractor" had begun replacing the more cumbersome "traction engine" by now). Of seven gas tractors entered by five producers (five steam traction engine makers competed as well under "Light Tractor" rules for those weighing less

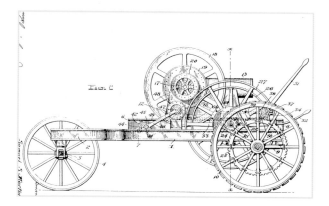

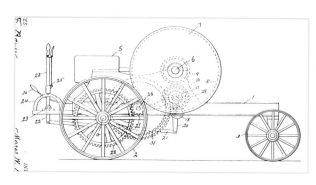

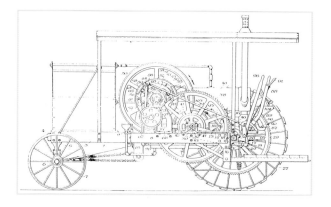

than seven tons), Johnston finished second, less than one point behind a Kinnard-Haines "Flour City" 30-horsepower four-cylinder tractor. Solid performance in Winnipeg generated sales north and south of the border in areas that most needed power farming. These results influenced planning for machines from every manufacturer.

Johnston was equally successful when his Auto Wagon came out. Akron Works manufactured these until 1912, when the company renamed the vehicle the Motor Truck and it went into its next full lifetime. Johnston, 32 years old in 1908, designed the engines that powered IHC into long-term truck success.

Samuel Morton filed his patent application on May 19, 1902, for his traction engine. The entire engine assembly, shown here as an unspecified single cylinder, rode on a movable platform. Moving the lever, 51, at the center rear of the tractor, brought the engine and its flywheels, 18, and friction drive wheel, 20, into contact with the traction pulley wheel, 27, which in turn drove the pinion gear, 24, inside the drive wheels, 10.

Moses Kouns improved upon the Morton Traction Truck design by making the rear axle of his version a solid, or continuous, rotating shaft, unlike Morton, who used stub axles. This increased frame strength and rigidity. He also showed, in this drawing, a gear drive system, 29, from the engine crankshaft, and 31, to the pinion gear. His enormous flywheels, 7, never saw production.

Ed Johnston and Charles Longenecker collaborated on the Type C Gear Drive tractors, starting in 1908. Johnston, overwhelmed with other work, sent the project to Longenecker at Milwaukee Works, who designed a new engine and completed the frame and gear drive, creating in the process a machine much simpler than Morton's and the first that IHC could really call its own.

1908 20-horsepower Friction Drive

The IHC big friction drives ran off their large single-cylinder Famous stationary engine. Moses Kouns, co-owner of Ohio Manufacturing, lowered the engines four inches to improve contact between the engine crankshaft-driven fiber friction wheel and the metal 51-inch diameter drive friction wheel (with the arched spokes).

By 1908, IHC moved some production responsibilities to its Akron Works, as demand for the Traction Trucks far exceeded what Ohio Manufacturing's Upper Sandusky Works could turn out. Production also began at Milwaukee Works at about the same time.

IHC used Milwaukee Works' horizontal stationary 10-, 12- and 15-horsepower engines on the Morton/Kouns tractors. Kouns lowered the engine 4 inches "to get a better bearing of the crankshaft-driven fiber friction pulley against the metal, 51-inch-diameter friction pulley and to give increased power for driving." He fitted a very costly double-gear in the differential to slow reverse speed to one-quarter of forward. Maurice Kane asked Johnston to develop a new two-cylinder horizontal engine, replacing IHC's current 20-horsepower Famous single, for an improved tractor Kouns proposed. Kouns recommended Johnston simply double the existing single, "believing it would develop 45-horsepower. This engine would handle four or five plows nicely, enough to satisfy purchasers."

What was not satisfying was continued friction drive-train slippage under heavy load. Morton's first customers learned quickly the machines didn't work for plowing. Kouns explained from the start that "When we went over 15 horsepower on a friction drive tractor for plowing, we had gone wrong." He remedied this in 1907 with the Type A gear-drive model in 12- and 15-horsepower versions, incorporating Kouns' and the New Work Committee's improvements. He urged production only of 12-horsepower models until it was thoroughly proven.

Type A tractors ran cast-iron gear transmissions, although some were sold with what may have been experimental—and expensive—steel gears. It carried over Morton's stub axle arrangement on 56-inch-diameter rear drive wheels. IHC shipped the first Type A, Number 1310, a 15-horsepower model with a 1907-built engine number CB158, to the IHC branch house in Aurora, Illinois, in early fall.

Throughout the rest of 1907, IHC marketed these tractors. Morton's 10-, 12- and 15-horsepower friction drive models became popular. Orders for 1908 exceeded Ohio's capacity, and IHC began assembling Morton and Kouns tractors in Johnston's Akron Works and Waterman's Milwaukee Works as well.

Ohio Manufacturing's methods were imprecise despite its investment in cast gears. Ohio matched gears only to individual tractors, not for the series. They had no standard pitch or diameter. Akron and Milwaukee built to IHC precision. Akron tried cutting gears to the nearest standard dimensions. C. N. Hostetter, a project engineer, recalled, "When the first new gears came through, some couldn't be driven into place at all, while others had teeth that refused to touch their mates." John Steward, Ed Johnston and his assistant, H. B. Morrow, designed a new gear train in Akron. At Milwaukee, H. A. Blacken completely dismantled the tractor to develop specifications. Thereafter, all IHC tractors were made from drawings instead of being assembled from samples (take a sample, copy it and build the next.) Johnston reinforced Morton frames, enlarged and strengthened bull gears, and improved cooling and brake systems.

This made the gear-driven Type A tractors strong enough and rigid enough to pull wagons or operate threshers off their belt pulleys, but they still couldn't plow as well as IHC wanted. Kouns tested a 20-horsepower gear-

drive with only moderate success pulling three 12-inch plows. IHC produced it anyway. Steward knew this was only a sales department solution, and he sent E. W. Burgess, an IHC patent attorney, to examine a Harpstrite tractor produced near Decatur, Illinois. Andrew Harpstrite mounted his moldboard plows directly beneath the center of his three-wheel tractor, which featured a large drum-drive rear wheel. Henry B. Utley, IHC's purchasing manager on the New Work Committee, suggested

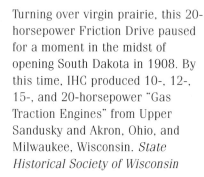

Turning over virgin prairie, this 20-horsepower Friction Drive paused for a moment in the midst of opening South Dakota in 1908. By this time, IHC produced 10-, 12-, 15-, and 20-horsepower "Gas Traction Engines" from Upper Sandusky and Akron, Ohio, and Milwaukee, Wisconsin. *State Historical Society of Wisconsin*

While Chicago Tractor Works was just a tent, Milwaukee, as the former Milwaukee Harvester Company's plants, were well established. Outside the Works in this 1910 photo were about 40 Type C Mogul tractors and one Type D Titan (at far left with its back tool box and partial right side rear fender visible). The two tractors without stacks through the roof were either Type A or B models. *Navistar*

1910 Titan Type D 45 Horsepower

Harry Waterman's triumph, the 1910 big Titan, sits next to one of his few failures, the 18–35, at left. Between 1910 and 1915, Milwaukee Works produced 1,319 of these powerful tractors, designed by P. W. Hawthorne and E. D. Eliassen.

Steward gather patents on every tractor and plow so IHC owned the technology to experiment or produce without infringement concerns, paralleling Deering's earlier idea. Steward judged many competitors "not worth having."

IHC considered mass producing some tractor parts as early as June 1907, but ruled it out when IHC Manufacturing Division Manager B. A. Kennedy learned that "to make this profitable it is necessary to have between 3,000 and 4,000 of certain parts and in the neighborhood of 1,500 other parts." Kennedy guessed right: IHC sold in the neighborhood of 600 complete tractors through 1908. By June that year, however, they understood the Type A still had shortcomings. Kennedy

watched them plowing and hauling freight in California and concluded that nothing from Ohio Manufacturing was strong or durable enough. On June 9, Kennedy met with Steward, William Cavanaugh and Edward Kimbark from the McCormick Experimental Department. They agreed on improvements to the tractors, performed at Milwaukee Works without advising Kouns of changes to his design.

Morton's stub axles allowed ground clearance, but they also permitted frame flex, limiting pulling ability. Waterman would "modify the machine so a continuous rear axle can be used in place of the present stub axles. This will necessitate increasing the height of the drive wheels about 8 inches or more, increasing (by only 2 inches) the front wheels to correspond; lengthening the bed 4 or 6 inches, and providing, in the case of the Type B tractor, that the base of the engine act as a stiffener to the beams of the truck." A solid, continuous rear axle strengthened and stiffened the tractor; 64-inch diameter drive wheels rotated on the live (rotating) rear axle. Milwaukee would revise the popular friction drive Mortons. They also would examine the gear-drive Type A tractors, attacking 20-horsepower versions first.

Kouns independently had made similar changes, revising a Type A chassis. Within days of the meeting, Kimbark learned that Kouns already had replaced his stub axles with an enlarged rear continuous stationary 4-inch square axle, and substituted 70-inch rear wheels on 18-inch hubs. He relocated drive pinions more directly under the gears, strengthening the tractor by increasing its mass, a stopgap method that would reappear in the future. (Ed Johnston would implement these changes for the Type C prototypes and production models a year later.)

This new Type B tractor did improve on the Type A. Following Kane's suggestion, Kouns substituted the two stub drive shafts with one solid full-width axle. (In addition, while the Type A and B had one forward gear, both models, from 1912 on, provided two gear-driven speeds.) IHC tested the initial Type B only with the 20-horsepower engine on 64-inch wheels at the end of 1908. (The first two-speed tractor sold from Upper Sandusky Works, however, was a 12-horsepower Type A, with friction reverse, on 16x56-inch wheels, Serial Number 1813, with 12-horsepower engine OB222 [or possibly OB227]. It was shipped to the Georgia Farm Machinery Company of Albany, Georgia, via the Railroad Express Agency office at Atlanta, Georgia, December 14, 1909.)

In January 1908, while Milwaukee manufactured Morton/Kouns-designed Friction Drive tractors, Experimental Department engineers James L. Martin and Charles I. Longenecker tested Lambert engines from Anderson, Indiana, in modified Morton frames. Kouns wanted "two 12-horsepower engines . . . set side by side, and so arranged, by means of a differential clutch, that either one or both engines can be used for traction purposes." John Steward was wary. Nothing Kouns had done so far demonstrated his ability to master this challenge.

The Type D Titan's cylinder heads show two different rocker arms, the right one original, the left one a factory replacement; the originals sometimes fractured. At far left, the gear shift is in neutral, the clutch lever, down, is disengaged and the brake pedal is not set. But the heavy tractor is parked on soft, level ground.

On June 1, 1908, Harry Waterman appointed young P. R. Hawthorne to design a new tractor at Milwaukee. By fall, Hawthorne's 45-horsepower two-cylinder, dual-crankshaft, Kouns-inspired engine ran well. (This ultimately went into production as the 45-horsepower Reliance, later renamed the Titan.) Hawthorne developed a throttling governor, where previous Friction Drives and Type A and B models used hit-and-miss types. (Hawthorne's governor was not reliable. For production, Milwaukee Works fitted hit-and-miss types. At this same time, Ed Johnston worked on his own two-cylinder opposed engine, which retained the hit-and-miss governor. This went into production as the 45-horsepower gasoline Mogul, with a fan on top of the radiator. Later models replaced the governor and cooling system.) Anticipating the future, Hawthorne's big twin ran on kerosene. He used automobile-type steering for the tractor frame, and a differential on the rear axle.

The preceding year (1907), Ed Johnston developed the prototype of a single-cylinder

1911 22–45 Horsepower Mogul

Built at Chicago's Tractor Works, this was Ed Johnston's largest effort. He created an engine for it by combining two of the 25-horsepower Famous single-cylinder engines (which he used in the Mogul Junior), mounted opposed to each other. Over the seven-year life span of this giant, Tractor Works turned out 2,437 Mogul 22–45s.

20-horsepower tractor (eventually the Mogul Type C Gear Drive) at Akron, with a gear-forward transmission but reverting to a friction drive reverse. He incorporated other Milwaukee Works improvements that were made on the Type Bs. However, the automobile and truck plants constantly pulled Johnston away to solve production problems; in his report to the Executive Council in January 1908, he commented that he'd done no work on the new machine for 10 weeks and it would take another $350 to finish it. The New Work Committee found money and time in April, when it decided to enter his tractor in the July Winnipeg trials. Johnston completed two or three running prototypes in 1908 and a few production models. Then the Executive Council transferred the project to Milwaukee's greater production capacity where Charles Longenecker took it over. Though it became the Type C, in New Work Committee reports it always was referred to as the "Johnston-Longenecker-Akron." The two engineers performed so many changes on the Morton/Kouns design that their Type C was IHC's first complete tractor.

On December 12, 1908, Alex Legge assembled the New Work Committee. Johnston and Waterman commuted to these Chicago meetings. Legge assigned them both to create a two-forward speed, maximum 45-horsepower, two-cylinder tractor prototype, as well as a 25-horsepower single. He continued this strategy for years, developing an intense rivalry between the two engineers and their departments that resulted in diverse solutions to engineering problems.

W. R. Morgan, J. M. Robinson, and J. H. McLane, regional sales managers for Canada, midwestern and eastern states respectively, supported Legge's contention that farmers wanted tractors capable of plowing 10 acres a day with a five-bottom plow. "Competitors' 30-horsepower engines pulled five plows, and the extra horsepower would be capable of running the largest Bell City threshers or even our eight-roll shredders when the corn is damp and tough." R .C. Haskins, southeast sales manager, found the 25-horsepower single very appealing. He agreed that two speeds, one for work and one for the road, were necessary. But not everyone praised Alex Legge's every idea. John Steward drew first blood.

"Listen! Who is more responsible for slow progress than Mr. Legge? He listens to Kouns. It is the friction drive which has kept us from going ahead." Purchasing Manager Henry Utley concurred, having seen two tractors at the Calgary branch, "returned because of failure of the friction drive. We have not got a plowing tractor. We should profit by the experience of steam outfits and of Hart-Parr, and build a large tractor."

Utley told the committee that while gas in the Midwest was 11 or 12 cents per gallon, in Western Canada it cost 35 cents per gallon. He wondered if "at such high prices, Canadian farmers might not stick with steam, or return to it. Coal sold for $2.50 per ton."

Harry Waterman tried to wrap things up. He proposed an engine with two parallel cylinders, using a friction clutch driving through gears to rear drive wheels 6 feet in diameter. He promised a running version by May, knowing that young Hawthorne's prototype could begin testing within 60 days.

Ed Johnston (nearly 30 years younger than Waterman,) let his cynicism escape. From his experience "and from what was said in this meeting, when the sales department said they wanted a 25-horsepower traction engine, they were speaking of requirements expected of 30 to 35 horsepower; our present 20-horsepower engine, when valves are tight enough and everything in good order, will deliver to the average operator 26 horsepower, but in working conditions the engine soon comes down to 23 horsepower. It is being frequently run up to 270 or 300 rpm, which overtaxes the engine, and it will not stand it for long."

He proposed making a "tractor of not less than 35 horsepower actual, a two-cylinder opposed engine. Such a tractor would serve as a general purpose tractor. In addition, we would want at a later date a mammoth engine for plowing." (To Johnston, a general purpose tractor could haul freight, belt to a thresher or pull plows. Cultivating was still done behind horses.)

Johnston preferred an opposed two-cylinder engine to parallel configuration "because it not only balanced explosions but is mechanically balanced at the crankshaft, and consequently there is less shake and strain." He promised a running prototype by April 1, 1909, aiming to beat Waterman by a

Introduced in 1909 as the most-powerful single-cylinder IHC tractor, with an initial production run of 100 models, the Type C arrived on 70-inch diameter rear wheels, 5 or 6 inches larger than standard on the earlier Type A and B friction-drive models. The Type C, offered as both a 20- and 25-horsepower model, used gear-drive forward/friction-drive reverse running gear.

month. (The Waterman/Hawthorne parallel twin would go into production first, in 1910, as the 45-horsepower Type D. Johnston's two-cylinder opposed tractor, first produced in 1910, would become the 45-horsepower Mogul. Until late in the testing process, both of these big twins would be often—and confusingly—referred to as 35-horsepower tractors.)

Ed Johnston tested his new 25-horsepower single prototype in Modesto and in El Cajon, California, in early March 1909. It failed. The New Work Committee met March 29, to consider plans to rebuild it. The session was so important that Cyrus McCormick Jr., brother Harold F., (IHC vice-president and Rockefeller in-law), Clarence Funk and

Alex Legge attended. Both Cyrus Jr. and Legge operated farms of their own, where prototypes often tested under close scrutiny from the two powerful executives. They ordered a nose-to-tail reengineering and reinforcement of the frame, steering and running gear. "The changes involve nearly every part of the tractor," Kimbark wrote in the meeting report. This work would prepare Johnston's frame for his upcoming 25-horsepower single-cylinder and 45-horsepower twin engines. Repairs to the tractor led him to design a new gear-drive transmission, delaying his finishing the Type C and the work on his uncompleted opposed-cylinder prototype. He also revised the engines to run on kerosene, as concerns over Canadian and U.S. gasoline prices continued. Type C assembly of the earlier versions resumed at the Milwaukee Works.

On April 13, the New Work Committee met at Milwaukee to set production plans for the rest of 1909. They re-examined Kouns' Type A stub-axle tractor with 56-inch drive wheels and compared it to Waterman's revised Type B continuous live (rotating) axle with 65-inch wheels. The committee preferred the Type B. Waterman said that manufacture of 175 tractors could begin August 1, 1909, and end around October 1. The committee also authorized building 121 Kouns Type As and 100 of the repaired Johnston-Longenecker Type Cs. Ten days later, the committee replaced the 65-inch wheels on the prototype Type C (with its engine mounted on a subbase) and used 70-inch wheels because "the large size (38-inch diameter) friction clutch pulleys could not be used with that machine." (while most Type B tractors were built on 64-inch wheels, Pennsylvania historian LeRoy Baumgardner discovered that a few examples were produced with the incrementally larger diameter. Prototype tractors often take parts from a variety of models and sources as engineers experiment with new configurations.)

Baumgardner also discovered Type A tractor Serial Number 1551, a 20-horsepower with engine UB364, sold to Dunham Farm, Wayne, Illinois, was shipped on August 13, 1908. This was gear driven, with "special 70-inch drive wheels, experimental." All the tractors with numbers surrounding it, 1550 and 1552, were shipped in late July; he theorizes IHC received the order for the tractor with larger wheels, pulled a numbered frame and completed the modifications, then shipped it, out of sequence with the others, after it was completed.

Tractor 1582, another 20-horsepower Type A, was shipped without an engine, to the IHC Akron Works, August 31; this too was a gear-driven "special truck, 70-inch wheels, experimental." These are the only two tractors listed on these particular production record pages fitted with gear drive transmissions; all the rest are friction drive models. This suggests that following a customer order, Ed Johnston at Akron's Advance Engineering decided to experiment with 70-inch wheels as he developed his prototype Type C.

Johnston's tractor failure led Legge in May to request additional Hawthorne-style machines, this time in smaller 20- and 25-horsepower versions.

Testing the big parallel twin revealed advantages to Hawthorne's continuous-but-revolving rear axle system, the "Milwaukee axle." (This placed the differential on the rear axle.) However, the other Milwaukee-produced and all Chicago tractors retained the counter-shaft-placed differentials, including Johnston's new Type C. Longenecker and Steward developed competing solutions (at Legge's instigation) to complaints about pulley belt interference with front wheels, further confusing the lexicon. The redesigned frames resulted in either a step-up front frame with the pulley mounted ahead of the engine (called the "long low sills" type, on which the frame rails over the rear wheels were lower and longer than those over the fronts; this also was the Johnston-Longenecker-Akron or the Milwaukee tractor), or a step down version with the pulley mounted off the crankshaft (the Steward-Johnston-Akron configuration, Johnston tractor, with "low short sills"). Waterman enjoyed the setbacks befalling his opinionated younger rival. He offered his vast Milwaukee resources for all tractor prototype building as well as regular production, saying he meant only to lessen Johnston's responsibilities so he might finally finish his opposed-twin.

Canadian organizers scheduled the 1909 Winnipeg Trials for early July. On May 24, Legge

1912 Type B Two-Speed Gear Drive
An uncommon machine produced only at the Upper Sandusky Works that formerly belonged to Ohio Manufacturing, this two-speed gear drive was produced over a long span, from 1910 through 1918. During that period, however, only 383 were assembled.

1913 M-A Auto-Wagon

One of Ed Johnston's greater successes was the Auto Wagon, IHC's first truck. IHC introduced the first ones, manufactured at Akron Works, in late 1907, though the Model M did not appear until 1909. IHC changed the name after 1912, calling these the International Motor Trucks, creating a separate division that continues independently today as Navistar.

approved entering eight tractors. Hawthorne and Waterman had six weeks to prepare and build the two latest barely-finished, Johnston-designed revolving axle machines. Waterman transferred his production foreman, L. B. Sperry, to the Experimental Department as night boss when workers went on two-and even three-shift schedules when assembly started May 22. In 40 days, crews completed two tractors. They tested them for one single day and shipped them to Winnipeg, painting them on the moving railroad cars. The larger Milwaukee twin arrived with the name "Reliance" painted on it and the Johnston opposed-twin appeared with an enormous induction-cooling radiator as the Famous 35-horsepower, forerunner of the 45-horsepower Mogul. Each was equipped with gear drive, two-speed-forward transmissions.

Entered in a new class without weight limits, they both bogged down under their own bulk. The step-up front frame ("low long sills"-type) 25-horsepower Longenecker Milwaukee, designated the Type D, won its class.

From August to November, Hawthorne replaced his new throttle governor with the older hit-and-miss system and removed a pressurized fuel/air intake, improving his prototypes' reliability. At a meeting in mid-September, Alex Legge organized a field trip to LaPorte, Indiana, to see Rumely OilPulls work. Steward, Johnston, Longenecker and Waterman joined him; their only favorable comment was that Rumely used fuels other makes had not demonstrated before. None of them favored either buying Rumely outright—a proposal Legge put out—or distributing their tractors in any

IHC market. They agreed that kerosene fuel deserved more study. So, it would turn out, did the matter of distribution.

On September 22, John Steward reported to Legge that the names Victor, Famous, Rival and Keystone were not yet registered by any other maker for tractors; he suggested the Famous line remain as it was, while renaming the Reliance line the Victor. At the last meeting of 1909, Steward advised against any further development on the Type C 25-horsepower "Longenecker-Johnston, as it is a form that cannot persist," meaning its friction reverse. "The Waterman [the Milwaukee Axle, axle-mounted differential] is more nearly in the line of ultimate progress." Waterman himself updated the committee on weight-reductions to his big Reliance, eliminating second gear from the transmission and removing the tank and pump for its air starting system. Finally, Deering Division manager A. E. Mayer warned Legge that "demand for a tractor larger than 20 horsepower was such that the regular output . . . must be disposed of before the trade knows we have a larger tractor." Otherwise, IHC never would sell its 12-, 15- and 20-horsepower models.

Lightened 20-, 25- and 45-horsepower Reliances spent all winter in Texas and Oklahoma. After those prototypes completed southern tests, the New Work Committee authorized production on May 25, 1910, officially giving them Reliance names on May 28. At the same time, the committee designated the Johnston-type tractors as the Famous Type C 20-, 25- and 45-horsepower models. On July 9, Clarence Funk reopened the name question, asking Ed Kimbark to check tractor brand name clearances for Ajax, Hercules, Titan, and Mogul. In August, domestic and foreign sales managers, meeting with production and manufacturing leaders, suggested renaming Famous tractors after McCormick and using Deering for the Reliances; exports should be "International" for Europe and "Champion" for South America. Then, on December 13, the committee abandoned Reliance, naming that entire line "Titan," the name in Greek mythology given the son of Uranus (heaven) and Gaea (earth) who was "of gigantic size and enormous strength."

Such was becoming the IHC tractor legacy: size and strength. In early 1909 at Amiens, France, an Upper Sandusky Works 15-horsepower Friction Drive that had been shipped to France in 1908 plowed two days without stopping for any service or repairs, to win outright the Diplome d'Honneur and 2,000 francs.

John Steward had projects going again at Deering Works by mid-1909. (George Ellis left about then to open his own business forming insulation board from flax in southern Minnesota.) Obsessed with making tractors more useful, Steward built a large-scale auto-mower created from 16-foot grain header-binders normally pushed by horses. He mounted this on the rear of a Type A and then a Type B tractor operated in reverse. Steward's "tractor binder" ran two harvests in mid- and late-1909, cutting 50 acres in a 10-hour day. On April 13, 1910, Legge approved five 20-horsepower prototypes and 10 of the 15-horsepower versions for testing.

Johnston's Akron Experimental Department nearly had finished revisions to his opposed-twin-cylinder Famous 45-horsepower tractor in the fall of 1909. Large tractors still were in demand in the North and West. Output of all manufacturers in 1909 reached about 1,000 gasoline tractors, 698 of which went to Canada, encouraging news to IHC's sales department. Johnston's products outgrew the machine tools at Akron, a plant adequate to produce Auto Buggies but not large castings for big twins. Based on Johnston's late-coming success with his big tractor, the Executive Council moved ahead into the tractor business, devising a solution to Akron's crowding. They agreed to construct a tractor assembly plant next to the McCormick Works in Chicago. Cyrus Jr. transferred Johnston there, naming him overall superintendent.

Unfortunately, when he arrived on January 30, 1910, there was no building yet and few tools with which to manufacture anything, even though McCormick, Funk and Legge had scheduled production of 25 Famous twins for this new facility. Johnston's staff of 10 resurrected scrapped McCormick Works tools and reconditioned them in a large circus tent erected near his office. Mobile cranes moved massive tractor castings, some pieces so large they upset the cranes struggling in and out of the temporary plant in front of the McCormick Works. Winter arrived; the staff continued riveting tractor frames in the unheated tent and assembling wheels outside in the snow.

Johnston's staff completed 50 big twins under inhospitable conditions before moving into its new home in January 1911, just after a New Year's Day storm destroyed the tent. The first buyers liked the powerful Famous tractors, officially renamed the Mogul 45s on January 25, 1911, just as they rolled out of the Tractor Works. The Mogul name came from 16th century Mongolian conquerors, although in England it had appeared on several heavy-hauling steam locomotives. Reports soon came back that parts of the huge machine needed reinforcing, due to the high stress loads of large plows gangs and intense, pounding vibration of Johnston's opposed two-cylinder engine. This was not uncommon with Johnston's projects. In an era when "engineers" without formal schooling were a combination of blacksmith, inventor, and mechanic, he had become an accomplished problem-solver. Still it was not engineering and some troubles didn't quite get solved with his educated guesses. Always in demand to solve problems not his own, always stretched thin with other obligations, he was not having a good decade.

Gasoline prices remained a concern. IHC began distributing Rumely OilPulls after all, especially overseas, where farmers demanded kerosene tractors and Rumely had no distribution. IHC expanded European sales. By 1910, to avoid protective tariffs on agricultural implements and tractors it sold in Europe, it opened factories in Sweden, France, Germany and Russia. (IHC was the first U.S. maker to sell a tractor in Russia, in July 1910.) It sold tractors in Argentina, South Africa, Austria, Mexico, Rumania, Brazil, Turkey, Italy, Uruguay, Spain, Peru, Switzerland, Chile, Norway and Serbia.

During a committee meeting on August 11, Steward's "tractor push binder" came under debate. William Cavanaugh, Johnston's assistant manager at Tractor Works, argued that "it operates fairly well only under the most favorable conditions. We have made an attempt to sell a few, and I do not believe one has been sold." No one supported continued experimentation.

"As sure as there is a God in Israel," Steward thundered in obvious frustration, "tractors will be adapted to that work, because they are qualified for it."

Clarence Funk and Alex Legge got Johnston's Tractor Works going in late 1910. (This was none too soon. In July at Winnipeg, Rumely took higher honors with its OilPull tractor, nicknamed "Kerosene Annie," than with any other machine, serving notice to steam loyalists and gas engine makers alike.) Mil-

waukee's Charles Longenecker completed his new fuel mixer and the other parts necessary to burn kerosene.

IHC had competition now; 56 companies produced or announced plans to manufacture tractors that year, 14 more than 1909. Just after Thanksgiving, 1910, Legge asked his managers to look far forward. Domestic sales managers pushed lighter tractors, from 8 to 12 horsepower. W. F. Yeslin, foreign sales manager, advocated two forward speeds universally, dumping Kouns' reduction gear reverse because in Argentina and Australia, where Steward's motor push binder and headers were popular, they were too slow. Steward sat silently for a while, surveying his short-sighted colleagues. Then he spoke.

"Looking away into the future, the tractor business is the biggest thing before this company and ought to add at least 50 percent to the volume of business we are now doing." Henry Utley immediately chimed in, "This development is so important that we could well afford to spend $50,000 to $100,000 working on a light tractor next season."

When the Experimental Department released its "Annual Report" on January 24, 1911, Office Manager W. R. Peterson addressed kerosene tractors. Until now, Titan or Mogul engines burned kerosene only by "attachments" fitted as original factory equipment or refitted to older tractors. With some difficulty, farmers could do it themselves. On May 1, a special tractor committee appointed by General Manager Clarence Funk, officially met for the first time. Here McCormick Division General Manager B. A. Kennedy heard that Chicago Tractor Works already was building 25 new 20-horsepower Type C tractors. These were Longenecker-Johnston machines with "about 70 percent of regular 20-horsepower horizontal engine parts, but distinguished from other kerosene jobs in that it is a complete engine, with an enclosed crankcase, new cylinder head and a throttle governor." Kennedy, pleased, had Milwaukee Works begin assembling 50 more. On May 19, the 25-horsepower Johnston single-cylinder tractor designed at Tractor Works appeared: "Both engine and truck are of new design. This machine is an attractive manufacturing proposition, weighing 2,000 pounds less than our 25-horsepower Mogul tractor, has an average drawbar pull of about 4,500 pounds, and the engine is designed to use kerosene as fuel." The Mogul Jr., though not quite Utley's "light" tractor, was born.

At Winnipeg for 1911, IHC alone entered one tractor in the "Light Weight" A class, winning by default. Its middle-level, Class B tractor took second. Organizers created two additional categories, including one for kerosene. The other, Class C, for tractors with more than 40 horsepower, counted 9 entries, for a total of 24 in all classes, a reflection of the trend among makers in 1911 to produce larger tractors. The winner there was Johnston's opposed-twin, finally tamed. IHC's Mogul 45 produced 64.52 horsepower, pulled 6,650 pounds from the drawbar, and plowed 2.74 acres in an hour.

Milwaukee's Harry Waterman set E. D. Eliassen to work in mid-1911, around the time of the kerosene change, designing a 30-horsepower-rated Titan. Eliassen used Hawthorne's Titan 45 as his model both for appearance and engineering. After testing through mid-1912, the New Work Committee authorized production on December 27. Longenecker intended this big kerosene-burning engine to use Hawthorne's compact air starter. One cylinder of this small opposed-twin fired like a normal internal combustion engine, while the other cylinder worked as an air compressor, building up 200 psi pressure in a holding tank. The operator released air into the right main cylinder, forcing its piston down while compressing the kerosene fuel mix in the left to make it fire.

The fifth Winnipeg test, in July 1912, was less consequential to farmers and producers alike; 19 manufacturers entered. IHC won the kerosene class following a two-hour test. Farmers knew two hours meant nothing in the life of a tractor. (This was the last significant contest; the 1913 meeting counted only 3 entrants out of nearly 40 manufacturers producing tractors. IHC and many others went to Fremont, Nebraska, instead.) Longenecker in Milwaukee improved his fuel mixer on the Titan 30, increasing engine output. Waterman wanted to know draw bar horsepower for all Milwaukee's tractors. His staff recorded 10 horsepower on the 20 horsepower Moguls and Titans, 12 horsepower on the 25-horsepower Moguls and Titans, and 27 horsepower on the Titan 45. After fuel mixer improvements, the New Work Committee rerated the Titan as an 18–35 on July 19, 1913, and followed with the Titan 45 as a 30–60-horsepower model on January 12, 1914. All throttle-governed Titans or Moguls could be retrofitted. At Winnipeg in 1912, average output of all

tractors brake-tested was nearly 50 horsepower; in 1913, it reached 60. Manufacturers meant for big tractors to make bigger power.

That Titan and Mogul lines existed in nearly parallel development with similar power ratings and almost identical features, flew in the face of the premise of IHC's consolidation. The Deering-versus-McCormick rivalries died hard; dealers for the old lines still wanted something different. The similarly named, closely performing machines, in their bewildering assortment, were nearly all ordered by a sales department that was still propelling IHC. As a general rule, Tractor Works churned out Moguls for the McCormick dealers, and Milwaukee produced Titans for the Deering branches. In communities where there was only one of the two IHC dealers, it might carry Titans, Moguls, Morton friction drives and IHC gear-drives, or parts of all four lines. IHC's tractor products were in place, meeting performance goals within the corporation and against the outside competition. Events ahead would clarify confusions and end duplications within the next few years. The roles of Milwaukee and Tractor Works became clearer and each week, the engineers moved IHC's big tractors closer to perfection.

Akron produced water-cooled and air-cooled versions, hence the M-A model name. The two-cylinder opposed engines measured 5-inch bore and stroke and produced 15 horsepower. Top speed was 20 miles per hour, and it would carry two tons.

1911–1917

Two

WITH ANYTHING NAMED TITAN OR MOGUL, "SMALL" IS RELATIVE

Even though Moguls and Titans steadily improved, farmers began looking elsewhere. Canada's influence on tractor design had waned as attendance at Winnipeg fell. Since 1900, great prairie steamers, and gas and kerosene sod busters had turned over grassland opened just a decade earlier. Manufacturers produced almost 11,500 tractors in 1912, and IHC built nearly 3,000 of them. Now, farmers who thought they needed a tractor wanted one to fit within their fences. Some midwestern and southern farms were only 5 acres, and few were larger than 40. Farmers knew they purchased cast-iron by the pound. Most recognized the value in working faster than a horse's walk, but draft animals were paid for and ate off the land they worked.

The New Work Committee paid attention to what farmers wanted, after IHC lagged behind on kerosene. Small companies might respond rapidly to farmer desires and quickly slap together a workable device from pieces gathered from various sources. To some makers, how well that tractor worked was inconsequential. When IHC's Special Tractor Committee met on January 6, 1911, its agenda was brief but not myopic.

While most of its regional sales departments were content with 20-, 25-, and 45-horsepower machines, the area east of the Mississippi still wanted smaller, lighter tractors. Purchasing Department Manager Henry Utley, also advocating weight reduction, suggested IHC buy a Universal tractor, which was built by Northwest Thresher Company in Stillwater, Minnesota. While Titan and Mogul 45s weighed 20,000 pounds, the 18-horsepower, two-cylinder Universal tipped the scales at 9,000 pounds and featured

1911 Type D Titan 25 Horsepower

They produced 1,757 of these during its four-year life. Farmers compared it to the Mogul Type C, which sold 862, saw a better machine, and bought them two-to-one.

1914 Titan 18-35

One of Milwaukee Works' few failures was the 18–35, authorized for production on December 27, 1912. A very complicated tractor, it weighed 15,800 pounds, with a two-cylinder engine that originally was rated at 30 horsepower.

Waterman/Hawthorne-designed tractors were compact because of Waterman's preference for parallel cylinders. Still, their weight and complexity caused problems. The New Work Committee discontinued the 18–35 on December 8, 1913, after only 117 had been shipped.

sturdy 10-inch-long pistons and a beefy 3.5-inch-diameter crankshaft. William Cavanaugh, however, felt IHC should use the Universal as the next heavy tractor; he still pushed for a lighter model, of perhaps 5,000 pounds, offering four-wheel drive.

Ed Johnston liked his assistant's four-wheel drive idea. A week later he introduced sketches of a 6,000-to-8,000-pound machine using his 35-horse-power two-cylinder engine. "The machine is gear driven through four tumbling shafts, the gear set located in the center of the machine and incased, and one differential. All four wheels turn for steering." Uncharacteristically, Harry Waterman pronounced it "a good foundation." "I have no doubt as to demand, considering it a better machine than the Avery tractors," Waterman advised. "But pay attention to the fact that in designing a general purpose tractor, we could not expect the same efficiency as obtained from our regular machines."

While initially opposed to multicylinder engines, John Steward reversed his opinion, forming a simplified lineup, advocating that IHC "build two sizes of tractors and use a four-cylinder engine on the larger size, cutting that in two and using half of it as a two-cylinder engine on the smaller machine. On this construction we would have to drive with all four wheels, or with that caterpillar plan."

Steward, one of IHC's most avid students of patents, saw reports of Holt Manufacturing Company in Stockton, California, and Northern Holt Company in Minneapolis. While the idea of crawlers had been in farming for more than 20 years, the name "caterpillar" came from Ben Holt's machines. (Within 5 or 6 years of this meeting, 11 manufacturers produced crawlers or half-tracks. By 1922, that number doubled.)

Columbia University Professor C. E. Lucke, hired as a consultant to envision future products, proposed a "gasoline-electric tractor," fitting a Type B or Type C model with a generator to provide electric power for cultivators or harvesters. "The tractor would be stationed at one side of the field and the wires handled automatically on reels winding and unwinding as the machines traveled to or from the tractor." Recalling English Fowler steam traction plows winched across fields decades earlier, John Steward advised "the plan was old."

Throughout the summer of 1911, projects came and went. The first 20-horsepower combined road roller-tractor went out for testing. Several European governments threatened to ban IHC tractors because of their noise; Deering Works developed mufflers for Titan tractors sold abroad under the Deering label. By November, the Tractor

Works began assembling 100 one-horsepower, air-cooled starting engine "attachments" for the 45-horsepower Moguls for testing, a few for Europe and the rest at home. "Starting is accomplished by friction contact with the flywheel. The engine is self-contained and can be detached and used for other light work when desired."

Committee Chairman Kennedy asked Waterman and Johnston each to experiment with more efficient engine cooling. Exposure to the Rumely OilPull tractors through European sales and domestic contests raised question of oil cooling. Waterman preferred water: "Gravity water systems are best," he said. "Radiator systems are next and oil cooling is least desirable of all, although it has the advantage of keeping foreign matter out of the system."

Ed Johnston, still competing with Waterman, reported to have tested closed systems. "We must have an enclosed cooling system. Two types of radiators are now coming through the shop and one is being made by an outside firm." Ten years after consolidation, engineering progress still came down to McCormick versus Deering.

Kennedy found one place where neither plant excelled. "At each plant it has been necessary to do

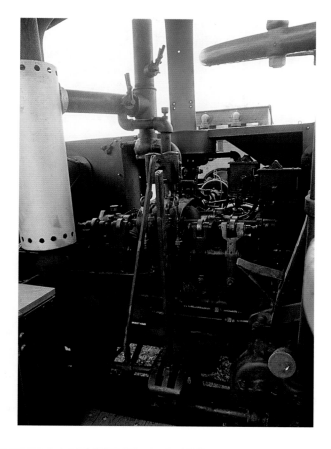

The long-lived rivalry between Ed Johnston at Tractor Works and Harry Waterman at Milwaukee included engine design among the targets for disagreement. Waterman and his experimental engineers favored two-cylinder parallel engines, while Johnston's twins were opposed-type engines, requiring extra room for the additional cylinders, heads and valve train.

This air-starting system was offered on both 18–35-horsepower and 30–60-horsepower Titans. The operator started this small engine, the left side functioning as a typical gas engine, the right making compressed air for a storage tank. When the operator released the tank, the compressed air flowed into the nearby cylinder, pushing one piston, and rotating the flywheel.

1913 Mogul Junior

Mogul Junior production began in 1911 and over its two-year life, Tractor Works produced 812 of them. In its last year, 1913, it was rerated, renamed as the Mogul 15–30, and given a drop front axle and other minor changes.

The Mogul Junior derived from Ed Johnston's large Mogul 45, using one of its two cylinders for its engine. It even adopted front and rear wheel sizes and overall appearance, though it weighed 15,400 pounds, about 4,000 than the big twin.

the painting out in the open and sometimes on parked flat cars, on account of congested conditions in the factories."

Johnston's 30-horsepower twin-cylinder tractor, authorized on January 19, 1911, was ready for testing in mid-April 1912. More promising were April 15 discussions on a "general purpose tractor capable of pulling three plows, with not less than two or three speeds, maximum of seven miles per hour, weight between 5,000 and 8,000 pounds and retail for about $1,000." Discussion around the table suggested something could be quickly produced by adapting the two-cylinder engine designed for the Cavanaugh-Johnston Tractor Works four-wheel drive that had begun prototype construction.

On May 6, 1911, Ed Johnston released plans to manufacture 25 horsepower Mogul Junior Tractors for 1912. This not-so-lightweight (16,300 pounds) kerosene model used one of the Mogul 45 engine's two-cylinders. A week later, John Steward's "light general purpose tractor" had completed field tests. It resembled the Harpstrite traction engine and Hackney Auto Plow (which Tractor Works also had pur-

chased for examination). Plows hung below the middle of the frame. Steward offered other differences from the big bore-and-stroke, slow-revving Titans and Moguls. True to his recent conversion, he used a relatively small displacement Brennan four-cylinder engine mounted transversely over the drive wheels. He estimated tractor weight at less than 7,000 pounds and manufacturing cost less than $600, using outside engines. Most committee members saw it work. In the next meeting, they discussed the options.

Waterman was skeptical of the durability of an automotive-type engine, such as the Brennan, with higher speed, higher compression, and higher power. He suggested that Milwaukee's new Hawthorne-Eliassen medium-bore twin might be preferable. Steward said he "viewed the farm requirements in a light tractor as precisely what is required of horses. The theory in my design was to build a tractor that would not absorb so much power to pull itself. In selecting the Brennan motor, it was understood that it is not the best type for this work, but nothing better could be found." If IHC were to build the engine, at less than $120 manufacturing cost, the entire tractor could be produced for $350. "By comparison, the cost of the Upper Sandusky tractors is approximately $522 for the 12 horsepower and $576 for the 15 horsepower."

Five days later, Waterman submitted his own proposal, unlike either Johnston's or Steward's designs. Milwaukee Works would build a 35-horsepower chain drive tractor following Titan general design. He would use the Hawthorne-Eliassen four-cylinder horizontal engine. This was made up of two of the new Milwaukee lightweight twins side-by-side, producing about 25 horsepower, and was capable of pulling three plows at 2.125 miles per hour and a road speed of 4 miles per hour. Waterman estimated its weight at 7,500 pounds and development expenses would run less than $8,000. (This became the 15–30 Titan "Flaming Four," when development testing produced only 30 horsepower.) Then Johnston offered to build, field test and make his tractor ready for manufacture for $7,500. The committee gave both men their projects and funding. By October, Johnston's tractor had added weight from the addition of a more durable IHC-built, four-cylinder engine, rated at 15–30 horsepower. (While this tractor never went into production with the four, this project and engine provided the foundation for Johnston's semi-unitized Mogul 20–40 prototype two years later.) However, a new candidate had entered the contest.

Harry C. Waite, an independent designer hired by Deering Works, devised a finely engineered

lightweight machine that went immediately into farm testing near Lewiston, Montana. Once its operators were trained, Waite told Deering he had another job waiting. IHC hired him rather than lose him, even though they were concerned by the manufacturing costs of Waite's tractor, quoted as $1,500 each in quantity the previous April. He agreed to omit wheel and chain roller bearings, revise his three-speed transmission to two forward gears and to reduce the tractor's weight. These cut costs to

These Titans used IHC's first four-cylinder engine, produced and assembled at Harry Waterman's Milwaukee Works. Immediately after renaming the tractor, Waterman and his crew began to design the next generation, the Titan 10–20.

On November 26, 1917, Leonard Sperry announced Milwaukee Works Decision 990. This changed "the name of the 15–30 Titan tractor to International 15–30 Horsepower Tractor." This came about as a result of the U.S. government decree following its antitrust suit against International Harvester, abolishing duplicate tractor lines. This was a late 1918 EC-series 15–30. *State Historical Society of Wisconsin*

1917 Titan 30–60

As big as Ed Johnston's Tractor Works-produced Mogul 45 horsepower tractor was, Harry Waterman's Milwaukee Works-built Titan 30–60 was more powerful. It was, however, physically shorter, because the Titan used a two-parallel cylinder engine, cutting nearly 4 feet from its overall length.

$850 in quantity. The committee asked him to produce another five development models, equipped to run on kerosene.

John Steward adopted Harry Waite. Embracing his new ideas resulted in the Steward-Waite tractor, "as a three-wheel machine, two-speeds—3.5 and 2.5 miles per hour—single-lever control, the carburetor air intake protected from dust by straining the air through water. All moving parts are to be absolutely covered. Also, to provide an attachment at a cost of $5 or $6 so that any standard grain binder could be operated by pushing it before the tractor." Like all of the engineers, Steward promoted his pet ideas.

Problems appeared with Johnston's 30-horsepower twin, the Mogul 18–35-horsepower tractor: "The main frame breakage was reported due to defective work in bending the channel." In Australia, the 25-horsepower Mogul Type Cs were breaking wheel spokes. Waterman thought this was because operators failed to keep them tight. Johnston recommended flat spokes that didn't need adjustment.

On November 29, 1912, Ed Johnston released specifications of his next small tractor, the single-cylinder kerosene 10–20-horsepower Mogul Junior. Milwaukee Works began releasing smaller, lighter tractors just before year-end. Decision D-484, dated December 27, 1912, announced a two-cylinder, 15,800-pound tractor using the Milwaukee-designed air-start device. First rated at 30 horsepower, it entered production as the Titan 18–35, with its own problems unsolved.

In late April 1913, the committee authorized production of the first 50 Johnston 12–25 horsepower "light tractors," badged as the Mogul 12–25 horsepower. This was the production version of his four-cylinder 15–30, but used the earlier two-cylinder engine with chain drive. (The committee ordered 20 Steward front-drive, center-plow tractors as well, at a cost of $500 each. It sent these out for additional tests after the first six prototypes performed well near Salina, Kansas, where Tractor

All dressed up with somewhere to go, this 1915 Titan 30–60 was equipped with optional acetylene lamps and road protection rims over the rear wheels. The big Titans always were delivered with extension rims on front and rear although the rears here were not fitted, suggesting this was headed for a show inside an arena or amphitheater. It is photographed just outside Milwaukee Works. *State Historical Society of Wisconsin*

The difference in proportions between the Titan 30–60 and the Mogul 30–60 (shown above) is clearly visible. Ed Johnston's choice to build an opposed-cylinder engine added nearly 4 feet of overall length to his Mogul, compared to Harry Waterman's Titan 30–60. This one tows an elevating grader. *State Historical Society of Wisconsin*

Works tested two Harry Waite prototypes and a Hackney Auto Plow. By early December 1913, Waite had moved to the Milwaukee Works and was an occasional contributor to New Work Committee meetings. In the year's last full gathering on December 8, the committee dealt with the troublesome 18-35 horsepower Titan and the air starting machinery on the 45-horsepower Titan.

"Approximately 117 [18–35 horsepower Titans] have been shipped out, a large number of these are unsatisfactory and several have been taken back. The design is such that it cannot be made satisfactory. Material is on hand for 200 machines; cost of manufacture last year was $1,674.53 each. With this situation confronting us, despite the obvious losses, it was decided that we discontinue permanently the manufacture of this tractor."

As for the 45-horsepower Titan, "a number of changes and improvements to get more power out of this tractor are under way. Cylinder bore has been increased and mixers redesigned. The air starting feature on this tractor was reported expensive to

1919 Titan 15-30
This was also known as the Flaming Four, because after dark, other farmers could identify one by of the flames shooting out the exhaust.

The Titan 15-30 was one of IHC's first smaller tractors, this one grown out of the 12-25. It also gave evidence of early IHC concern about dirt—the final drive chain gear was completely enclosed, and the fan belt and pulley were protected behind a screen and framework.

manufacture, also unsatisfactory. Several cases were mentioned where the air starters had been replaced by the small starting engine used on the Mogul line." No longer was Waterman immune from failure.

By the end of 1913, while there were 80 companies in the business, barely 50 produced machines. From them, just 7,000 tractors were produced and sold, about a third fewer than 1912. Weaknesses with the Titans had gained perspective. IHC was eliminating manufacturing failures such as the 18–35 horsepower frames and marginally developed ideas such as the air-start system. Sales problems and matters of public acceptance of the tractors were different issues. It was a demanding period for farm equipment makers and for farmers themselves. Following nearly three decades of hard times, from 1870 into the 1890s, farmers had come back. The depression of 1873 had ended by 1879; grain production increased, as farmers fed a growing population, including a quarter-million emigrants fleeing famine and hardship in Europe and Asia. Abraham Lincoln's 1862 creation of the U.S. Department of Agriculture acknowledged the significance of farming. The Grange and various Farmers Alliance movements from the 1870s gave voice to their concerns. These organizations briefly united farmers in demanding more equitable economic systems and regulation of the monopolies they thought took advantage of them. The Sherman Anti-Trust Act of 1890 was a direct result.

Transcontinental railroads reached the Pacific Northwest in 1893; crops moved faster, farther and cheaper than before. This opened trade around the Pacific Rim, bringing cotton and grain to Asia and returning profits to America's farmers. Prices rose steadily beginning in 1897 and they continued, sometimes taking dramatic jumps. In 1910, farm journals tentatively labeled the first decade "The Good Years." Yet, even as they saw "The Great Years" ahead, editors and writers raised a chorus of discontent. They wanted tractor makers to produce machines they felt farmers needed: Better built, more maneuverable, more reliable, easier to start, less cumbersome to operate, less costly to purchase. "The Country Gentleman" and "The American Thresherman" in their editorials called out to International Harvester (which held one-third of the market by 1911), and to Avery, Rumely, J. I. Case, Minneapolis Threshing Machine Company, Emerson-Brantingham and Hart-Parr. Not only did these makers react, but dozens of other independents jumped into the business. By the end of 1914, there were 61 firms in the United States and Canada producing farm tractors. The sensation of a Golden Age was nearly universal. It was only a sensation.

IHC began eliminating products. Late that year, L. B. Sperry circulated that Milwaukee Works took the 20- and 25-horsepower Type D Titans out of production. In early June, Sperry introduced a new Titan 15–30 horsepower four-cylinder tractor weighing 9,300 pounds. Still, it was not major manufacturers who answered magazine cries for compact, lightweight tractors. Small makers like Bull Tractor of Minneapolis produced a 5,000-pound 5–12-horsepower tricycle. The Little Bull retailed for $335 and by the end of 1914, the company had sold 3,800 of them; IHC slipped to second place in sales behind the upstart. Robert Hendrickson and Clarence Eason, designers of the Wallis "Cub," furthered the benchmark and took credit for introducing the "unit-frame" tractor. In response, Alex Legge encouraged Addis E. McKinstry, the new manager of Experiments, to design and build a four-wheel, 8–16-horsepower tractor, to weigh 5,000 pounds, to run with a two-cylinder engine cast "en bloc" with mechanical valves. Legge meant for the two-cylinder engine to distinguish the machine from the Tractor Works' Mogul 8–16, (a project in development based on the one-cylinder hopper-cooled engine,) and intended "the

work be rushed, as it is necessary to have a tractor of this size to complete the Titan line, to satisfy local agents" who had to compete with Bull and Wallis.

Legge, McCormick, Deering, and the Executive Council faced a dilemma. IHC dealers wanted product. Yet they still competed with each other more than outside rivals. By mid-1914, the U.S. Justice Department had begun to pound the conglomerate. According to Barbara Marsh, author of A Corporate Tragedy, IHC invested $28 million in new plants and new products, including tractors and trucks during its first eight years of consolidation. Sales rose from $56 million in 1905 to $101 million in 1910. Its assets, worth nearly $173 million, ranked it as America's fourth-largest company. Because George Perkins was a generous donor and influential Republican Party fund-raiser, President Theodore Roosevelt blinked when he looked past IHC's size and tactics.

Roosevelt's successor, Democrat William Howard Taft, didn't inherit Teddy's IHC-blindness. In 1912, the Justice Department filed suit against the

The Flaming Four used seven carburetors. One at the top controlled gasoline mix to start the four-cylinder engine. Once the engine was warm, the operator switched to kerosene, and there was one kerosene carburetor per cylinder. When the engine began to overheat, the two additional carburetors controlled a water-injection system to cool the engine, eliminate pre-ignition, and make the fuel more dense

Manufacture of the new "small" Titan 10–20, introduced at the end of 1915, backed up production at Milwaukee Works, which was also making Titan 15–30s. On August 1, 1917, the just-formed Gas Power Engineering Department moved 15–30 assembly to Chicago Tractor Works, leaving more capacity for Titan 10–20s to be built. (This is a 1919–1922 model with full rear fenders.) *State Historical Society of Wisconsin*

This studio view of the Milwaukee Works Titan 18–35 shows what a complex machine it was. The solid flywheel was one example; Rumely had abandoned solid flywheels several years earlier because as bearings wore, the flywheel became a resonator for all sounds mechanical, amplifying the sound of an engine self-destructing. *State Historical Society of Wisconsin*

company as its 10-year voting trust expired. The government charged that IHC "monopolized the harvester and binder markets, destroyed competition by forcing dealers to sign exclusive contracts, created a patent monopoly and reaped excessive profits."

IHC was additionally damned because in 1895, Cyrus' brother Harold had married into the Rockefeller family. John D.'s Standard Oil Company was under constant Justice Department scrutiny. This relationship was too much for Taft to ignore. In 1913, the McCormicks, accepting the wisdom of outside profes-

sional management, urged Clarence Funk (whom they always felt was a Deering loyalist) to resign. When he left to become president of Rumely, they promoted assistant general manager Alex Legge to Funk's job. Legge first worked for McCormick in 1891 collecting bad debts for the Omaha, Nebraska, branch. He came equipped with good judgment and excellent business sense as well as his long-held loyalty.

Cyrus Jr., attempting to avoid the government pressing its suit to trial, divided IHC in two companies after Funk left. One half, called International Harvester Corporation of America, took care of tractors, trucks and other new product lines as well as foreign manufacture and sales. Then he reorganized existing harvester, binder and other old product lines as the International Harvester Company of New Jersey. This fooled no one. The Federal District Court judge ruled in 1914 that when IHC was formed in 1902, it controlled 85 percent of the harvester and binder production and sales, a fact no one denied. While the judge ruled that IHC's treatment of smaller competitors was just and fair, he still ordered it to dissolve.

Courtroom procedures occupied corporate time and resources; however business, especially tractor business, went on. Chicago Works, accommodating pressures to produce smaller tractors, released its 12–25 horsepower two-cylinder Mogul in March and the single-cylinder Mogul 8–16 in September 1914.

Farming tumbled from its profitability peak in 1910, sinking into a recession that began with Wall Street banking worries in 1907 and bottomed out with a disastrous partial crop failure in 1914 (one that did in Funk's Rumely.) IHC delivered 3,831 tractors in 1912, just 1,930 in 1913 and barely half that, 1,095, in 1914. The corporation, still pushed by its sales departments, offered 16 different models in 1913; six of those sold fewer than 40 tractors each. In 1914, there were 17 models, but only the Titan 45-horsepower Type D and the Mogul 12–25 sold more than 100 each.

While appealing the antitrust verdict bought them time, IHC's divisions prepared for enforced change. On August 20, 1914, Sperry issued Decision Change #D-609, indirectly resulting from the ruling. "In order to have the four-cylinder Titan tractor consistently rated when compared with other I.H.C. types, it has been decided to change its rating from 15–30 horsepower to 12–25 horsepower." The Titan used IHC's first four-cylinder engine, laid horizontally. This was done so Deering and McCormick branches had similarly rated tractors to sell at comparable prices. Milwaukee then set about designing its Titan 10–20.

By early September 1915, an era of fierce internal competition passed. In late June, John Steward died of heart failure. He was 74 and had worked at Deering and IHC until two weeks before his death. Harry Waterman, Milwaukee Works superintendent, retired and Paul Schryer replaced him. In Chicago, the Executive Council named Ed Johnston manager of the Experimental Department of Gas Power Engineering, in charge of design of tractors, engines and trucks. H. B. Morrow replaced Johnston as superintendent of Tractor Works.

On September 14, 1915, the New Work Committee "decided to restore the original rating of 15–30 horsepower as applied to the four-cylinder Titan Light Tractor . . . This change was requested by the Sales Department as this machine will deliver ample power at all times to carry this rating."

Throughout 1916, Milwaukee Works changed the transmission and introduced the valve-in-head engine, as part of their own 8–16-horsepower tractor project. This justified sales department horsepower boasts.

Ed Johnston, in his new job, signed off on the next significant decision from Tractor Works on October 14, 1916, announcing the 8–16 Mogul tractor (later renamed the four-cylinder International 8–16.) Chicago engineers designed the 3,000-pound tractor using their new in-line, vertically mounted four-cylinder engine. Chain driven through a three-speed gearbox, it ran on gasoline, benzol, motor spirits, naphtha or kerosene.

Production considerations brought about the next improvement on August 1, 1917, soon after the Executive Council moved the Milwaukee Works Experimental Department to Chicago and consolidated it with Tractor Works Experimental. This group adopted the name Gas Power Engineering Department. It moved Titan 15–30 production from Milwaukee Works to Chicago beginning with the 1918 model year, "to relieve the crowded condition of Milwaukee Works," caused by scheduling production of its new smallest tractor, the Titan 10–20.

On April 6, 1917, the United States entered the World War that had begun nearly three years earlier in Bosnia. By 1917, the Justice Department's antitrust battle with IHC was nearly over. The Justice Department had encouraged other antitrust defendants to

propose resolutions to their own suit, even letting them schedule actions to their benefit. IHC had lost plants, sales branches and products in Germany, France and Russia to nationalization before the United States joined the conflict. McCormick offered to sell its three old-line harvesting machinery subsidiaries. (This was a benefit; harvesters were its corporate loss leaders.) Cyrus Jr. suggested reuniting the divided companies as International Harvester Corporation once again. On October 12, 1917, Ed Johnston noted that "it has been decided to change the name of the tractor to 8–16 International."

Prior to peace in Europe on November 11, 1918, IHC surrendered. The most painful terms of its agreement was to own and operate only one sales facility in each town. IHC released 4,778 dealers, most of whom quickly joined John Deere.

Two weeks after the European Armistice, on November 26, L. B. Sperry posted Milwaukee Works Decision 990, changing "the name of the 15–30 Titan tractor to International 15–30 horsepower Tractor. Change to become effective as near to December 1st, 1917, as new nameplates can be procured. This is done because there is only one tractor of this size now manufactured."

That was the bad part of IHC's surrender. The good news was very good: IHC could make use of all those pooled funds and facilities to strengthen its growing tractor business.

This was the maiden voyage of Ed Johnston's first unit frame tractor, the Mogul 20–40, on February 18, 1914. The frame, a gray iron casting, housed the transmission, which supported, on pads, the horizontal four-cylinder engine, 19A. The entire unitized frame was 97 inches long, with another 56 inches of front extension members, 21, to the front axle. Ed Johnston supervised assembly of 10 of these Mogul 20–40 prototypes. Not only did this introduce IHC to unit frame construction, it brought three-point suspensions as well with the automobile steering-type front axle (25, 26, 27 and 28) supported at one point by the pivot and pin, 23 and 24. The numbers on this print, one of only two photos known to exist of the 20–40, relate to descriptions taken during pretrial depositions from Ed Johnston, David Baker and others involved in a patent infringement suit in the early 1930s. *National Archives & Records Administration*

1915–1928

Three

No Sooner Peace than War

The rivalry between Ed Johnston's Chicago Tractor Works and Harry Waterman's Milwaukee Works was a highly advanced, forward-thinking strategy. Two separate design teams developing identical products is a technique common at the end of the twentieth century. Instead, in 1915 IHC's practice of near duplication reinforced Justice Department objections to McCormick's and Deering's monopoly. It was its own biggest competitor. However, the lawsuit and other factors changed all of that.

1918 International 8-16
On October 16, 1916, the Executive Committee approved production of Ed Johnston's revolutionary new small tractor, the Mogul 16. Impressed by the smoothness of Harry Waterman's four-cylinder Titan 12–25—and always in competition with him—he designed this new machine to use a four as well.

Milwaukee Works began designing the two-cylinder Titan 10–20 in late 1914 as one of Waterman's final challenges to his younger rival, giving the Titan slightly more power than Johnston's Mogul 8–16. Waterman ran the first test model in April 1915 and authorized two more development tractors for tests until year-end around Milwaukee. Then he retired. His successor, Paul Schryer, shipped the Titan development models off to Texas for winter work. Problems with inadequate power and premature chain wear, and tests of magnetos delayed the Titan's production. Schryer built another seven test samples. Then in November 1915, Milwaukee redesigned the two-cylinder engine with removable cylinder barrels, a new high-tension magneto, and a stronger transmission. Eight more prototypes followed before January 22, 1916, when Schryer finally signed off on production, which began on February 28.

This was worth the effort to International Harvester. The beginning of war in Europe two

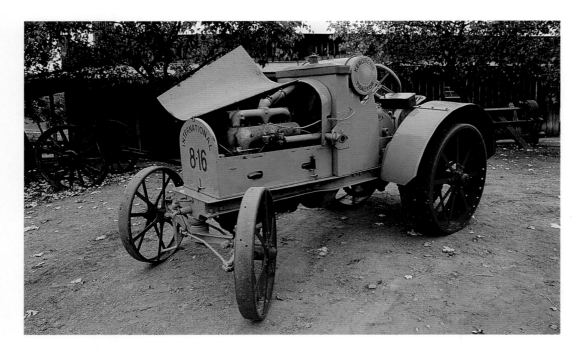

stalled; it introduced the 7–20-horsepower rated Big Bull, weighing 4,500 pounds and selling for $585.) For 1916, Ed Johnston, now manager of experiments for the Gas Power Engineering Department, increased cylinder bore and replaced the single-speed forward transmission with a two-speed unit, renaming it the Mogul 10–20. The Executive Council approved production in November, one month after approving the other 8–16 four-cylinder (International) Mogul (on October 16). IHC wanted this Mogul to share an engine with the Model G truck, but oil leakage problems delayed introduction both for the truck and tractor, which, as Guy Fay reported, was set aside until design of its own engine was completed and tested.

This other 8–16 tractor represented a tremendous advance for IHC. Its compact dimensions made it maneuverable and practical for small acreage farmers. Its tapered nose appealed to orchard operators and its shape, reminiscent of contemporary automobiles, brought 8–16s to the attention of industrial users. It was too radical for some conservatives, but for those buyers, IHC had more traditional 10–20 Mogul and Titan tractors. When Henry Ford rose on the horizon as the next major

Johnston's original idea was to have the Mogul/International 8–16 share the four-cylinder engine with the Model G truck. But oil leakage problems kept the engine in the test lab long beyond the cut-off date for use in the tractor, and he designed a new one instead.

1915 Mogul 8-16
This was IHC's money-maker in 1915. That year, the company sold 5,841 tractors. More than 5,000 of them were these Mogul 8–16s, designed by Ed Johnston. In its last year of production, 1915, it still had only a single forward speed. Plow guides were options.

years before increased demand for food and textiles, a need met in the United States by farmers attracted to smaller machines. In 1915, IHC sold 5,841 tractors; more than 5,000 of those were Johnston's Mogul (one-cylinder) 8–16. (Bull Tractor had not

The tapered nose with no openings for a radiator made sense to orchard owners while its overall shape, which reminded many of contemporary sporty automobiles, appealed to industrial tractor users, both groups being early supporters of the unconventional-looking machine.

Even though development problems delayed manufacture long after its approval date, it proved to be one of Ed Johnston's most fertile designs. From this rail frame, chain drive platform, he spun off crawlers and multiwheeled experimentals to test new ideas and supply new markets with IHC tractors.

challenge to IHC's peace of mind, it was the unremarkable Titan that fought off Dearborn's assault.

On October 7, 1913, Henry Ford's first Model Ts drove off the assembly line at his Highland Park, Michigan, plant. His workers produced a car in three hours moving along the 250-foot-path. Significant as this was, it was only one of Ford's warning shots fired toward other U.S. manufacturers. For tractor makers, the first signs of war appeared long before 1913, as early as 1905 when Ford experimented with prototypes called "Automobile Plows" on his farm in Dearborn. His chief tractor engineer, Joe Galamb, had created in the spring of 1907 a horizontally mounted four-cylinder tricycle tractor using unit-frame construction, relying on the engine as part of the structure. Once finished and patented though, Ford forgot about it. He sent Galamb and his assistant, Gene Farkas, to pursue lighter weight, Model T-based ideas. When Galamb learned about Hendrickson and Eason's unit-frame Wallis Cub tractor almost a year before its introduction in 1913, it sent him and Farkas into productive frenzy, creating what became the Fordson in 1916. With this small, lightweight, unit-frame tractor as his ammunition, Henry declared war on the horse. However, as the series of interlocking peace treaties in Europe quickly embroiled a dozen countries in a war started over a political assassination, so did Henry's attack. Every other tractor maker wanted to defeat draft animals as well. They all became victims of the assembly line juggernaut called Henry Ford & Son.

Even though Ford claimed he didn't care about other tractor manufacturers, he was competing against International Harvester and everyone else. In 1916, there were 165 companies claiming to be tractor makers. A portion of these, Advance-Rumely, B.F. Avery, Aultman-Taylor and others, continued to produce simple variations on what they had done in previous years—heavy, slow, ponderous things, with an occasional all-purpose or motor-cultivator-type machine introduced to respond to changing times. Others, inspired by Ford's well-publicized efforts to transform his Model T into a tractor, tried similar, automobile-based attempts. A core group, including IHC, followed a middle ground, taking from both extremes technologies of value and ideas with merit.

France and Germany, a horse's life expectancy was 7 to 10 days. In 1900, there were more than 23 million horses on farms in the United States. In 1910, there were a million more, yet there were only 3,650 tractors at work. The value of tractors became as apparent to those at home as the need for cutting, harvesting and binding equipment became in the Civil War. Farm journals pushed for useful small tractors, and city newspapers picked up the tractor idea, engaged by its novelty.

In 1850, 70 percent of the U.S. population worked in agriculture; by 1910, it was 33 percent. The population had increased, yet far fewer people fed and clothed the others. In 1917, Great Britain planned to convert all green lawn to food production. There were only 600 tractors in the U.K. then. By the end of 1918, there were 3,000, and a year later, nearly 7,000 in all had opened up almost 1.4 million acres to cultivation. In France, 4,000 mostly American-made tractors worked to restore farming land nearly destroyed by war. To plow an acre of land behind a horse meant the farmer walked nearly seven miles, taking as many hours. The Department of Agriculture reported 34,371 tractors working on U.S. farms in 1916. In North America, 70 active companies (of about 150 claiming to be in business) manufactured 29,760 tractors, nearly 80 percent of them two-plow rated to work at more than two miles per hour. A tractor towing two, three or four

This was the Tractor Works production line assembling International 8–16 tractors. Its two weakest links are visible here, the chain drive and its rail frame, which allowed the entire tractor to twist under heavy load. Many farmers complained its center radiator cooked their feet during summer work. *Navistar*

Gas Power Engineering Department built its own dynamometer test car to measure drawbar pull and horsepower in the back yard of Tractor Works. The car was based on the frame of a Mogul 12–25, but the engine was replaced with a water brake to allow variable resistance against a tractor without wheel lugs. *State Historical Society of Wisconsin*

Wartime needs for food and cloth increased farmers' profits but also induced them to increase production. The war drew nearly every available horse and able-bodied male to Europe. On battlefields in

1920 Titan 10-20
The traditional Titan 10-20 proved to be IHC's weapon against the Fordson. Unremarkable, traditional and unsophisticated, the Titan 10-20s couldn't hold up to comparison against Ford's more advanced Fordson. Farmers who worked with them came to hate both of them, but when the dust settled in 1928, Ford was gone. Alex Legge had deeply discounted hundreds of Titan 10-20s to remain in business.

plows proved amazingly more efficient to newspaper writers who had never seen steam traction engines pull 15. Horses that sold for $49 in 1900 brought $109 in 1914 and $139 in 1918. If bombs and rifle shots didn't get them in France, they still could be worked to death, their hearts failing under the load of heavy plowing in Kansas or Georgia or Maine. Tractors would save America, the editors wrote, and they could save the world.

North American makers turned out 62,742 machines in 1917, shipping 14,854 to Europe. In 1918, wartime uses of steel and other material threatened all domestic industry. The U.S. Government Priorities Board began to speak of rationing steel, limiting first-generation development prototypes to 10, second generation test models to 50 and total production by all manufacturers to 315,000 tractors, hoping this would be enough to continue to feed and clothe the world. In fact, the final count reached only 132,697, and the Armistice in November brought an end to allocations in December. More than 100 new companies, seeking to ensure the right to profit from the war in Europe—or to continue adequate supplies of other raw materials—entered the tractor business, bringing the census of supposed makers to more than 250.

Sitting on IHC's New Work Committee or Executive Council was like living in nearly constant turmoil interrupted by brief calm. The corporation's bold new channel-frame tractor, the four-cylinder

Nearing the end of production, Milwaukee Works stockpiled its later Titan 10-20 models (full fenders indicate production between 1919 and 1922) on an upper floor of the plant. All the radiator filler covers are open to warn factory personnel to not run the tractors. *State Historical Society of Wisconsin*

1926 Model 20 Industrial/H.P. One Man Grader/Trackson tracks

Lurking behind and inside the H. P. One Man Power Grader and the Hadfield-Penfield Rigid Rail Tracks is an early version of McCormick-Deering's 10–20 in Industrial form.

1926 McCormick-Deering 10–20

IHC's Executive Council authorized production of the small unit-frame 10–20 Gear Drive tractor on January 20, 1922, as an International model. Part of IHC's "Two Tractor Program," this was the little cousin to the International 15–30 Gear Drive introduced a year earlier. On August 22, they both were renamed after the founders.

Mogul 8–16, conceived in 1914 and first born in August 1916, was reborn later in 1917. Its problems required two engine transplants (first, to remedy failures involving splash lubrication and enlarging the crankshaft diameter to strengthen the engine; next was to address horsepower shortcomings). Tractor Works, by this time managed by Ed Johnston's successor, H. B. Morrow, had to completely revise the front end steering knuckles, bearings and bushings, and accommodate a name change even before the model's introduction. It always used in-line vertical four-cylinder engines, coupled to three-speed gear transmissions driving the rear axle by chains. As the International 8–16 (its name changed on October 12, 1917), it offered farmers America's first production power take-off (initially tested on 50 prototypes and approved April 4, 1919). It provided engineers with a test vehicle to experiment further with four-wheel and six-wheel drive. Engineers developed crawler tracks, and in June 1919, extra-width, reinforced steel wheels for rice field work. Later, cast-iron wheels wrapped in rubber blocks produced by Firestone Tire & Rubber appeared, but they failed to survive testing. In addition, the International 8–16 developed and proved IHC's own assembly line production, in quantity, beginning in 1918.

By then, its cousin, the Mogul 10–20, was approaching retirement, and the Titan 10–20 should have been. IHC discontinued production of the Mogul in 1919, yet, for a number of reasons, the Titan continued until 1922. Ford's competition and frustrations with the smaller tractor left the company little choice. The 8–16's lubrication system led a small tube from the transmission case to the external final drive chains. It vented to outside air, allowing dense, fresh air to mix with warm lubricating oil vapors inside the case, sometimes igniting and fracturing the case. Legge considered substituting a gear final drive already in development, approving this version on September 27, 1920. But even this decision was only a Band-Aid to a severely injured project.

A year earlier, in mid-September 1919, Alex Legge had written to Harold F. Perkins, IHC's vice-president, assessing the manufacturing problems that held up output of the 8–16. Cyrus McCormick Jr. accused engineers of delaying the project with modifications and improvements, and blamed the sales departments for not selling the tractor hard enough. Cyrus Jr. supported manufacturing's proposal that

A tremendously popular tractor, IHC produced 25,021 of these 10–20s in 1926. Introduced at $850, it cost more than the Fordson, but this machine became the IHC's main weapon against the Ford. Using a unit-frame construction, it housed the engine, transmission and gear final drive within the single-piece cast iron tub.

"By the time the tractor reaches this booth," the caption in the October 1923 National Geographic magazine read, "everything is in place except the wheels, which are put on just beyond the booth. Grey paint is sprayed on by compressed air. After the wheels are put on, the line passes through a drying tunnel 110 feet long, in which the temperature is maintained at 150-degrees." *Navistar*

The gear drive unit frame tractors gave IHC a rigid platform from which to expand into crawler manufacture. They did so with this TracTracTor 10–20, introduced in 1928. Experiments with crawler tracks on International 8–16 rail frames proved the necessity of unit frame stiffness. *State Historical Society of Wisconsin*

Truck and Tractor Works management get decision-making priority over all other departments. Legge questioned production delays, reminding Perkins (and Cyrus Jr.) of the $1.25 million just spent to create Chicago Tractor Works' foundry, meant to greatly relieve the production bottleneck. Yet this did not increase the 25-per-day production of 8–16s to the 100-a-day level that was ordered. In its design, its engineering innovations, and now in internal politics, the International 8–16 took on new significance.

Johnston and Morrow warned that 8–16 channel frames were too flexible to hold tolerances necessary for severe loads. Under peak stress, twisting frames allowed gears to disengage. Johnston ordered a complete redesign on January 20, 1922, calling for a "Platform made in one piece [a unit frame] and heavier metal; cylinder head and crank chamber changed to give larger water passages," and a half dozen other supports, reinforcements and enlargements each meant to strengthen and stiffen the tractor. Then, instead of spending the money to make new casting patterns and to revise the production line that assembled the 8–16s, those efforts and resources went into two new machines, in a new line eventually named for the founders.

Gas Power Engineering approved production of the first of these new machines, initially authorized as the "12–25 Four Cylinder International Tractor with gear final drive, burning kerosene," on October 1, 1920. This was shortly after the gear-drive decision for the 8–16, which eventually became the McCormick-Deering 10–20. Almost on the eve of production, the Naming Committee changed its designation to the International 15–30 (later renamed again to the McCormick-Deering 15–30). Ed Johnston approved an optional PTO on the following Valentine's Day. Six months later, IHC made the PTO standard equipment, while increasing the belt pulley diameter from 16.75 inches to 19, increasing its speed from 2,600 feet per minute to 2,960. While Waukesha produced serial numbered engines for the tractors, on July 21, on the eve of production start up, Johnston ordered Paul Schryer's Milwaukee Works to begin numbering the 15–30s at T G 101 (for Tractor, Gear-driven). In its second year of life, on May 26, 1922, Milwaukee began producing a vineyard version, without the belt pulley but with "special rear wheel shields which completely cover the top half (approx.) of the wheels, joining the motor hood and fuel tank with as smooth an outline as possible. The air cleaner [is] to be mounted inside the rear wheel fenders," at the request of the Los Angeles and San Francisco branch houses. A "Special California Type" came a week later, fitted with 12x40-inch rear wheels and 24-inch diameter fronts, with the relocated air cleaner and without the belt pulley or radiator curtain "unless specially ordered as an attachment."

When the original International Gear Drive 15–30 arrived in 1921, it had adopted several pages from Henry Ford's lesson book. First, the new tractors were, like the Fordson, the Wallis Cub and Ford's 1907 prototype, unit-frame modular construction machines. Tractor Works had built two prototypes, one with a channel frame, the other of one-piece unit-type construction. The channel frame version flexed as much as the 8–16 had, unpredictably popping out of gear under heavy plowing. The unit-frame model remained rigid and in gear.

The International was renamed the McCormick-Deering 15–30 on August 22, 1922. It and the McCormick-Deering 10–20, introduced in 1923, housed the engine, transmission and gear final-drive, all pre-assembled elsewhere, in the single-piece cast-iron tub onto which production line workers bolted front axles and rear half-shafts. (The Executive Council retained the International name "for use on tractors supplied to foreign countries where the name International is preferred," possibly in response to the reinstitution of antitrust proceedings in July.)

Evolution continued, and on July 18, 1923, Milwaukee began producing "low-wheel, Orchard type" 15–30s, fitted with 12x42-inch rears and 6x28 front wheels and spark arresters in place of regular mufflers. The following May, the California Orchards inherited the Los Angeles-San Francisco vineyard fenders, and a note in the margin of Milwaukee Works Decision 1559 reported that the first tractor so built was TG-14894 on November 10. IHC offered solid rubber tires, 10x50 rear and 4x34 front, on French & Hecht wheels, available on January 19, 1928. The following September 4, for model year 1929, Ed Johnston signed off on the "increased power" 15–30, whose improvements were gained by enlarging engine bore from 4.5 to 4.75 inches and raising rated speed from 1,000 to 1,050 rpm. This increased power version rated output at 22–36 horsepower. The tractor designation remained 15–30 despite sales department efforts in mid-1930

to order "name plates, transfers, stencils and literature for the Model 22–36." However, their undated, handwritten Change Order Number 1926 was never signed, and the only 22–36s so badged were those for export. In that new configuration still under its old name, IHC offered its full line, including three orchard varieties, a "regular, California and Low Wheel" and Industrial 15–30s, later becoming Industrial 30s.

A similar pattern followed the smaller 10–20, first authorized for production at Tractor Works under Decision 631 on August 25, 1921. It too initially appeared as two prototypes, one with a channel frame and the other as a modular unit-frame construction, with identical test results. As with the 15–30, the 10–20 was a kerosene-burning gear-drive tractor, whose four-cylinder vertical engine measured 4.25x5-inch bore and stroke and ran at 1,000 rpm. From the first approval, it carried a power take-off from the transmission as standard equipment. On September 2, 1922, just in time for the first production run, the Naming Committee retitled the machine a McCormick-Deering for sales in the United States and Canada, while keeping the International trade name for foreign sales. Tractor Works reaffirmed manufacture approval, signed by its new manager, A. C. Snodgrass, on

One unique feature of the TracTracTor 10–20 was the twin "camel humps," the two domes which housed track brake and track clutch mechanisms that were necessary to slow tracks for turning. Because there are very few ways to make a crawler work, Caterpillar Inc. filed a patent infringement suit against IHC based on this model.

1927 Deering 10–20 with C.L.M. diesel
In February 1924, Tractor Works and the Executive Council agreed to provide 10–20 gear drive tractors to foreign markets, named either McCormick or Deering as requested. France's long-time agent, R. Wallut, requested Deering badging, and the first one for export was produced September 7, 1924.

December 29, 1922. Snodgrass authorized orchard versions, with similar mechanical changes as appeared on the 15–30 models, on October 13, 1923.

Name considerations reappeared once more in February 1924, when Tractor Works signed off on a decision "to furnish for the foreign trade 10–20 Gear Driven Tractors with the names McCormick or Deering," when requested. Margin notes reported that the first "Deering" tractor, Number 18594, was built September 7, 1924. Snodgrass, as Tractor Works' manager, approved a narrow-tread 10–20 on October 16, 1925. The overall 48-inch width over the rear wheels was 12 inches less than the regular production models, with the first, N T 501, assembled February 3, 1926.

This relatively orderly progression of prototype development, testing, eventual mass production, continued evolution, improvement and enhancement, was steady and deliberate. However, disorder, unsteadiness and improvisation followed a parallel path behind the scenes.

Both within and outside the confines of IHC's various plants and committees, experimentation continued almost ceaselessly. As early as 1900, John Steward and his young assistant, George Ellis, had devised a type of independent power take-off to provide forward travel as well as cutter power to the

Deering Auto-Mower destined for the 1900 Paris Exposition. Ed Johnston had done something similar for the McCormick Auto-Mower, but with the addition of a reverse gear and independent power take-off. (Although, of course, Deering's inability to operate its cutter independent of its reversible engine proved a liability.) The audiences during these demonstrations were huge.

Fifteen years before that, however, the English steam traction engine maker, Aveling & Porter, showed a chain-driven linkage run from the flywheel to a front-mounted Bell reaper, pushed ahead of the engine. Farm Implement News published a line-cut drawing, illustrating the rig, in its December 19, 1885, issue. Aveling & Porter apparently demonstrated the "Steam Reaper" at the 1878 Paris Universal Exposition.

Sometime after the Auto-Mowers were shown, in 1904 or 1905, still in France, grain harvest workers went on strike in the Brie region. Between the strikers' efforts to interrupt harvest and labor-sympathetic weather conditions, a large portion of the grain was knocked down, leaving fields of crops that the binders of that day could not salvage. According to Farm Implement News of February 12, 1931, an implement manufacturer from Auneau named Albert Gougis had devised a tractor "equipped with a connecting rod directly transmitting the power of the motor to the operating mechanism of the machine." (The machine being his McCormick grain binder.) The "connecting rod" was a shaft connected by two universal joints, a power-take-off shaft driving the binder. "After starting the motor, you first put in operation the reaper through the power take-off, then by engaging your clutch, you gradually start forward. In a difficult place of soft ground, you can change the speed of the tractor and as the reaper mechanism continues to run at the proper speed you overcome difficulties without trouble. In the event there is any clogging, you throw out the clutch, thereby stopping the tractor and as the reaper mechanism continues to operate it will clear itself in a moment."

According to historian Guy Fay, Gougis invited IHC officials, including Ed Johnston, to examine his tractor and his "independent" or "live" PTO system. Unfortunately for Gougis, another inventor recalled a pickup for traditional horse-drawn harvesting equipment that accomplished the job of handling the downed grain, resulting in an inexpensive attachment (about 35 francs, not quite $2) to existing equipment instead of the purchase of a Gougis tractor and shaft-driven binder (about 7,000 francs). Without further economic impetus to push development, the PTO idea stagnated until around 1917, when Bert Benjamin happened to think of it.

Bert R. Benjamin had graduated from Ames College in Iowa with a degree in mechanical engineering and went straight to work for McCormick Harvesting Machine in 1893 as a 23-year-old draftsman, working in the McCormick Works Experimental Department until 1899. He spent that year in manufacturing as chief inspector, before going back to experimental until early 1903, when he was reassigned to manufacturing, again as chief inspector. Then in 1910, he returned as superintendent of McCormick Works Experimental Department. Throughout the years, Benjamin specialized in implement design.

In September 1917, Benjamin was in Napanee, Indiana, watching three of his International four-horsepower "Binder Engines" harvest hemp, a product in great demand by the military for a variety of uses. A Titan 10–20 pulled one binder through medium hemp, 6 to 8 feet tall, four horses pulled another through similarly dense material and an eight-horsepower-rated Happy Farmer tractor pulled a third through 10-to-13-foot-tall hemp. Benjamin watched the harvest process and made observations in writing to IHC's General Office on September 27.

"The hemp dust and leaves interfere with the auxiliary engine (that powers the binder) in different ways, so there is probably about 25 percent to 30 percent loss of time from the complications of the outfit." In addition, in soft ground, the nose of the binder sunk under the weight of its four-horsepower engine.

"The tractors (operating ahead of the dust) are running with very slight loss of time, and the leaves and dust do not interfere with the power of the tractor." The time wasted cleaning the binder's radiators and air intakes and the duplication of fuel costs led Benjamin to some conclusions. He sized up the farm owner as someone capable of buying two or three more tractors and who would do so if the free-breathing tractor engine also drove the binder by power take-off shaft.

Nearly a year later, October 21, 1918, Benjamin's McCormick Works tested a prototype PTO, IHC's first, installed on another prototype machine, operating the cutter bar of a mower attachment and a sweep rake lift. It worked well enough to encourage the relatively orderly progression of prototype testing, production, evolution and improvement that IHC had done with so many other products: On March 29, 1919, Tractor Works Decision 451 authorized manufacture of the 50 PTO-equipped International 8–16s. Tractor Works listed it as an option on the International 15–30 on February 14, 1921, and finally, on August 3, Bert Benjamin's power take-off became standard equipment on the renamed McCormick-Deering 15–30 and new 10–20 as well.

Once Henry Ford had supplied something like 4,260 Fordsons to England's Ministry of Munitions, he felt he was able to begin production for American farmers around April 23, 1918. He still owed the English and Canadian governments 2,740 tractors, but he felt a strong desire for the same recognition at home that he had achieved abroad. In that vein, while the first 3,200 tractors left the United

War surplused thousands of them after the Armistice. Europe still needed food and cloth, and farmers, thinking the war-time economy would never end, expanded throughout 1919 and 1920.

During 1920, the USDA reported that 162,988 tractors were sold, the biggest year yet; 35 percent of these were Fordsons while 15 percent came from IHC. There were 229,334 farms using tractors that year, representing just 3.6 percent of all farms. To Ford (and the others), that meant the other 96.4 percent were potential customers. But in 1921, crop prices fell as European farms got back to work. Tractor production, except among a few firms, virtually stopped. By year end, manufacture dropped to just 35 percent of the peak reached during 1920. That January, Ford had cut his Fordson's price by $165. IHC followed during the spring and summer, dropping the $1,200 Titan 10–20 to $900. The $1,150 International 8–16 went to $900 and the 15–30 decreased from $2,300 to $1,750. General Motors entered the business through its Samson Tractor subsidiary, but by year end, Ford had sold half of the 34,000 tractors produced, IHC had sold one-quarter and GM's sales were nearly negligible.

Horses were still cheap, and crop prices remained low. During the winter, farmers repaired old equipment or sat on their hands. The market stagnated until February, when Ford, determined to keep his new Rouge tractor plant running, cut the Fordson price from $625 to $395. IHC followed, reducing the 8–16 another $230, and the Titan down to $700. To make his tractors look as good a bargain as Ford's, IHC President Alex Legge threw in either a plow or other implement. All the other manufacturers fell in line with industry-wide reductions averaging the same as Ford's $230.

These lower prices moved farmers off their hands. However, the late, very wet spring had even more impact. Farmers who had hoped to get fields seeded using horses were delayed so much that only tractors could get the fields worked in time to make a good harvest. In that same season, Ford made one of his few mistakes. Early in the year, he announced that his company would become a full-line producer, offering a complete assortment of Fordson implements. Within a few months he reversed the decision, letting dealers select for themselves the implements they sold. It left the Fordsons vulnerable to equipment mismatches that damaged their

Waukesha provided engines for the 15–30 until 1923 model year, when it also was renamed the McCormick-Deering 15–30. While designed at Tractor Works by Ed Johnston and his staff, the 15–30s were manufactured at Milwaukee. Vineyard, Orchard and "Special California Type" variations appeared as early as 1922 and on into 1923.

States with no identification on them, those that followed were stenciled with the machines builder's name.

His self-promotion ability galled the competition. IHC protested both to the Ministry of Munitions and to the U.S. government against Ford's proposal to be the official tractor of the war, to provide one standardized machine to the exclusion of all other manufacturers. They accused Ford of maneuvering public sentiments so as to ensure his own uninterrupted supply of ore and coke to make his steel.

All the publicity created a demand for the small Fords, a hunger that Ford planned to satisfy through State War Board allocations. But his own U.S. production got off to a slow start, and other manufacturers began to fill farmers' needs. Congress passed the Food and Fuel Control Act to regulate prices and guarantee minimums for all commodities. The winter of 1918–19 was mild, enabling farmers to work later in the fields in the fall and go in earlier the next spring. Those farmers with horses felt no need for tractors because of the luxury of good weather and plenty of time. Those without enough horses were soon surprised when the Department of

reputation. Yet it was GMC that quit first, in 1922, having "invested" $33 million in a business it had entered only to challenge Ford.

In 1923, Ford reached its peak, producing 101,898 tractors, capturing 76 percent of the market. It left 9 percent, 12,057 machines, to IHC. All the other 73 producers combined made up the remaining 15 percent. In 1924, Ford slipped slightly, to 70.9 percent, 83,010 tractors, while IHC grew to 16 percent, with 18,758 machines. Competitors failed rapidly and dozens ceased production during 1924 because they either produced inferior machines or made good equipment but could not afford the loss that Ford endured. Those who remained only garnered 14 percent of the total.

IHC dealers practiced aggressive salesmanship, seizing every Fordson demonstration as a chance to show how limited they were compared to the IHC tractors. This, and a still-suffering economy, further eroded Ford's market share in 1925. By year end, he'd still sold 64 percent of the annual production, but IHC had risen to one-fifth of the 164,097 produced. Ford chose to not improve or update his tractor, preferring only to get them into the hands of former horse farmers, "to ease the drudgery," he said. The Fordson revo-

lutionized farming, proving that a small, lightweight tractor could be mass produced and sold cheaply, and proving that it could replace the horse. IHC used the period of the World War and Ford's tractor war as a time of further experimentation. Only one of the efforts, a Motor Cultivator originating in 1915, did not succeed.

In 1927, the U.S. Supreme Court refused to reopen the Justice Department case against International Harvester, ending one of the two great challenges to the company's existence. Between January 1 and June 4, 1928, Henry Ford built barely 8,000 Fordsons in Dearborn. On that day, he ceased U.S. operations and transferred all Fordson tooling to Cork, Ireland. His aggregate production during 1927 and 1928 gave him 31 percent of the market. In 1927, IHC claimed an equal amount, and in 1928 the company claimed 62 percent of the business. That year, experiments that had been begun long before began paying off. IHC introduced its Trac-TracTors, crawlers based on the McCormick-Deering 15–30 and 10–20. Another experiment, dating back to the Mogul and evolving from the unsuccessful Motor Cultivator, was introduced in 1924, and sold 24,899 copies in 1928. It revolutionized farming as thoroughly as the Fordson. IHC's Farmall then went ahead and plowed Ford under.

1915–1932

Four

PRECARIOUS FAILURE AND SOLID SUCCESS

John Steward and Harry Waite had planted a seed together. Yet by the end of 1915, when it first bloomed, Steward was dead and Waite's own tractor company had failed. They had envisioned something capable of all the jobs routinely performed by horses, a concept encouraged in farm magazine editorials.

Steward's successor, Ed Johnston, and his assistant, David B. Baker, developed the general purpose Mogul. R. W. Burtis, another Tractor Works engineer, redesigned horse-drawn grain drills, harvesters and other implements to work behind the Mogul during 1915 and 1916. Still, the Mogul was too clumsy and bulky to do delicate, precise row crop cultivation.

While IHC didn't introduce this model as the "Regular," the tractor adopted that name once variations such as Narrow Tread and Fairway versions appeared. The arrival of the F-series made some differentiation necessary.

Even as Baker developed the Mogul, he helped Carl W. Mott, Philo H. Danly, John Anthony and Ed Johnston on something they all called the Motor Cultivator. They completed their first one in late 1915. Baker added a draw bar, believing that cultivating machines had possibilities beyond a single purpose.

Another fan of the Motor Cultivator was Bert Benjamin at McCormick Works. Benjamin liked multiuse machines and he appreciated the Motor Cultivator's simplicity. Raised on a farm, he did field work from age eight till he left Iowa, engineering degree in hand, to move to Chicago at 22. Benjamin's assignment at McCormick entailed adapting horse-drawn tools to power farming. He knew that behind a horse, these implements needed wheels to ease the load. But college had taught him to see how wheels might not be needed with tractor powers.

Tractor Works operators tested the Motor Cultivator through the summer of 1916 at an IHC farm in Aurora, Illinois. They kept it centered in

1918 Motor Cultivator

Primarily the work of David Baker, the Motor Cultivator first appeared at Tractor Works in 1915 when Baker, Carl Mott, Philo Danly and John Anthony completed the first one. Ed Johnston and Baker conceived the idea. because the Mogul 8–16 and 10–20 were not suitable for crop cultivation.

For experimental purposes, David Baker added a drawbar, believing even cultivating machines should do more than one task. Baker and Johnston specified a very popular four-cylinder LeRoi engine for power, mounting it directly over the drive wheel for traction.

the rows with foot levers that shifted the spindly front wheels. To turn, they released an engine lock and cranked the steering wheel. This rotated the entire engine, transmission, and drive wheel assembly.

The engine sat over the rear drive wheels, behind the operator's head. Mott and Baker learned that Motor Cultivators easily overturned on sidehills. The balance was top-heavy above the machine's narrowest point. They added weights to the front wheels as counter balances, which made pedal steering harder and less responsive. This was cut-and-try engineering, seat of the pants work, which was what Ed Johnston and David Baker knew best. Johnston, after grammar school, joined his family's harvester business at 14. He apprenticed in every department until he got to Johnston Harvesters experimental department. In 1894, he joined McCormick at age 24. Baker, a city boy with manufacturing experience, started at McCormick at 15. They both learned by doing and, when necessary, by redoing it.

Johnston's Motor Cultivator was the focus of many New Work Committee (NWC) meetings. Ed

One of the problems with the Motor Cultivator was its top-heaviness; its high-mounted LeRoi engine made the cultivator unstable. To counteract that, engineer David Baker tried a heavy cast crawler drive mechanism. *State Historical Society of Wisconsin*

Johnston somehow slipped it past exhaustive review procedures that IHC applied to subjected other projects. The sales department liked the idea and, based on past successful Johnston designs, argued that this one would work as well. The NWC ordered 300 from Tractor Works for 1917 after testing only two or three prototypes. Baker, Danly and Mott continued working as manufacture began. Tractor Works completed 58 by July, too late to be useful for the 1917 season. Sales halted production

At about the same time that Benjamin first mounted a corn picker on a wheel-type Motor Cultivator, Gas Power Engineering made progress in revising his Cultivating Tractor. This photograph, made in mid-November 1920, shows the "heavy" Farmall prototype, in which the front is now the narrow end. *State Historical Society of Wisconsin*

Eighteen months after the previous patent for a drawbar-equipped cultivator, the Heavy Farmall appears with its Power-lift (45) and early versions of steering brakes, 91, 92, 140, 141. It does not take much to imagine the side drawing with the seat reversed and the large steering gear, 134, elevated to protect it from impact if the machine worked the opposite direction.

Philo Danly, as Ed Johnston's collaborator with Bert Benjamin, produced this reversible Farmall in late 1921 and early 1922. With its engine mounted lower through the frame, its balance and maneuverability were greatly improved. However, power-lift remained, 115, as did steering brakes, 48.

This was Philo Danly's last "heavy" Farmall. By the time Henry Doolittle applied for this patent, Bert Benjamin's "light" Farmall was in prototype assembly. While this is still crude compared to what was finally produced, its compact size and extremely simple configuration were worth protecting.

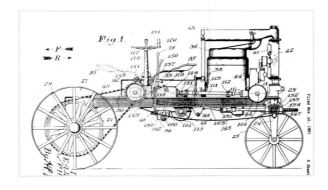

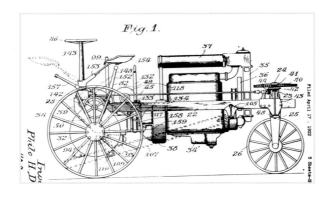

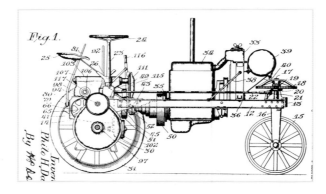

at 100 units; IHC shipped only 31. On August 22, the NWC ordered 300 more for 1918. Then, in early September, Addis McKinstry, IHC's vice president for sales, recalled 1917 models to Tractor Works. Baker and the others changed the engine's governor and cooling fan, and they refitted heavier, cast-iron front wheels.

For the first time, IHC had used customers for final testing. There was a reason. Johnston, neither stupid nor malicious, anticipated shortages in raw materials because of World War I in Europe. U.S. involvement was inevitable by 1917; IHC reasoned that keeping existing machines in production was

easier to justify than introducing a new one when rationing hit raw materials. Still, early buyers found the same problems as Baker and Mott: It was top heavy, prone to overturn, its LeRoi engine was underpowered, and it was geared to move too slowly. This put Baker in a difficult position. A more powerful engine would add weight where they least wanted it, further jeopardizing its balance.

Henry Ford also influenced fate in 1917. As he readied Fordson production for American farmers, he wanted implements. Ford considered draft horses his real competition, so he asked IHC for advice. Alexander Legge, directing the U.S. War Production Board, seized the mutual opportunity. He sent Bert Benjamin to Dearborn, loaning his Deering Works chief to Ford until mid-1917. Benjamin helped change to Fordsons to use McCormick-Deering equipment and designed a Fordson line of implements.

Back in Chicago in late 1917, he invented a kit to make Fordsons into cultivating tractors. Then Ford dropped plans for implements, leaving selection to his dealers. This was frosting on the cake; Benjamin had studied Ford's assembly line production and its high-speed automotive-type engines, both of interest to Legge. Now IHC would sell implements to Ford dealers too. Progress on the Motor Cultivator idled in place.

Sales liked the Motor Cultivator, but manufacturing didn't. McKinstry's sales staff always wanted the next new thing. As the economy tightened, manufacturing's Harry Utley endorsed a two-tractor, large-and-small-machine plan. The Motor Cultivator's priority dropped to third. Utley, resistant, never created enough tooling to meet a 300-machine order (issued with options to add 200 if all 500 were completed by late February 1918.) The 1918 machines incorporated the changes retrofitted to 1917s, allowing higher engine speeds without overheating.

The new model, with more parts of cast-iron, weighed 3,400 pounds (instead of 2,200) with a PTO, a belt pulley, and hitch, each an element of IHC's new "Triple Power Plan." Mott, Danly, Baker, and Anthony tested mowers and a sweep rake lift mounted on units without cultivating blades. Mott experimented with a crawler drive in early summer, to improve traction but also to lower the center of gravity. It added too much weight and the NWC retired the idea after a few prototypes. Tractor Works completed 160 by July 15, ending the year at exactly 301, including the 1917-rebuilds.

This slack pace resulted from steel shortages during World War I; the government allowed manufacturers 75 percent of 1917 quantities. It didn't review allocations until December 1918. On August 22, about 10 weeks before the Armistice, the NWC reduced production for 1919, knowing IHC would get less steel. McKinstry calculated that it cost $500 to build each cultivator, plus transportation, commissions, sales costs and overhead. (This hurt; six-cylinder Avery two-row Motor Cultivators sold to the public for $540, and GMC's Samson Iron Horses cost $450.)

A week later, IHC canceled 1919 production altogether. It delivered 213 in 1918 (67 left-over 1917s redone as 1918s) and 84 in 1919. The last 62 sold for $450 through mid-July, 1920. The final report, written charitably toward Johnston and Tractor Works, judged the Motor Cultivator "could not be produced at a cost which it was estimated the farmer would pay."

In response to Alex Legge's request on February 10, 1922, for a "cheap tractor," Benjamin, Danly and Baker quickly responded with a very quick, crude construction. Yet in demonstrations at Hinsdale on June 24 and 25, this homespun prototype turned the tide. On July 29, just 10 days after this prototype was photographed, the large Farmall died. *State Historical Society of Wisconsin*

Shorter, lighter and better balanced, this early 1922 Farmall prototype is not yet the "lightweight" Farmall, but it shows steps in that direction. Ed Johnston assigned Philo Danly to work with Benjamin. Danly, expected to report to Johnston all of Bert's ideas, took his job with Benjamin very seriously. *State Historical Society of Wisconsin*

machine as well, for cultivation. Benjamin's efforts to mount shaft-driven implements on Johnston's Motor Cultivator, however, only emphasized its mechanical failures. As C. W. Gray wrote in a 1932 internal tractor history, "This attempt illustrates [how far we went] to fit attachments to a tractor not fundamentally suited to receive them." Benjamin's efforts to mount shaft-driven implements on Ed Johnston's Motor Cultivator emphasized its mechanical failures.

Others manufacturers offered machines representing less compromise and better value. Traylor Engineering sold its 6–12 tractor for $750, with the same four-cylinder LeRoi engine. The Traylor 6–12, a traditional four-wheel configuration, could cultivate and plow. Its tools hung under the center, as with the Steward-Waite tractor and the Hackney Auto Plow.

On June 11 and 12, 1919, Johnston took Motor Cultivators to Blue Mound, Illinois, for the first strictly cultivator show in the corn belt. Avery, Moline, and Allis-Chalmers showed machines, along with an Emerson-Brantingham prototype. J. I. Case Plow Works introduced a rail-frame 12-horsepower cultivator with two tall drive wheels at the rear, steered by a single wheel in front, engine and cultivators in the middle. Case offered it only

1923 Farmall Prototype
By the time Bert Benjamin's idea reached this stage, his concept of a "Combined Tractor Truck" had evolved many times into the Farmall. It was Alex Legge who said that no matter what it did, "it must at least look like a tractor."

Bert Benjamin was primarily an implement designer. His Farmall project grew out of early changes in David Baker's Motor Cultivator. Once Baker and Ed Johnston moved the engine off the single drive wheel, it stabilized their machine. But it still drove backwards, that is, facing this direction.

Cost and selling price were crucial, and would remain deciding policy factors throughout the history of the company. In 1920, IHC wanted farmers to buy not only a "general purpose" tractor (large or small) for plowing and harvesting but a second

in mid-1919. Far lighter than a unit-frame Wallis Cub, it suggested a new direction in machinery design.

In his memo to Alex Legge on July 27, 1916, Bert Benjamin described "the next step toward getting considerably more production from one operator." That step came in the form of IHC's next tractor innovation, called the "Farmall."

Benjamin had envisioned a highly adaptable "Combined Tractor Truck" of two-to-four-ton capacity, powered by a 15-to-25-horsepower kerosene engine. It would carry "a combined harvester-thresher, power direct from engine, with speed independent of the tractor, could carry and operate a grain binder and shocker, a corn picking device with a box for loads, a hay loader and rack for hauling hay, or a water tank, pump and sprinkler device for fire protection on the farm."

Benjamin described something fanciful. Alex Legge was more practical. He insisted that whatever this "next step" did, it "must at least look like a tractor." The conservative Scot understood that Midwest farmers might shy away from something that looked too different from their expectations.

Mott and Johnston dropped the 1919 crawler drive and, in early 1920, they reoriented the engine to the direction of travel and moved it slightly forward on the frame. This immediately improved the balance. They left the narrow-end rear wheel to do the steering but, using a differential with sprockets and chains, they drove front wheels converted to tractor wheels. They introduced the automatic differential brake. Benjamin set cultivators closer to the single steerable wheel since the larger wheels no longer swiveled. In NWC reports, they referred to this as the "Cultivating Tractor." In late 1919, Johnston, seeking to better differentiate this latest version, asked for ideas on a new name. Ed Kimbark suggested "Farm-All," recorded in the November 10 Tractor Works records. By early 1920, this became the Farmall.

Benjamin nearly had completed his long-term study of farming methods and implement design. He took his research and ideas to Tractor Works. Johnston assigned Philo Danly, Mott, Baker and Anthony to design tractors for Benjamin's new implements. Danly, serving as Johnston's eyes and ears on the project, took his assignment seriously

and developed machines that met Benjamin's goals. One, designed with David Baker, used a Waukesha engine fitted with a reversible operator's seat and a transmission with three speeds forward and three reverse.

These new ideas got little support. Johnston was too busy developing the International 15–30 and 10–20 gear drives to support the sales department's Two Tractor Program. IHC still had a 12-25 in the works and research was under way on updated steam tractors. The ongoing agricultural depression, slow sales, and Motor Cultivator losses left little money to hand-build more than two prototypes and test them with their own implements. (The Model A Farmall, using an L-head truck engine from Akron, appeared around February 7, 1920; the Model B arrived June 30, using a new engine that carried through to production.)

Benjamin campaigned for the reversible Farm-All. He wrote Legge on October 15, 1920, that prototypes performed 11 separate farm operations using a single operator. He adopted automotive-type

By late 1919, Tractor Works, assigned to work on this project, referred to it as the Cultivating Tractor. Ed Kimbark, Engineering Department secretary, named it the Farm-All on November 10, 1919, and within a couple months, it became the Farmall.

1924 Farmall Regular

One big concern with the Farmall was how it would affect sales of 10–20 Gear Drive tractors. In Texas, the Houston branch manager told IHC if the company didn't build the tractor, he'd find backers and produce it himself.

engines from 8–16s, pricing his machine at $900, even though the International 8–16 (at $1,000) did only four tasks, with one individual (horse teams would have to plant corn, cultivate fields, and do the other jobs.) Benjamin filmed a demonstration, running the Danly/Baker prototype in both directions at IHC's Hinsdale, Illinois, test farm, and showed the film at the December 13 NWC meeting. The audience included Cyrus Jr. and Harold F. McCormick, Legge, McKinstry from sales, Utley from manufacturing, Johnston and three Chicago office sales managers, J. G. Wood, J. A. Everson and J. F. Jones.

Following the film, Johnston, surprisingly, announced support for the Farmall. "Farm power, increasing production per man," he said, "was the coming thing in agriculture industry." Harry Utley disagreed: While he liked the PTO, he felt the machine and its special implements were too heavy, complicated and expensive. He didn't believe all-

purpose machines even were desired. Farmers wouldn't sacrifice good equipment to switch.

Johnston warned that running a modest experimental program, to build five tractors and implement sets by hand, would cost $150,000 to $300,000. Knowing that doubling the tractors would not double the costs, he advocated enlarging the test fleet. J. F. Jones, the Chicago office sales manager who would become the Farmall's arch foe, felt that farmers wouldn't take to it because it was "built on exactly the wrong lines." He suggested replacing it with something heavier. McKinstry, still doubtful, supported adding five more prototypes because "having gone so far, we should not abandon the program."

Legge remained neutral. He operated a farm about two miles north of the Hinsdale facility. He and fellow "hobby farmers" Harold and Cyrus McCormick recognized the Farmall's value. Still, cash was tight; the 12–25 and the steam tractor

By September 1924, Ed Johnston's Tractor Works had turned out 205 of Bert Benjamin's general purpose tractor. Johnston had not favored the tractor, partly because his Tractor Works had enough other work to do, and partly because it wasn't his own idea.

claimed development funds. IHC remained at war with Ford, and after the Motor Cultivator, the only way the McCormicks could support this program was slowly and from deep in the shadows.

Benjamin became an apostle. He wrote letters, he cornered anyone he encountered with any influence. He converted Johnston's staff to the machine, its implements and the work it could accomplish.

Around Christmas one of Benjamin's engineers, C. A. Hagadone at McCormick Works, sketched a lighter-weight version of the Farmall at about half the 4,000-pound approved model. On January 21, 1921, the NWC canceled the five heavy prototypes and ordered "two of the modified, lightened Farmalls." This was the first time Ed Kimbark's Farmall name appeared in official IHC papers.

The lightweight Farmall provoked several changes. It ran in one direction only, steering in front; two powered wheels pushed from the rear. By May 1921, Tractor Works enclosed final drive housings and moved cultivators to straddle the single front wheel. This allowed farmers to rapidly adjust steering, to cultivate without damaging crops within the contours of a row. Engineer Arnold Johnson, working with Benjamin on implements, called this enhanced "dodging facility" a turning point, telling C. W. Gray that engineers were never "enthusiastic about the manner of connecting various attachments, but when they saw the cultivator on the front of the tractor they felt at last they were on the right track." Still, McKinstry's sales department found nothing in this new, fast tractor that it could sell as an advantage over horses.

Throughout 1921, Benjamin kept looking. He sent Harry Utley an outline of costs, overhead, expenses and income for a farmer operating a 160-acre hog farm. Replacing horses with a Farmall turned feed lands into cash crops. Benjamin calculated a net income of $3,500 versus $3,000 if farmers with a Fordson still needed six or eight horses for functions Farmalls could serve. Legge circulated this letter around the Executive Council, whose members already called the Farmall "Benjamin's tractor." Bert didn't stop there. His time at Ford gave him his next load of ammunition.

"Take a Fordson," he wrote to Legge in late May, "combine the front two wheels into one so it will go between rows, raise the rear axle, and set the wheels out to straddle the rows, we will then have, first, the plowing outfit, second, a cultivator. This

1927 Fairway

The first Fairway models used what were essentially standard steel front wheels without the guide rim. These were too narrow and cut into the lawns they were meant to protect, leading Tractor Works to devise these wheels, nearly 50 percent wider.

can be sold to farmers for $700 . . . Either this company or Ford will soon be putting out [this] modified form. It seems important that Ford does not take the lead . . ."

During June and July, Legge held two NWC meetings to consider Fordson and Farmall developments. (While 186 companies claimed to be tractor manufacturers in 1921, and 97 actually produced at least one, IHC considered Ford its only competition.) For the first time, Legge called various departments on the carpet for foot-dragging. While McKinstry was a Johnston loyalist, sales cared little for this new machine and never attended field tests to see farmers' reactions to the prototypes. Johnston, criticized for engineering's slow development of new implements for the Farmall, deflected accusations to the Executive Council for failing to make final design decisions. Utley replied that initially he'd had little faith in the project, because McKinstry and sales showed no interest. McKinstry reiterated that his regional managers felt farmers wouldn't accept anything that forced them to re-equip completely.

Legge listened patiently, waiting till the close of the July 21, 1921, session to speak: Farmall implement development would continue at McCormick Works. Other implements for International 8–16 and International 12–25 tractors (in development) would come from Deering Works. Tractor Works would expand development to 100 Farmall prototypes for 1922. Seemingly resolved, the issue broke open again on August 26. Utley pointed out that "the new cultivating devices to go on the Farmall tractor change the machines so materially that he favored having a single Farmall tractor brought out and approved before building 100 of these." The council murmured pleasurably: The farm depression still dampened sales, and Ford's price war had hurt income. But now, two Farmall champions, the McCormicks, moved in the shadows and in late December, Legge ordered manufacture of 20 Farmalls with mowers, corn planters and several other tools.

Bert Benjamin believed he still was swimming against the tide. In fact, by the end of 1921 the flow was shifting into his favor. IHC's Executive Council, and its manufacturing and sales managers were coming around. Only Ed Johnston resumed a wary posture. His motivation was basic: The Farmall was not his, but came from an implements division engineer who stepped into Tractor Work's territory. Development money for Farmall projects did not go to him. Johnston knew there was little wrong with the idea. The McCormicks, Legge, and now Utley and McKinstry all liked the idea, but they felt the real thing was not quite ready for production.

On February 10, 1922, Alex Legge reconvened the Special Tractor Conference' to discuss "the feasibility of bringing out a cheap tractor." The battle with Ford was at full pitch. Benjamin proposed IHC fight back by reducing Farmall power and weight. Naysayer J. F. Jones still saw no value in any Farmall, heavy, light, or now, cheap. He urged Tractor Works to find ways to "bring the cost of the new 10–20 tractor down as much as possible."

Benjamin prevailed. The defense held again that with so much spent so far, the committee should build "one or two more tractors along the lines [Benjamin] proposed and then determine the merits" of his light Farmall.

Still he did not rest. He, Danly and Baker continued to improve their design, sending drawings to Henry P. Doolittle, IHC's general patent attorney, to protect the work. Benjamin even tried to sell Doolittle.

"Time saved in cutting grain with a Farmall," he wrote, "was 12 1/2 percent, or one hour in eight, by turning square corners at full speed, avoiding loss of time in turning, and because a smaller headland was required."

Acknowledging its belief in Legge's support of Benjamin's tractor, IHC's directors unanimously elected him president on June 2. (Harold F. McCormick became chairman of the board. McKinstry became president of IHC of America, the sales arm of IHC.) Legge, irked by poor prototype quality, wrote Harry Utley on June 23, 1922, accusing manufacturing of undermining Farmall development. "About the only thing we have demonstrated so far is that we have done a very poor job in putting Farmall prototypes together, which suggests that you should strengthen your engineering staff to the extent that you avoid letting out into the field things that have to be rebuilt."

On June 24, Legge went to Hinsdale to watch Benjamin's light, cheap Farmall, and the next day, even before the Executive Council meeting ended, Utley left for Hinsdale himself. What they saw converted them both. Benjamin's new machine, lighter by 800 pounds, no longer was reversible. It provided three forward speeds but only one reverse. While the differential and turning brake mechanisms carried over, Danly, Anthony and Mott completely changed the steering and pushed the cultivators to the front of the tractor. At the next NWC meeting, July 29, the large Farmall model was abandoned. They stopped funding the 20 prototypes (one of which had worked at Utley's Downers Grove farm since May 4. Fifteen of the 20 were returned to Tractor Works and scrapped. Utley's tractor (No. Q291) one Hinsdale prototype (No. Q209) and three others disappeared in record keeping.)

Addis McKinstry, J. F. Jones and the rest of the New Work Committee visited Hinsdale throughout early August, each returning to Chicago converted to Benjamin's tractor. At the August 30 meeting, Jones announced, "This was the first time that I would vote to proceed with the development." Only Johnston discounted Benjamin's advances, assuming the critic's role that Jones had abdicated. Johnston argued, "The Farmall must have power

Fairway models appeared almost immediately—some developed with their characteristic flat, wide wheels—out of the initial 205 tractor production run of 1924. By 1927, tall vertical exhaust and intakes had disappeared.

1929 Farmall Regular

The University of Nebraska tested its first Farmall in mid-September 1925. It was, as C. H. Wendel described it, the first true row-crop tractor to be tested there. Months earlier, in a move to help cash-strapped farmers buy its tractors, IHC had accepted a row crop—corn at $1 a bushel—in exchange for equipment.

enough to pull two 12-inch bottoms. This machine could not weigh less than 3,000 pounds, and may run higher. The cost of a smaller Farmall would be so near the larger Farmall that the price would make the small model uncommercial." No one agreed.

On September 14, McKinstry proposed assembling two more lightweight prototypes with implements to set final performance and appearance characteristics "prior to starting manufacture." The committee agreed and at the same time killed further research and development on other motorized cultivators, the steam tractor prototypes and the general purpose 12–25.

These radical changes in attitudes came about not only because Benjamin's lightweight "cheap" Farmalls impressed his challengers. Early in the summer of 1922, Bert Benjamin's battles with Ed Johnston came to a head. Johnston's failure with the implement-inspired Motor Cultivator contrasted harshly against implement engineer Benjamin's success with his Farmall.

C. W. Gray's history of the Farmall, written at the Executive Council's request, avoided the politics and dramas of 1922 that he otherwise discussed in other years. His draft version and later "sanitized" editions betray no secrets. He mentions "grapevine

information that sometime during 1922 Mr. Benjamin issued an ultimatum that he must be given free rein." Or he would quit.

It's not unreasonable to imagine that Benjamin, worn out from battling committee and engineering chiefs, contacted Henry Ford through Gene Farkas and Joe Galamb, with whom he'd worked five years earlier devising Fordson implements at Dearborn. (There is no evidence in either IHC nor Ford archives to confirm this, however.) But even if Ford never offered a job, even if they never spoke, Benjamin had only to hint to Legge such a possibility. Cyrus Jr. and Harold McCormick would have done anything to keep him from Dearborn, as they did when they named Benjamin assistant to the chief engineer of International Harvester Corporation, overseeing all further Farmall development. The balance of power in engineering shifted during the summer of 1922.

In late February 1923, Legge told the Executive Council that Benjamin's tractor came closer than ever to meeting the ideas and answering the objections of everyone who had a say. He solicited opinions as IHC prepared a final testing run in 1923. He reminded council members that Tractor Works already had its hands full producing the new 10–20 Gear Drive model. Benjamin's Farmalls, he explained, would come from Johnson's Engineering Department, made by hand, as previous models were done. His implication was clear.

Legge and the group unanimously approved making 25 of the tractors, with "no radical departures to be made in design." A chastened Ed Johnston promised that engineering department production would begin in mid-May and be completed by early September.

He and Legge calculated mass-production costs and found it was nearly the same as the 10–20 Gear Drive. Legge ordered Johnston to stop experimenting with other final drive systems so they could set Farmall specifications. Legge needed sales and manufacturing to determine prices and promotional methods of the tractor, which got its "Farmall" trademark registration in Washington on July 17, 1923.

Johnston completed 26 models long before his deadline and by August 9th, they were working. Four remained at Hinsdale, one went to Cyrus Jr.'s farm in Wheaton and another to Utley's in Downers Grove. Thirteen were shipped to branch houses for evaluation by farmers in Georgia, Mississippi, Tennessee, Texas and Wisconsin. Almost without exception the results were good and the tractors held together. Reports to Legge said it had "plenty of power," and "splendid ground-gripping qualities." Benjamin interviewed operators on the Durham Farm in Wayne, Illinois, where one hand told him: "In cultivating young corn four or five inches high, we can do a better job with the Farmall because it handles so easy that practically all our time is utilized watching the cultivator shovels. With a two-row cultivator pulled by three horses, we pay so much attention to the horses that we cannot do a good job cultivating."

On October 9, McKinstry recommended Utley's department produce 100 Farmalls for 1924, presenting both his confidence in the machine and reservation about how the Farmall would affect 10–20 Gear Drive sales. Legge and Johnston, encouraged by the reaction among southern testers for the Farmall, advocated higher production even though they worried about its appearance. While it did "at least look like a tractor," it was not attractive. A cotton farmer from Texas who owned two put it concisely: "It's homely as the devil, but if you don't want to buy one you better stay off the seat."

Tractors authorized for 1924 production gained improvements including increased rear axle diameter, starting gears of steel, main frames of rolled tubing and strengthened bull gear housings. Tractor Works also enlarged kerosene fuel tanks to 13 gallons.

Selling for $825, IHC lost substantial sums on these early machines because these tractors were hand built. The company accepted these losses, however, as introductory and promotional expenses. In late February 1924, the NWC and Executive Council, still moving cautiously, ordered 200 Farmalls built to expand testing. On leap year, February 29, Tractor Works shipped QC-501 to Taft, Texas. Soon after, Benjamin sent the owner the first "skeleton" wheels, open metal frameworks soon known as Texas wheels.

Benjamin spent two weeks with 501 in Taft. The owner asked him for a four-row cultivator and, working with a local blacksmith, Benjamin fabricated a prototype. The owner called in his neigh-

bors to watch as he covered 100 acres in 14.5 hours compared to 18 acres the previous 10-hour day with his original two-row cultivator. Benjamin took plans to McCormick Works for production for South Texas cotton farming.

By September, Tractor Works turned out 205 of Benjamin's tractors and improved, strengthened, modified, or revised 16 more features, ranging from simplifying the steering gear, to fitting a muffler in place of the overhead exhaust pipe, to simplifying the gear shift, and further strengthening the transmission case. When J. F. Jones, proposing manufacture of 300, questioned one more time the effect of the Farmall on 10–20 Gear Drive sales, it was Ed Johnston who answered him.

"There has been a constant cry for a tractor to meet Ford's," said Johnston. "It is impossible to meet Ford on price, therefore, we have to produce something of greater utility to justify our price. The Farmall will do this. If the Farmall is the tractor that will kill the 10–20, it would be far better if we ourselves kill it."

NWC and the council agreed to produce 250. Dealers in some branches were told to not promote the new machine but to push 10–20s and 15–30s, delivering Farmalls only when buyers insisted;

1929 Badger Shovel on Farmall Regular

Very few references exist for Industrial Regulars, but a series of IT serial numbers appearing in 1929 and showing up on machines like this Badger Shovel lend credence to the idea that Tractor Works produced, for at least one year, an industrial version.

branches in other areas were told they could not get one at all. In the cotton-growing south, McKinstry's staff encouraged sales.

Legge put this strategy in perspective: "The Farmall was going into the cotton states," he said, "and if we did not push it elsewhere, there was little danger of hurting 10–20 sales. On the other hand, it would pick up business that we had never had."

During the Executive Council meeting on March 21, 1925, Benjamin continued sparring with J. F. Jones, offering another cost analysis. He'd examined cotton production with mules at $110 a bale against $83 a bale with the Farmall. "You see that operating by Farmall makes it possible to save the crop for the United States instead of losing it to Egypt, southern Russia, India, the Argentine . . . producing there with cheap labor at $95 a bale." In April, J. F. Jones went to Texas to see for himself.

Outside of San Angelo, he watched a demonstration with P. Y. Timmons, manager of tractor sales; Jim Ryan, Houston branch manager; Joe Foley, Dallas manager; Guy Fisk, Amarillo branch manager; several implement engineers; and Bert

Machines like that had to be the inspiration for subsequent government regulators such as the Occupational Safety and Health Administration (OSHA). Exposed chains, shafts and tracks surrounded the operator.

Benjamin. As the afternoon wound down, the group began discussing the Farmall. Timmons repeated J. F. Jones' concern that it might adversely affect 10–20 sales. Fisk, Foley and Ryan agreed they "had little use for 10–20s in cotton country. They were not adaptable to all row crop operations."

Jim Ryan didn't hesitate: "If you don't adopt it for production, we'll organize a company in Houston and build it down here." Jones, parroting Ed Johnston's comments to him eight months before, announced that "if anyone was going to build a tractor that would affect the sale of the 10–20, let's do it ourselves." An official photo taken at the demonstration showed Jones near the planters towed behind the tractor. Benjamin, at the engine, stood a long way away.

On May 5, Jones stressed the need to have 1,000 Farmalls ready by the end of October. Within a month, the number increased to 1,500 and at the end of July, McKinstry added another 1,000 to the plan for 1926. Good crop harvests in 1924 made farmers ambitious over the winter, increasing demand for the 10–20 and 15–30 models and creating interest in the Farmall. In September, the council ordered Tractor Works to solve the two chronic Farmall complaints about broken studs on the differential and troubles with the steering. These were significant, because IHC was ready to begin full production.

Just as IHC committed fully to the Farmall with a big production run, corn prices dropped, due to crop surpluses. In late winter 1925, IHC began to accept corn, valued at $1 per bushel, in exchange for farm equipment. By May, prices rose. The Executive Council, preoccupied with a Justice Department appeal to the U.S. Supreme Court to reopen the 1912 antitrust suit, dropped the corn program.

On March 19, 1926, Utley reported to the Executive Council that Tractor Works produced eight Farmalls a day, having met outstanding orders for 1,708 tractors. IHC priced them $100 above 10–20s to emphasize their greater potential. The build order climbed to 2,954, and Utley expected daily production to reach 15 by July 1.

IHC could make this jump because in June 1925, it opened the Farmall Works. It acquired this facility, in Rock Island, Illinois, in 1924 from Moline Plow Works; it had been its tractor plant.

Legge told McKinstry to "make no larger capital expenditures at Tractor Works to increase production on the 10–20, but proceed at once with the development of the Rock Island plant layout for floor space for an output of 100 a day." McKinstry reported that to equip Rock Island to produce 50 per day would cost $2.45 million. Legge hesitated, feeling this was too large an expense. There was still some doubt, as if IHC's Executive Council was hesitant to push the success, feeling it prudent to conserve IHC's resources and preserve its reputation, should the Farmall unexpectedly fail as the Motor Cultivator had done.

By November 5, 1926, near the end of another record crop harvest, Rock Island settled at 20 to 25 per day. Threshing had begun throughout the Midwest when hard rains and high winds hit in storms lasting days. Harvesting and threshing stopped, fields flooded, and unharvested grain shocks and bundled stacks sprouted. Some states' grain harvests were entirely ruined. Crop prices slipped rather than rising from destroyed supplies; predictably, tractor sales fell. While U.S. makers produced 178,074 tractors in 1926, they sold only 122,940 (46,441 as exports); 4,430 of the U.S. sales were Farmalls. McKinstry estimated 1927 would reach 6,600, while district sales managers felt 7,500 was more realistic. Legge wondered aloud if IHC should "get up our courage and perhaps go to a bigger schedule." He took the gamble and guessed right: Rock Island manufactured 9,502 throughout 1927.

Tractor Works introduced a narrow-tread model for export on May 5, 1927, just as Rock Island production reached 35 a day. (In fact, more of these went to the southeastern United States than overseas.) Before the end of June, the Supreme Court denied the Justice Department's final appeal. IHC was freed to return its full attention to business. In March 1928, just after the Executive Council learned that the Oliver Farm Equipment Company had two cultivating tractors testing near Corpus Christi, Cyrus Jr. predicted Farmall production at Rock Island would reach 125 per day by June 1. The Works met his goal on June 4, even as Alex Legge reminded Cyrus Jr. of continuing complaints of breakages of transmission cases and front axles.

Legge's prescription was drastic. Believing the problem lay in manufacture, not design, he threatened to shut down Farmall Works until manufac-turing guaranteed the strength and quality of its products. Ed Johnston hurriedly developed malleable steel castings, and put 100 of them out for tests, particularly to watch the permanence of the mounting bolts and those that held the halves together. Johnston also re-engineered the front bolster, with stronger versions introduced in mid-July 1928.

Production for 1928 reached 24,899 Farmalls, 35,517 in 1929, then 42,093 in 1930, (with daily production runs reaching 200 on January 27, 1930). As the U.S. Census released figures counting 920,378 tractors on farms, IHC celebrated on April 12, when Rock Island's Farmall Works completed manufacture of the 100,000th copy of Benjamin's tractor. (Within two months, the corporation celebrated again as the 200,000th Johnston 10-20 Gear Drive, with Cyrus McCormick Jr. at the wheel, rolled out of Tractor Works.)

But in 1931, the agricultural depression, made worse by a long drought in 1930 that destroyed crops, caught up with what began on Wall Street in October 1929. Farmall sales collapsed by two-thirds, to 14,093 for the year. (Competition fell away too; where there had been 186 registered tractor makers in 1921, in 1929, there remained 33.)

IHC, and in particular its 200,000 gear-drive 10–20s, defeated Henry Ford even as it learned from him. Ford returned, importing some 1,500 Fordsons a month from Cork, Ireland, starting in November 1929. IHC staked its claim as the dominant tractor maker in North America. However, other farm equipment makers were not standing by idly.

Benjamin and Johnston, ever perceptive, recognized the trends for both smaller and larger machines. As the January 9, 1930, issue of Farm Implement News reported, "Three-plow standard type tractors have added to their stature because the Great Plains wheat farmers discovered that they could handle another 100 acres or so with wheatland disk plows, duck-foot cultivators, rotary rod weeders, and combines, if their three-plow tractors only had enough more power to pull an extra foot or two of disk or to carry the combine up slopes."

In early 1930, projects began to appear around Gas Power Engineering, referred to in NWC notes and Executive Council minutes as the "Increased Power Program." These weren't describing changes forced onto 10-year-old 15–30s and 10–20s.

1930–1935

Five

THE LINES EXPAND . . . AND INTERMINGLE

"*Progress*," Ed Johnston explained to the Executive Council, "has put our competitors in a position to increase the horsepower for the size of engine and to improve the fuel consumption. We are suffering in the trade." He urged adoption of a program to produce a more powerful Farmall, and even a smaller one. By January 11, 1930, that project was named the Increased Power Program.

Johnston found himself preaching to the converted. Council members promptly approved three sizes, counting the current Farmall and the proposed increased power Farmall as one. The

1930 Increased Power Farmall

The Executive Council approved an Increased Power Program on January 11, 1930. With these prototypes, Johnston tested cambered front wheels and the duck-billed steering column that appeared in production in 1932.

second was the intermediate Farmall, powered with an increased power engine for the 10–20 tractor. (Johnston gained approval to build two of these.) Third was the large Farmall, to be powered by the increased horsepower 15–30 tractor engine, later referred to as the F-40.

The "increased" power came through from a new head, intake manifold, and piston design without changing bore or stroke. The engine also would use a water pump with a more effective thermostatic control. Johnston would strengthen frames as well. Some Industrial Model 20s in Europe had broken; to him, increased power meant an improved tractor. In August, he created a wide tread for the Farmall, from 10–20 parts, for crops around San Francisco.

The Gas Power Engineering Department (GPED) experimental shops worked long days. Carl Mott, Philo Danly and Gus Engstrom turned out new engines and strengthened unit frames on IHC's wheel tractors. David Baker received two increased-power 15–30 engines

Johnston's staff increased power by designing a new cylinder head, intake manifold, and pistons, yet didn't change bore, stroke, or engine speed. He also adopted a water pump to better cool the engine, strengthened the frame, and placed the gas tank inside the larger fuel tank.

and frames, and built Model 30 TracTracTor prototypes. On September 15, NWC approved five more. Baker produced two industrial wheel-type prototypes derived from the Model 15 crawler, and the committee approved pilot programs of five more crawlers and industrials in early October. Two weeks later, October 23, the programs grew to 50 each.

Johnson's dictum that increased power meant improved tractors became a goal throughout GPED. He, Baker and the entire engineering department pushed for ball bearings in all moving parts. Based on experiences with the Farmall, and the No. 20 TracTracTor, tighter tolerances for seals gave longer lives for rolling surfaces. Baker informed the committee these changes added $10 to the cost of each 10–20 and $15 to the 15–30 (referred to internally as the 22–36.) On this tractor, he added, the bull pinion and bevel gear assemblies gave trouble, because close tolerances were not possible with taper roller bearings.

Alex Legge, asked by President Herbert Hoover to help stabilize farmers' market prices, resigned from IHC's presidency (though he remained on its board) to head the Federal Farm Board in June 1929. Legge occasionally returned to Chicago for meetings of particular interest to him, especially as efforts in Washington failed to make progress.

On December 1, 1930, Alex Legge defined the experimental Farmalls in terms farmers understood. The increased power model would handle two plows, the intermediate (powered by the improved 10–20) was three plows and the large (15–30) Farmall was for four. Then he wondered if the power increase was enough. David Baker idly suggested fitting four-speed transmissions into large and intermediate models while dropping the two-plow original. John L. McCaffrey, IHC's 38-year-old assistant manager of domestic sales, and new to the NWC meetings, disagreed, saying that his boss, Maurice F. Holahan, manager of domestic sales, "felt we should put out the increased power Farmalls only at this time." The NWC immediately began to build 25 increased power models and 25 intermediate Farmalls.

On February 12, 1931, the NWC Tractor Sub-Committee first discussed strategy for dropping the

increased power 22–36. Its replacement, the W-40, would use the latest 49-horsepower engine. The 22–36 (still in catalogs as the 15–30,) cost IHC $825 to manufacture. With 20 percent more horsepower but only 8 percent more weight (roughly 400 pounds), manufacturing added about $40 to the cost. Baker and Leonard Sperry built 10 preproduction W-40s and sent them to the branches at Houston, Little Rock, San Francisco, Amarillo, Salina, and Jacksonville. Two remained at Hinsdale.

Two weeks later the Naming Committee gave final designations to the increased power Farmalls,

referring to the two-plow model as the F-20, the intermediate as the F-30 and the large Farmall as the F-40. The increased power 10–20 became the W-30. The NWC ordered no more experimental F-20s or F-40s built. It wanted just 10 F-30s, 10 W-30s, and updates on "regular" Farmalls. Sperry asked for two W-40 chassis for experiments with "high compression, heavy fuel engines."

Alex Legge held a special conference on IHC's tractor development and business in Phoenix, March 12–14, 1931. Legge had resigned from Hoover's Federal Farm Board on March 5, greatly

By December 1, 1930, Alex Legge had defined these Increased Power Farmalls as two-plow tractors. He approved building another 25 prototypes immediately. Every measurement on these prototypes fell midway between F-20 and F-30 production models. By late February 1931, these prototypes officially had a new name: F-20.

This is the right-side view of the Increased Power Farmall prototype, which evolved into the F-20, photographed on May 15, 1930. Gas Power Engineering recorded the weight of this experimental tractor at 4,140 pounds and identified it as Q-943. This is another of the 25 prototypes. *State Historical Society of Wisconsin*

frustrated and defeated by his inabilities to help farmers and turn around the world economy. He returned to the presidency of IHC and immediately got to work where he knew he made a difference. He and Executive Council members watched Johnston's entire line-up, from No. 15 TracTracTors to W-40-standard-tread wheel tractors. In each category that IHC built, GPED showed direct competitors as well, from Holt 15s to Case Model Ls. GPED's tractors showed well. But this did not have the effect on Legge that they hoped.

"Up to 1914, the tendency of tractor design has been entirely toward larger machines of greater horsepower," he said. Recognizing this strategy was not economical for the average farmer, IHC frequently "went right about-face, to the small tractor, and in 1914 we made our first, the one-cylinder 8–16 Mogul. The same economic conditions govern us today, and we must not make our tractors too heavy, too high in cost and too expensive in operation." Legge asked his participants for their preferences.

Charles R. Morrison, IHC director for domestic and Canadian sales, asked for everything, especially the Model 15 TracTracTor which his departments renamed the T-20. He wanted the two larger versions to follow, a T-30 and T-40, to match the Farmall lineup.

Bert Benjamin proposed returning to the two-tractor plan. He suggested that a 24-horsepower increased power Farmall, along with the intermediate Farmall, would take care of 90 percent of IHC's current business. The other 10 percent came from California, where TracTracTors would fill their need. Discussion bounced between Morrison's and Benjamin's extremes. Members approved large-scale production of the F-30 intermediate-sized Farmall and the increased power F-20. Two matters remained.

David Baker reported progress in engineering the high-compression, heavy-fuels projects, particularly with the Hill diesel engine from Michigan. One prototype ran at Phoenix with pump-wear problems that they solved on the spot. The NWC agreed to build five more for intense testing. Baker mused that "if this Hill diesel engine came through with satisfactory performances, our troubles on the increased power 10–20s and 15–30s would be behind us, as those two tractors would use the Hill engine." Legge urged Baker to get to work.

Finally, Legge mentioned a Caterpillar patent infringement suit against the TracTracTors, and IHC. Henry Doolittle suggested they "not recognize any infringement and inform them to proceed with the suit." Alex Legge concurred but added that, as he was acquainted with Caterpillar board member C. L. Best, he would write to Best, suggesting a visit "with a view to settling this in a friendly way." However, Legge's contact with Best was only the beginning of something that would go on for more

than a decade. Caterpillar's board was not interested in settling these questions outside of court, and threw back in IHC's face what it called Legge's efforts to circumvent legal process.

On July 14, Board Chairman Cyrus McCormick Jr., signed off on improvements to the "regular" Farmall, including raising output by three horsepower, adding a four-speed transmission and enclosing the steering gear. GPED halted work on the T-30 and F-40. The T-40 would use the W-40 six-cylinder Fort Wayne FBB gas engines. By September Legge turned up the heat, ordering engineering to produce 100 W-40s and T-40s, 10 with the FBB converted to kerosene, 10 diesels and as many as possible as soon as possible with a four-speed transmission. Johnston

1932 TracTracTor T-20

Derived not from the troubled TracTracTor 10–20, but rather from the new small Farmall F-12 model, this crawler first appeared on Valentine's Day 1930 as the T-15. A prototype run of 25 convinced Gas Power Engineering it needed more power. GPED renamed the crawler the T-20 and experimented with other engines.

A mixed shipment loads onto several rail cars outside Tractor Works on December 13, 1935, after a light snowfall. Here F-20s swing into place. *State Historical Society of Wisconsin*

20, so that "a sufficient increase in horsepower can meet the situation."

A month later, on September 26, 1931, Johnston asked Baker to lay out and design a new one-plow Farmall, an F-10, with their modified unit-frame at the rear for the engine, transmission and running gear, while extension rails, mounted onto the unit-frame, supported the front axle. This would be the first practical application of a little-known but significant project from back in 1914, their Mogul 20–40. This tractor also played a role in Caterpillar's suit against IHC.

Always well dressed, Ed Johnston maintained the appearance of calm, even though near-constant stiffness and pain he endured from his rheumatism often made him cranky. The pain, and the crankiness, were always increased by stress. Johnston was stressed.

In September 1931, Caterpillar Corporation filed a lawsuit against an International Harvester dealer, Reinharts, in Winnemucca, Nevada, and IHC. The suit claimed IHC infringed on 84 items in 23 patents held by Caterpillar and others. The culprit was IHC's new TracTracTor Model 20. The crawler and its entire development, back to a unique Mogul 20–40 in 1914, was Johnston's idea and design. Caterpillar said it was theirs.

In the law offices of Wilkinson, Huxley, Byron and Knight, IHC's patent attorneys, Charles L. Byron deposed Johnston. They got right to the point.

"Track laying tractors were sold in small quantities, especially in California, and during my trips out there I investigated . . . and found they were commercially not successful, on account of their chains and track rollers were not durable. I conceived the idea of a multiple-wheel tractor to have about the same performance as the track laying tractor and of getting all of the mechanism enclosed, whereby dirt could be kept out and the oil could be kept in."

Johnston first sketched an eight-wheel variation of the International 8–16 on July 1, 1915, his idea being to provide about the same performance as a track layer. Following ground contours, the wheels rose and fell independently on wheel-carrier frameworks connected to the transmission housing. With engineering designer Gustaf W. Engstrom, Johnston and the McCormick Works

assigned Gus Engstrom and Carl Mott to design and manufacture IHC-built diesel engines for the 40 series and smaller engines for the 30 series models.

Increased power was on Legge's mind, but not just as a marketing and sales tool. In late August, he notified the NWC that "of 1,000 TracTracTor Model 20s put out, there are a few which have been sold and these will be returned or they will be involved in litigation if a slight increase in power is not available." Setting Holt's Model 20 as a target and taking that target literally put them at risk. David Baker worked fast, using parts from F-30 Farmall engines and new ones peculiar to the Model

Experimental Department completed the first prototype in the spring of 1916.

"We had plenty of mud holes in the back yard of the Tractor Works . . . and I recall testing the tractor in those mud holes and later at Hinsdale [September 1, 1916] and still later at Healdsburg, California," early in January 1917. Johnston built five more, three of which also went to Healdsburg. He and Engstrom took their drawings to IHC's in-house patent chief, Charles E. Lord, who filed them. About 18 months after the first six-wheeler was completed, Johnston and Engstrom developed several crawler versions. Caterpillar's attorney, Charles M. Fryer, questioned Johnston about those in his cross-examination.

"We made several," Johnston explained, "some equipped with tracks and some with four wheels, by changing the wheels and substituting sprockets and idlers for the wheels, the same identical tractor carrying the track." After testing around Aurora, Illinois, for several years, Johnston ordered the 6 six-wheel prototypes, the 10 four-wheel drive versions and the full-crawlers scrapped at McCormick Works.

(One Aurora farmer fell in love with a four-wheel drive prototype and refused to sell it back. He used it for years. When a part failed, Tractor Works Experimental Department had to build or cast him a replacement, one at a time. It cost too much and brought about IHC's rigid policy of getting prototypes back.)

"Track layer type tractors were more complicated and expensive to build than the conventional wheel type tractors, the demand for these was very limited, and after testing these, it was the decision of the company to refrain from entering into the manufacture of that general type at that time."

There were other considerations. The 8–16's rail frame was not rigid enough to withstand the crawler's stresses. Superior traction twisted the rails, throwing tracks, popping open final drive seals and covers, allowing fluids to leak or become contaminated with dirt.

Johnston never mentioned another reason IHC decided to not produce the 8–16 variants. The challenge to building a crawler tractor (or even one with six wheels) is steering it. Track clutches or brakes disengage power and slow the speed of one side,

1932 F-30 with P&H diesel
Diesel power was becoming desirable to both farmers and manufacturers. While IHC introduced the F-30 models in 1931, its first diesel tractor did not appear until April 1932, as the TD-40 crawler. An early owner replaced the original engine with a P&H two-cylinder diesel.

forcing the faster set of tracks or wheels to come around. Ben Holt's track clutch-track brake was patented in 1907. Holt's system allowed crawlers to turn very tightly by completely stopping one track as the other continued. In 1917, Holt, 10 years into his 17-year term, would not likely cooperate with IHC. Johnston and Engstrom selected differential-type steering for the 8–16s, which slowed the inside track while speeding up the outside. Turning was not nearly so tight, though it kept power on both tracks. Harry Waite drove his tractor through friction drives and clutches. Waite's company failed in 1916, and he sought financial backing for a new effort. While John Steward had liked working with Waite, IHC had found Waite and his ideas too expensive long before Gus Engstrom tried to steer his crawler.

Risk of infringement on Holt and Waite patents derailed the 8–16 projects. Johnston and his Tractor Works engineers waited, and began experimenting with 10–20-based crawlers in 1924, when Holt's "Traction Engine" patent expired.

The next day Byron and Fryer grilled Johnston about his Mogul 20–40 from 1914 and 1915,

learning more of the same: The one-piece frame that he, David Baker and Anton Dressler developed also proved too expensive for manufacture in 1915. This basic design was the efficient and cost-effective solution to a number of problems in farm tractor development. Johnston reintroduced it with the gear drive 10–20s and 15–30s, and it required little modification to serve as the foundation of the TracTracTors.

The case went to trial in Reno, Nevada, (the nearest U.S. District Court to the Reinhart dealership) on September 11, 1933. Caterpillar's concern boiled down to page 40 of Judge Frank Norcross' findings, in paragraph 118:

"Other than International Harvester Company, the manufacturer of the tractors charged to infringe the patents in suit herein, there is no manufacturer of track-type tractors in the United States manufacturing and selling track-type tractors other than the plaintiff, Caterpillar Tractor Co. . . ."

Caterpillar, believing IHC was powerful enough to drive Henry Ford and General Motors from the tractor business, wanted to avoid competition from this force. Judge Norcross found IHC

Pawling & Harnischfeger built cranes in Wisconsin and produced its own diesel engines to power them. P&H was not a regular repower supplier to the agricultural tractor market. This 50-horsepower, 287-cubic-inch two-cycle diesel also fit well into the F-30. It offered greater power on less costly fuel.

guilty of infringing on 18 claims in six patents. On March 8, 1934, Norcross awarded Caterpillar "injunctive and compensatory relief" and court costs. IHC was out of the crawler business. Wilkinson, Byron, et al, filed a stay of execution of the court orders and an appeal the next day, reinstalling IHC in the business.

The principal market for crawler tractors was central California, as much for its sandy soil as for the peat around Sacramento and Stockton. This productive land fostered the birth and success of C. L. Best and Benjamin Holt and their crawlers. The Trackson Company of Milwaukee, Wisconsin, produced two types of full-crawler conversions, both available for IHC's 10–20 and for the Fordson.

The late 1920s had been a fertile period for tractor development. The McCormick-Deering 15–30 and 10–20 gear drive models offered the Gas Power Engineering Department (GPED) a rigid platform for experiments and new product invention. Johnston kept his engineers busy devising a variety of orchard and industrial models.

They experimented with a half-track conversion from Moon Tracks of San Diego, California. These were not perfect; front steering wheels slipped or plowed in soft or wet conditions, and their turning radius was larger than that of a wheeled tractor. Full tracks were the only solution. As California grew in population and agricultural significance, IHC no longer could ignore crawlers. Demand increased after Ford withdrew from U.S. markets in 1927. West Coast farmers had no alternative to Caterpillar. By April 30, 1928, Johnston had a 10–20 crawler, which IHC introduced as the TracTracTor. Nearly every New Work Committee (NWC) report referred to the Holt 20 as its target. Johnston turned his first commercial crawler with steering clutches mounted outside the tractor frame, under dome-like structures nicknamed Camel Humps.

After completing 10–20 versions, the NWC ordered 200 and Johnston built the first 15–30 pro-

totypes along similar lines in mid-1929, matching the 10–20 in all but scale. David Baker devised a new system with steering brakes set into the rear of the 10–20 chassis, below the operator's seat. One prototype ran 217 hours on a "crawler dynamometer." Removable access covers made service easy yet protected intricate mechanisms. This was a substantial enough improvement that on November 12, 1929, IHC scrapped $18,000 worth of existing tractors and parts rather than sell them.

Baker's revision went in production as the No. 20 TracTracTor. IHC produced 472 crawlers in both sizes and versions by year-end, when Johnston had two smaller prototypes undergoing tests, one in Arizona, the other around Chicago. This was his No. 15 TracTracTor, which "compares favorably with our principal competitor in weight, width, length, balance, clearance and convenience of control," referring to the Holt 15.

Baker's redesigned No. 20 embodied "correct principles of clutching and braking on fast moving shafts." Johnston urged immediate manufacture. "Being designed without the handicap of using the

1934 F-12 with 1-row Corn Picker

The idea of mounted implements grew out of Bert Benjamin's experiments with Ed Johnston's Motor Cultivator. By the time IHC produced its F-series Farmalls, Benjamin's Deering Works had a full line of "attachments" for F-12, F-20 and F-30 models.

IHC produced its No. 10 single row corn picker, meant for mounting onto the Farmall tractors, from 1931 to 1936. Mounted pickers, towing a wagon behind, made one-person farming possible. F-12 tractors went into production in January 1933 as IHC's small, one-plow Farmall.

regular 10–20 frame and transmission," he said, "was more satisfactory from all standpoints."

J. F. Jones also urged quick production. "We cannot afford to go through another season without a TracTracTor. We must give our dealers something to sell to tide them over until we can give them something better."

Shortly after Caterpillar filed its infringement suit in September 1931, IHC's Executive Council, pleased with Leonard Sperry's ongoing IHC diesel developments, revised the 100 T-40 order from 10 to 90 crawlers equipped with the new diesel engine. Baker released to production the I-30 Industrial with a four-speed transmission, and he began a rapid experimental development program to replace the Model 20 Industrial with the I-20.

Johnston inquired about a rubber-jointed crawler track made by Roadless Traction Ltd., of Hounslow, England, showing photos on October 30 of installations on Fordson and Case tractors.

1934 TD-40
Early production diesels from IHC, Caterpillar, and other manufacturers suffered excessive engine wear. Still, demand was very high for these powerful, fuel-efficient engines in tractors meant for heavy work.

By August 8, 1933, IHC had delivered 45 of these diesel crawlers and had a backlog of orders for hundreds more. The solution to engine wear problems came in a switch away from paraffin-based lubricants, which proved incompatible with diesel fuel.

In April 1932, Tractor Works began production of its first diesel crawler, the TD-40. Here, in July 1935, assembly line workers fit the track frame assembly to the unit frame that supports the engine. IHC had a policy that all its engines must start with a crank, so its diesels fired first on gasoline. *Navistar*

1935 TA-40

TracTracTor 40-size crawlers were developed to court a growing oil and pipeline business, but that usage required extensive modifications, including longer tracks mounted rigidly to the front of the unit frame to support a crane. Agricultural uses needed the opposite.

Johnston liked its quieter operation but was concerned about track durability and cost; Roadless demanded a steep royalty of nearly $40 per tractor. Legge questioned if IHC did not take this opportunity now, might they lose it later? Johnston acquired one for test, paying $500 for the complete system.

In IHC's view, the infringement lawsuit from Caterpillar over the 10–20 TracTracTor was becoming moot. Though IHC had introduced the small crawlers three years earlier, on October 1, 1928, it had produced only 486 to date. The first versions, with external track clutches, gave problems and quickly were replaced with the No. 20 model. By Thanksgiving 1931, information from the branches told Chicago that only 400 were in private hands. Owners were dissatisfied.

Field improvements made the 10–20 as strong and reliable as the No. 20, but cost IHC $250 per tractor in parts and $100 for freight and labor. Yet fixing a complaint of inadequate power was impossible without aggravating the main objection: The front end lifted from the ground under any load, a problem requiring major redesign. IHC faced a dilemma. Its reputation was at stake. It had to satisfy the owners. It had resolved to stay in the crawler business, believing it would win the suit.

IHC heard that its No. 20 crawlers also were not strong enough, especially in sandy soil regions around Amarillo, Spokane, and Denver. Worse, the No. 20s suffered premature track roller wear. Tractor Works had produced 1,000 but some 240 remained unsold. Manufacturing had devised another field repair kit. But tests showed the new T-20 to be superior in every way—in power, balance, traction, lubrication and dirt sealing. Furthermore, the new crawler represented no infringements on any patents.

The Executive Council concluded that it must replace the first two versions with T-20s. It would sell the new models at wholesale. Manufacturing would salvage engines, clutches and radiators to use in wheel tractors. The 240 unsold No. 20 models also would be stripped. Carcasses would be destroyed. To save freight, dealers would perform the salvage, keeping the proceeds. Alex Legge, the

ever-frugal Scotsman trained in the trenches of debt collection, had another thought, distributed to NWC members by letter on December 7.

"We are going to leave a lot of stuff scattered around the territory, which will serve as monuments to the inefficiency of this organization." He proposed very generous trade-in allowances to dissatisfied owners, allowing near-even exchanges for T-20s. IHC then would update the older models and sell them for a very low price, say around the cost of the kit and labor. "This would result in the stuff being used until it is worn out, and people are always willing to put up with something that is not 100 percent if they get it at a bargain."

This was classic Legge, but it set a precedent as classic IHC. The corporation, stuck with an unsuccessful design in an effort to meet a growing need, made good. After all the buy-backs, trade-ins, scraps, strips, replacements and resales, IHC lost something approaching $120,000, absorbing the loss as a cost of keeping its reputation. It also removed from the market all infringing TracTracTors.

In late February 1932, Ed Johnston conceived a wide front axle for F-30 narrow-tread tractors, using wheels and the axle from the 10–20 and its successor W-30. For this photo on October 19, 1933, he had a Narrow Tread Wide Front High Clearance model. Rear wheels were 60 inches tall, while fronts were 46. *State Historical Society of Wisconsin*

1935 Farmall F-30 HV

The Farmall high-clearance idea first arose in New Work Committee meetings in mid-September 1933, when P. Y. Timmons, power farming equipment sales manager, informed the committee that sugar cane had made a comeback in Louisiana, and farmers there needed a tractor with high ground clearance.

Johnston summed up his crawlers in advance of their funeral. "It was a compromise to provide a crawler-type based on the wheel tractor. The draw-bar pull could be much improved by loosening up the tracks as [we] found desirable with the T-20 when it was put out, but even so it was inferior to the T-20 and was not suitable for hilly land and loose ground."

In January 1932, the NWC dealt with variations on old themes, modifying the regular narrow Farmall as a new Fairway tractor, replacing the front wheels that often cut into the bunkers with a wide front axle. Ed Johnston in late February created a similar configuration as a wide-tread front axle for the F-30 narrow-tread tractor, as a no-additional-charge option. This would use wheels off the 10–20 and W-30 tractors but would not fit an F-20. By April, his engineers devised a wide front axle for the F-20 that also would fit the regular Farmall.

David Baker continued work on the F-10 one-plow tractor. Tractor Works released the first of these smaller semiunit-frame models as the F-12, with the earliest prototype, No. Q2071, shipped to Houston for tests on May 13, 1932. Tractor Works manufactured 19 preproduction models in early August. Production began October 5. Competition nipped at the Farmall's heels. The Regular's output dipped to 3,080 for 1932, though IHC tractor prospects were bolstered by production of 2,500 F-20s, as well as 1,500 of the F-12s.

On August 1, 1932, IHC broadened its industrial point of view, pushed by P. Y. Timmons, power farming equipment sales manager. Observing oil pipeline construction, he proposed IHC pursue this new activity. Leonard Sperry outlined a few, substantial modifications.

"To mount a boom and winch for handling pipe or to meet other oilfield service, we must have tracks that are rigid at the front instead of oscillating. We must carry the track forward to the front of the tractor, to prevent it from tipping as the boom with its load will swing from forward to sideward." Timmons returned September 30 with another challenge.

"Because of other tractor manufacturers, we must offer low pressure tires," he said. "We can purchase wheels from French & Hecht, which are built to fit our tractors and are sold to our dealers. The tires have inner tubes and carry about 12 pounds pressure, not the zero pressure (solid rubber) tires tested in Florida. We will ultimately furnish Goodyear tires when they are ready." He then reiterated his interest in rigid tracks for the TA-40 Trac-TracTor and asked for a larger crawler.

"Build a third size TracTracTor, a T-80, for example," he suggested. "Approximately the horsepower of the Holt 65, and use the large six-cylinder Waukesha engines until we have a diesel engine to use." To impress his point, Timmons predicted annual sales of 500 to 750 of the T-80s.

Addis McKinstry agreed. "We are in the 'crawler' business to stay," he said, "and it is necessary for us to cover the whole field."

Alex Legge moved the diesel project along in early November 1932. Ed Johnston reported that the only serious difficulty encountered on the 12 four-cylinder prototypes was "excessively high temperatures in the piston heads, resulting in destruction of the lubrication and burning the top piston ring, causing, in turn, excessive wear, loss of power and high consumption of the lubricating oil." Leonard Sperry felt he had solved these problems, and estimated that only Caterpillar, which had introduced its first commercial diesel Model 60 a year before, was farther along in diesel development.

McKinstry enlarged the program to encompass a 95-horsepower six-cylinder model for the T-80. Variations in bore and stroke of a smaller block would offer 30 horsepower for the T-20 tractors, 38 horsepower for F-30 and W-40 tractors, and 55 for the T-40. Legge encouraged a 100-unit preproduction program for the T-40. At year-end, when the

NWC cleaned up loose ends, it heard from Leonard Sperry.

"The unexpected has become the accepted," he observed. "It is entirely possible that pneumatic tires may be developed to meet many agricultural operations, as they are now meeting industrial tractor needs. Allis-Chalmers is advertising pneumatic tires on farm tractors. There is a possibility that these tires may cut into crawler tractors sales. Caterpillar is experimenting with pneumatic tires on wheel tractors it has purchased."

The NWC, ever aware of Caterpillar's role in influencing IHC product development, approved low-pressure pneumatics for the increased power 10–20s, W-30s, and the Farmall Regular, as well as the F-12 tractors. They offered F-12s as orchard, industrial and fairway versions. Sperry recommended providing a fourth, with a much higher

1935 W-30

By late 1930, the New Work Committee knew it must update 10–20 and 15–30 gear drive tractors. A program of Increased Power models included these two wide-fronts. In late February 1931, the Naming Committee gave final designations to a number of revised machines, dubbing the 10–20 as the W-30.

Bearing serial number FB7262CNW, this was the first high-clearance cane, narrow-tread, wide-front axle tractor produced. Coming up with this machine required a new front axle, as the original F-30 narrow front was cast and could not simply be arched for greater clearance.

Increased Power for 10–20 tractors meant the same as for the Farmalls, just subtle improvements in head and intake manifold design, different carburetors and a water pump to better manage engine cooling, all deceptively simple ways to increase horsepower.

speed gear, determining that 10 miles per hour now seemed sensible.

In the new year of 1933, the committee addressed ongoing problems large and small: Magnetos and impulse starter couplings for four- and six-cylinder Farmalls; a clutch-release hitch for Farmall tractors that disengaged if the plow hit something; low-pressure pneumatic tires for the F-12; worm-steering gears for the F-20 and F-30; kerosene engines for the F-12; continued pressure on Sperry and GPED for diesel engines; electric starters; relocated air cleaners; new engine crankcases to provide better lubrication to the bottom end and tops of the F-20 and T-20 engines; corresponding widening of the tractor frame with hood and fuel tank to match; elimination of engine side doors to clean up appearances of the same tractors; further development of prototype I-12 industrial tractors; six-cylinder kerosene engines for T-20s; prototype clutches for the F-12 produced in-house to replace outsourced Rockford units; production considered for one T-80 TracTracTor per day at $2,834.03 manufacturing cost, to compete favorably, but at higher price due to its high weight, with Caterpillar's gas 70.

"Now comes the momentous question," John McCaffrey, now U.S. sales manager, said to the meeting on April 7, 1933. "Can the large size Trac-

TracTor be marketed at a profit?" Export sales staff felt it was pointless to proceed until diesels were ready. Timmons argued "the T-80 [would] complete the crawler line and secure and retain dealers handling these tractors." McCaffrey had a last word, as would be the case often in future years: "Without this size tractor, we are handicapped in the crawler trade. It is needed for construction, for industrial uses. If we have not got a large TracTracTor, we are not in the crawler business."

The very last word came from Legge on April 19: "Approving the program to build a sample T-80 does not mean a definite commitment to the line of manufacture."

"The committee," Ed Kimbark read in a letter from Harold McCormick during a June 20, NWC meeting, "are impressed with the advantages of the construction used in the F-12 Farmall, compared to the Regular, the F-20 and F-30. Designing this form of chassis, having high wheels and one-chamber gear case should be combined with designing modern, higher-speed four-cylinder engines, for tractors of the two-plow and three-plow sizes."

Leonard Sperry went pale. Was this an order to redo the entire line? His portion of GPED was overextended as it was. Ed Johnston scrambled. His resources also were stretched thin. The F-12 meant a lot to him as IHC's first mass-production application of the unitized tub he created with the Mogul 20–40. He advanced the benchmark established with Benjamin's Farmall.

But he had no money, no personnel and no time to develop new tractors, even ones based on his idea. Johnston investigated the changes required in shipping packaging for F-12s and Farmall implements. He found about 90 percent were affected. The high-wheel design presented obstacles to attaching existing Farmall implements. While tractor manufacturing costs were less using a unit frame, the F-12-type case reduced clearance for cultivating, and brought wheel rims and their dust closer to the driver. The changes required in present implements outweighed the advantages. Johnston intentionally defeated himself to avoid killing his staff or turning out another hurried project.

Sydney G. McAllister, NWC chairman, reminded members on August 8 that although

1936 Farmall F-20
Nonadjustable wide front axles
were not too common on F-20s. Ed
Johnston devised the wide front
axle after the New Work Committee
urged him to create one for the F-
30 narrow-tread in February 1932.
By April, he had a wide front that
would fit both the F-20 and the
earlier Farmall Regular.

IHC delivered 45 TD-40 TracTracTors, and portable power units took another 45 of the 100 available diesel engines, there were dozens of unfilled orders. Johnston pointed out that all manufacturers continued to suffer problems with excessive wear on cylinder sleeves, pistons and rings. He was prepared to predict a life of 1,500 hard hours, but he heard that Caterpillar was ready to guarantee 3,000. (This wear problem continued until manufacturers shifted to West Coast-refined, nonparaffin-based lubricants, as Caterpillar did in solving the problem.) Demand for diesels, in crawlers, power units and standard-tread W-30 and W-40 tractors, kept pressure on Sperry and Johnston.

The four-plow tractor idea returned in discussions on September 11, 1933. Based on semiunitized F-12s, with speed ranging from 2 to 20 miles per hour, P. Y. Timmons wanted this with the diesel engine. Relentless, he returned a week later, pushing a rapid development program for Cane Cultivator and Plow tractors based on F-30-N narrow-tread models. Sugar cane had come back in Louisiana, and planters needed tractors with high ground clearance.

Sperry agreed the F-30-N Farmall offered the "advantage [of] straddling the bed in cultivating instead of running between the beds as the 10–20 must do," but the narrow-front axle was cast and couldn't be arched. A new one could be designed and produced. McAllister approved another accelerated development program. Suddenly, everything Johnston and Sperry supervised was rushed. They never had enough time or personnel, although they always got enough money to do the projects thoroughly. Their work and IHC's product inventory expanded geometrically. Sugar cane versions of F-30s rose high off the ground; heavy-track version of the T-40s sported front bumpers, double oil pumps, a raised seat, a larger diameter clutch, and crankcase protection plates for "trail-builder" uses; Orchard, Industrial and W series standard-tread variations of the Farmall F-12 got tested and went into production.

GPED developed and released T-20 TracTrac-Tors with IHC's own six-cylinder engines. This removed outside engine suppliers from tractor manufacture. GPED lengthened the front end of the 15–30 (22–36) standard tractors 3 inches to accept remaining FBB gas engines until the four-plow tractor was approved for manufacture. Johnston and Sperry released a series of experimental F-20 replacements based on the F-12. A dozen times in the last six weeks of 1933, Ed Johnston repeated, "The Gas Power Engineering Department could not do much on it at this time, without an increase in the engineering force, for the reason there are so many developments under way." It became his litany.

Then, for a few brief days everything stopped. For a week, beginning Sunday, December 3, 1933, IHC did little work. Alex Legge, defeated by the Farm Board's failures to energize a depressed economy, and still saddened over the loss of his wife, Katherine, nearly a decade before, worked in his garden early. At 10 a.m., he felt so ill he went to bed and called his doctor. He died at 11:15, of a heart attack as he pruned his lilacs. Legge chaired the last New Work Committee meeting of his life, No. 735, on November 17, 1933. After the funeral on Wednesday, December 6, the McCormicks and the board of directors elected Addis McKinstry president. He would serve only until New Year's 1935, before retiring.

During one of McKinstry's first NWC meetings, on January 15, 1934, the Naming Committee labeled the improved gas-engined 22–36 tractor the WA-40. Diesels became the WD-40. McKinstry signed orders to produce 20 of each per day for two years. GPED completed W-40 detail drawings on March 1 and sent them to manufacturing, and the first development models, 7 WAs and 3 WDs, rolled out of GPED on May 1.

The worm-steering gear prototypes worked well in tests so the NWC made it standard equipment on all F-20 and F-30 tractors, as of January 19, 1934. NWC renamed the "Trail-Builder" TA-40 and TD-40 crawlers the Cruiser-type TracTracTors, with the track pivot relocated further rearward, creating leverage that held the nose down. About 250 TA-40 Cruisers went to government contracts.

On April 24, NWC dealt with proposals to develop marine adaptations for its new diesel engine. These meetings mark the earliest appearances of the newest McCormick, Fowler, to the Executive Council and the NWC. Born in 1898, he was Cyrus Hall McCormick's grandson. After graduating from Princeton at 23, he drifted through sev-

Over the years, Gas Power Engineering continued to improve and update the F-20, adding worm steering gears and new crankcases, to allow better lubrication within engines, by early 1934. Soon after, GPE began developing its replacement, the F-20X or F-21.

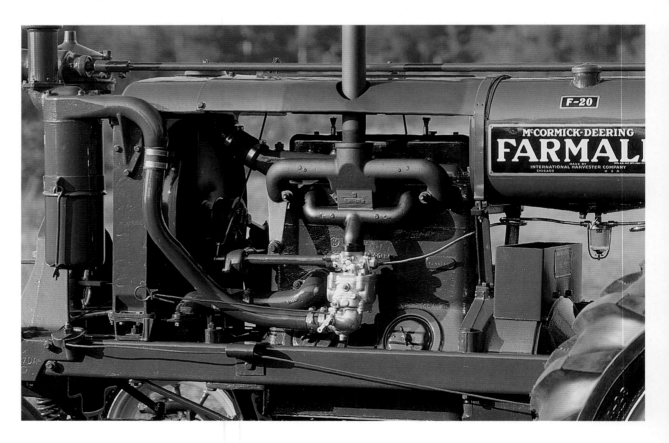

eral interests, psychology (inspired by his mother's fascination with Dr. Carl Jung), music and accounting. He ran a small business until Alex Legge suggested it was about time he came to "The Company." Fowler started in 1928 in the apprentice program. He spent five years learning manufacturing, engineering and sales. By 1933, he was assistant sales manager, and in 1934, he became head of foreign sales. On his first vote, he joined the majority for marine development.

In early May, Johnston and Sperry told the NWC that W-40 tractors were out testing and they'd determined costs to manufacture the 6,495 pound, WA-gas version at $848.32. This, they calculated, could retail for $1,350. The diesel represented a $581.83 premium. Weighing 7,029 pounds, the WD cost $1,330.15, with retail set at $2,225.

In late May 1934, IHC found itself again needing to repair its reputation, as with the early crawlers. A combination of design, manufacturing and field service problems produced an ill-fitting air filter for the diesel engines, the gas F-12s, and some of the TracTracTors. Climate-related, it appeared only where drought conditions brought on intense

dust. Otherwise, there was no problem. Ed Johnston explained:

"The numerous complaints of excessive wear of the F-12 engines are largely due to dirt entering through inefficient air cleaners. The design of the original made it extremely difficult to assemble the cleaning element uniformly into the cleaner. It results in excessive wear of pistons, sleeves, rings, bearings and crankshafts which in turn results in excessive oil and fuel consumption and loss of power." (Sperry defined acceptable oil use as one quart per 10-hour field day after 300 hours of use; these tractors used one gallon a day.)

The policy was to make it right: Replace faulty air cleaners with new ones, make engines air-tight by, if necessary, thoroughly overhauling the engine and replacing worn parts. GPED designed new pistons with four rings instead of three. One source of the dirt was residual sand and metallic chips from Milwaukee and Tractor Works castings. McKinstry ordered installation of a filtering system for the lubricating oil used to run in engines prior to installation. IHC had these systems in operation at the Fort Wayne gas engine plant and at Farmall Works.

"I think each individual identified with this

1936 Farmall F-12

No sooner had field service technicians completed their "First Change" repairs to thousands of F-12s on farms than more problems arose with IHC's engine in the tractor. This time the heat shield on the exhaust manifold failed to properly heat the intake manifold, allowing unvaporized kerosene to wash the cylinders.

undertaking," McKinstry said, "must be impressed with the amount of money involved." McKinstry kept records but released no totals for this repair; it would have been premature. He learned from Legge and quickly found his voice, using it to satisfy customers and to ask his managers to work more carefully and more wisely. It worked.

After completing the first prototype T-80, Holahan and McCaffrey decided it was too large, apparently based on Caterpillar's poor sales of its gasoline 70. McCaffrey proposed a TD-65 as a more reasonable alternative. McKinstry agreed.

The pressure from domestic sales to provide a tractor for every farm and crop strained GPED by

mid-1934. Johnston's durability and stamina earned him promotion to vice president of engineering. He couldn't slow the flood of new work; for each project completed, two new ones were waiting. Engineers returned from one test trip, filed reports, and left on another. The W-40s would start production even as 1934's Midwest drought slowed demand. Johnston and Sperry hoped for an opportunity to catch up.

When the costs for working at this pace came due, the price was high. At noon on June 27, 1934, McKinstry and Johnston shut down the 12 series tractor production line, halting manufacture completely. It was the only way to get parts changed before 12 series tractors left the plants. Repairs cost much more in the field. This delay permitted outside makers of new air filters and elements to deliver adequate supplies, so Tractor Works could remedy the problem before shipment. Production resumed on July 9.

The entire program, including parts, repairs, overhauls and F-12 plant shutdown, cost IHC $750,000. Only in four regions, Central, Southern, Southeast and East, did 19 branches need help. The 36 others did not. The service department trained sales agents and sent them out to make repairs. Manufacturing estimated that perhaps 10,000 diesel, F-12 or crawler tractors needed service, from simply tightening or replacing air filter canisters and elements, to full top-to-bottom engine rebuilds, transmission repairs, and, in the case of crawlers, track replacements.

Ed Johnston had harped about keeping dirt out and oil in. A sales organization hungry for products and concerned with manufacturing costs continually postponed his efforts to make tighter machines. Johnston argued for pressure lubrication; he got that with the T-20 and T-40 crawlers. Yet, even as this unprecedented "recall" was going on, sales argued that "the appropriateness of pressure lubrication on farm tractors as compared to splash lubrication had not yet been fully demonstrated."

In early August, David Baker sent a new four-plow tractor, the CW-40, the third series W, to Hinsdale. Johnston, intent on avoiding recent problems with tractors released too quickly, asked for another year for testing and development. McKinstry reminded him that this CW-40 was the 22–36 replacement. The C-version only incorporated the latest seals and air filter. Test harder, McKinstry said; delay was not approved.

GPED staged final sign-off tests of the third preproduction W-40 series in early October 1934, in Phoenix. Johnston set the test there to guarantee challenging conditions. The only problems came in the transmission. While it never failed in tests, the heat and dust taxed it. In Johnston's ideal world, GPED would have upgraded the transmission before 22–36 improvements but no one envisioned the power of the diesel. Larger gears won't fit; designing a new case and testing a transmission would add two to three more years. Delay was not approved, McKinstry had said.

While GPED was overworked, Bert Benjamin had not rested on his laurels. In early October 1934, at Hinsdale, he showed NWC and executive officers "a new means of attaching implements to the F-12 tractor," demonstrating both a No. 90 plow and a middle-buster. Predictably, Morrison, Halohan and McCaffrey, (he, most vocally) wanted all of it immediately, and available universally.

Benjamin and Sperry had resolved to introduce this new hitch for plowing after harvest. They could deliver F-12s earlier because hitch modifications were small. Implements were the problem; the list to be offered grew like weeds. With tractor production at 2,000 per month and the 1935 fall harvest 10 months away, tractors and enough implements had to be in dealers by July. In late November, Holahan convinced everyone that tractors without implements were preferable to new implements without a tractor. It gave sales time to advertise, he said, and farmers time to anticipate.

On December 26, the NWC agreed to develop I-30 models for government airfields, with complete shielding to keep dirigible ropes from entangling in moving parts. They would develop a set of I-12s with revised orchard fenders for similar use. The TD-65 and the stillborn TD-80 got a shot in the arm when John McCaffrey learned construction and industrial users had expressed a need for crawlers and other machines with 100 and even 125 horsepower. He urged sending the one completed T-80 to Spokane, but McKinstry said no. "This would be objectionable from an expense standpoint, and because it would bring requests for that size TracTracTor, which, at present, we have no intention of building."

With McKinstry's admonition about no delays burning in their ears, Johnston and Sperry wrote to McCaffrey. Having watched him for nearly two years by now, they recognized an enthusiast. They advised him that their large six-cylinder diesel "with recent modifications could be run safely at a speed of 1,500 to 1,600 rpm, and could be depended upon to develop the horsepower required. The Engineering Department could turn over specifications for this engine in two months."

In John McCaffrey, they imagined the preservation of their world, if not a renaissance for engineering. They hoped to build for him high quality machines, tested thoroughly and put into production when they were ready. McCaffrey was not the only one who would let them down in the decades to come.

1935–1940

Six

S.S.D.D.
(SAME SITUATIONS, DIFFERENT DECADE)

"Should we stop production of the kerosene-engine F-12 tractors?" Leonard Sperry asked.

IHC had started manufacture of the F-12 using a Waukesha-built engine designed by Fuller & Johnson, because its own was not yet ready. After IHC began using its own engines, problems quickly developed.

The first New Work Committee meeting of 1935 began with a case of history repeating itself. Trouble developed again with piston ring wear, particularly oil control rings, just months after the improved parts "First Change" was done by field service technicians.

The kerosene manifold didn't heat the fuel enough to vaporize it completely. Liquid flowed past piston rings, diluting lubricating oil. Worse, Sperry sampled manifolds and found 40 percent where the cored hole missed the carburetor. Ed Johnston uncovered another cause out of IHC's control—bad fuel, consisting of heavy oil, to which distributors added high-test gasoline so it would ignite. This mix broke down; some elements were not consumed and these thinned the oil. It was a geographic consideration. There were no problems in Texas, yet nearly every tractor sold in Little Rock and more than half from Memphis required an overhaul and a new crankshaft.

The committee considered interrupting production. John McCaffrey voted no.

"We are practically current on orders," he said. "Three out of four F-12s are kerosene tractors. Better we face having to send changes later than to not ship tractors again." Johnston and Sperry created a new manifold and a revised

1937 O-12

In April 1935, the New Work Committee changed tractor paint from varnish to a synthetic enamel paint, because it held up better on exposed metal surfaces outdoors. By summer 1936, new tests showed enamel red lasted longer than the enamel gray, and IHC officially changed color on November 1, 1936, for all 1937 production models.

The first 0-12 was built on January 29, 1934. Between then and the end of production in 1939, IHC produced 2,991 of the 52-inch-tall, 50-inch-wide orchard tractors. As pneumatic tires became widely available, Leonard Sperry recommended increasing road speed to 10 miles per hour on these, industrial and fairway F-12 models.

1937 F-30-V

By early 1937, plans for the F-30 successor, a machine known as the F-32 or the 3-F, were far enough along that the New Work Committee was anticipating F-32 prototypes by early 1938. It would have 33 drawbar horsepower, yet weigh only 200 pounds more than the F-20.

carburetor with a smaller venturi and a new fuel nozzle. They covered both pieces with a heat shield to deflect radiator fan blast. They fitted these "Second Change" kits to tractors still in the assembly line. Sydney McAllister authorized the modifications and heat shields added

to WA-40s that would start production April 1 as well.

In early February, GPED's managers examined the new hydraulic power-lift built into the F-12 Farmall. They mounted the pump close to the power take-off (PTO) shaft, which drove it. They had studied an implement lift from a John Deere Model A tractor. Deere provided hydraulic lift but used gravity drop. Like Deere, IHC mounted its lift on the rear axle, giving the patent lawyers worries. GPED engineers proposed relocating the lift ahead of the rear axle, but patent attorney R. D. Acton doubted "the interpretation 'forward of the rear axle' differed enough from Deere's placement 'at the rear of the tractor.'"

Meanwhile, in the Tractor Works back yard, McAllister, McCaffrey, Charles Morrison and a dozen others watched the first T-65 operate. Johnston ran out the prototype T-80 as well. Next was the new prototype F-20X, built along F-12 lines. This was Johnston's newest application of the semi-unit frame design of his Mogul 20–40.

Test results from Phoenix's trials with WD-40s and revised kerosene-powered WA's encouraged McCaffrey, and Sperry and Johnston, to start production of 500 each of the two versions at about 25

per week. When A. W. Seacord of domestic sales learned of production plans, he informed manufacturing of 4,300 advanced orders for four-cylinder diesel tractors for 1936.

In late March, Sperry presented sales with an advantage the F-12s offered over John Deere models: GPED's new power implement lift also placed downward pressure to set the implement into the ground after it was dropped. The new lift was ready for testing.

Another F-12 invention eventually spread to the rest of IHC tractor lines, the Quick Detachable, or "QD," Draw Bar, proposed in October 1934. By April 1935, GPED had working prototypes, but due to scheduling confusion, didn't try advanced versions, even though production was to begin August 1. The engineers feared sales was rushing something not yet completely proven into production. McAllister, alarmed, sent 15 QDs to Wisconsin, Minnesota, and the Dakotas for immediate testing. Manufacturing needed results urgently so it could extend or cancel its order with the foundry for castings.

The interrelationship between engineering, manufacturing and sales created a new production plan. Manufacturing accelerated the pace of all tractor lines in late April 1935, to develop a steady schedule instead of letting market responses create peaks of productivity or valleys of plant inactivity. This stabilized the labor population as well. But now stockpiling tractors created another problem.

"When tractors stand exposed to the weather more than 30 days," Seacord told NWC members, "it is usually necessary to repaint the tractor, at a cost of about $5 each. This occurs whether the exposure is in storage at factory yards or outside at branches or with dealers." GPED proposed using new "synthetic paints which must be sprayed, and which require a somewhat different provision in drying ovens, and will allow an exposure of four to six months. If the tractor is shipped or sold during that time, it can be wiped off with an oily rag and the appearance will be substantially that of a new tractor."

In addition, Seacord continued, "The question of color of the new paint was discussed. The new factory equipment will permit changing the color to red or any other color at any time without affecting the equipment." He added that paint color was not up for decision at that time. When they began testing the new spray techniques, however, experimentation with other colors would soon follow.

On May 21, Fowler McCormick, as foreign sales manager, joined Ed Johnston's NWC meeting called to discuss re-establishing tractor manufacture in Europe. Johnston's prime candidate was the F-12.

Charles Morrison, IHC vice president of sales and a booster of high-clearance models, heard about the new F-32. Then he asked New Work Committee members, "Does the F-30 just fade out of the picture?" It would do just that after September 1939.

1937 WD-40
The first WD-40 was built on April 16, 1935. John McCaffrey, director of national sales, urged immediate production of 25 per week. However, diesel engine technology was still a "work in progress" with IHC and most other manufacturers at the time. GPED changed the fuel injector angle just before 1937 model year.

EVOLUTION OF THE STYLED FARMALL

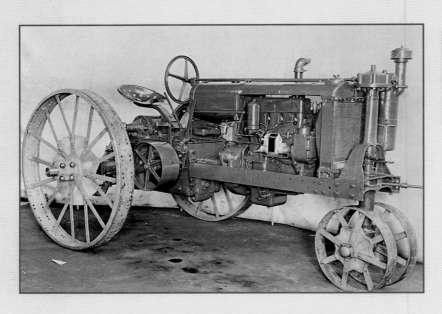

This was one of the first five F-21 prototypes, photographed March 1, 1936, a month before field testing began in Phoenix. It weighed 400 pounds more than an F-20, weight coming from 54-inch diameter rear wheels with heavier spokes, a frame lengthened 6 inches and a new transmission providing a road speed of 15 miles per hour on pneumatic tires. *State Historical Society of Wisconsin*

By early August 1936, the prototype for the new line of styled Farmalls was called the New F-20. Engineering changes and sheet metal designed by Raymond Loewy created the Intermediate New F-20 or the F-22, as shown in this October 21 photograph. Engineering proposed a four-horsepower increase over the F-20; sales would accept less if it could have the tractor sooner. *State Historical Society of Wisconsin*

The influence of Raymond Loewy and IHC's competition is apparent in this F-22, photographed May 19, 1937. The Oliver 70 Row Crop appeared in 1935, with full side panels and sleek lines. It sent designers running back to their drawing boards. On this version the forward frame rails grow almost seamlessly out of the unitized transmission case. *State Historical Society of Wisconsin*

Field work at Hinsdale showed a later refinement of Loewy's lines. By this time, late October 1937, GPED had reduced the weight to only 156 pounds more than the F-20 and cut back the wheelbase to slightly more than 1 inch longer. John McCaffrey and sales began to change their minds. *State Historical Society of Wisconsin*

When GPED reminded McCaffrey its F-22 had everything he wanted—adjustable tread, 21-mile per hour road speed, good clearance, brakes and steering wheel, standing platform, foot throttle, more power, and better looks, he balked. It was too good; no one else offered so much. On April 27, 1938, engineering began removing body panels, and the F-22 was renamed the 2-F. *State Historical Society of Wisconsin*

When Gas Power Engineering renamed the F-22 the 2F, it changed the ongoing F-30/F-32 into the 3-F. This was a 33-drawbar horsepower, three-plow tractor weighing 200 pounds more than the F-20. Photographed on August 8, 1938, this was approved for production six days earlier, the same day IHC discontinued F-14, F-20 and F-30 production. *State Historical Society of Wisconsin*

When tested at University of Nebraska, the WD-40 provided less than one-horsepower advantage over a faster-running kerosene WK-40, 48.79 versus 48.53 brake horsepower. Fuel economy, however, showed a big advantage to the diesel, returning 14.56 versus 9.87 horsepower hours per gallon.

"In Germany we are shut out from importing tractors," McCormick explained. "There are several quite large manufacturers there; the internal trade is good. In France, it would be a great advantage when trade picks up to have a tractor for sale which was manufactured there.

"We have several million marks in Germany," he went on, "which cannot be sent out of the country and which would be available to start manufacture. Industrial knowledge and ability are available there." McCormick was unsure, however, about engines. "One thing to be considered," he said, "is whether we can ship engines into the country in which we are to manufacture, at least for a time. Or can we purchase a suitable engine in that country?"

McAllister favored opening a factory in Germany. Fowler McCormick agreed, "But we cannot tell anything about Germany until we know what the government will do."

On September 18, the NWC again confronted the issue of the names under which it manufactured its products. "These machines (industrial tractors, power units and TracTracTors) are now designated in the domestic trade as McCormick-Deering and in export trade as McCormick or Deering, as required. Our industrial distributors are somewhat confused by the name McCormick-Deering. The name International is used domestically on motor trucks, and the sale of industrials or crawlers is handled by many of the same distributors." The NWC agreed to name industrial-use TracTracTors as Internationals but to keep those used for agricultural applications under the McCormick-Deering name.

The committee also addressed other issues. Export sales asked for kerosene-burning versions of the WA-40. Model 22–36 engines were back in production in PD-300 power units as stationary power for farms and industrial locations. Export requested 500 Improved 22–36s to meet inquiries for a powerful kerosene or distillate tractor. These would use the less expensive four-cylinder ball-bearing splash-lubricated engine in place of the six-cylinder pressure-feed engine that had appeared in the heavier WD-40 chassis.

Just before Christmas, McCroskey pushed for accelerated development of new crawlers, and

redesign of existing ones. "In California, our biggest potential market, 1,500 old original Caterpillars went out of production in 1928. On 40 percent of the farms in the Pacific Northwest, this size [T-30 and T-60] will pull a harvester-thresher. The question," McCroskey continued, "involves the simplification of the T-20 along the lines being carried out in the design of the T-30 and T-60 (previously the T-65 but renamed to combat Caterpillar's new 60). This covers, among other things, turning brakes on the cross-countershaft and a pivot of the tracks on the axle of the driving sprocket." He emphasized that he "did not favor planetary steering devices, but preferred a positive declutching configuration. In making that statement," McCroskey added, "I recognize it is not the province of the sales department to dictate the design . . ."

But sales department personnel did influence IHC product design and selection during this period. When engineering designed the T-30, NWC agreed it would be built for agricultural uses; it did not need to be strengthened for bulldozer work. At this meeting domestic sales reversed itself, and asked that the crawler be built stronger.

To do that, Johnston had to find three or four extra horsepower, potential he knew existed in a future 4.5x6-inch four-cylinder engine. He already had 33-brake horsepower, which led sales to label the new crawler the T-35. Power for construction uses moved sales to a frenzy. McCaffrey, recently named director of domestic and Canadian sales, reiterated that more horsepower was necessary.

"We must do what Caterpillar R.D.4 does," he said, "or be seriously handicapped." Estimates for

1937 International Industrial 30 with Galion E-Z Lift Grader

This 1937 Galion Patrol Leaning-Wheel Grader, Model P318, was manufactured by Galion Iron Works and Mfg. Co., Galion, Ohio. It measures 29 feet long overall and stands 9 feet, 8 inches to the top of the cab. It carries a 10-foot blade. It was sold originally to the California State Highway Department in Sacramento. Galion is now owned by Komatsu.

1938 O-14 with Orchard Plow

IHC produced only 639 of these O-14 models during 1938 and 1939, with production beginning June 27, 1938. Tractors sold for $825, with rubber tires but not including the No. 4 IHC Orchard Plow shown here.

production tooling reached $725,000 for the crawler and $441,000 for its engine, utilizing some equipment in place for other diesel manufacture. This got Sydney McAllister's attention.

"The TracTracTor business is in the red," McAllister said. "We should have a better picture of the potential markets before we contemplate putting a million or more dollars into another size."

Ed Johnston intervened. "If it is a question," Johnston said, "of staying in the Crawler-type business, we should proceed."

McCaffrey added that "It was necessary to have four sizes to stay in the crawler business in a worthwhile manner."

Opportunities in the crawler market, and efforts

to tap them most profitably, would be recurring issues on which McCaffrey and sales would always have an opinion.

The over-worked NWC met again to hear Sperry's update on European manufacture on January 2, 1936. Touring Germany since Christmas, he learned that a German fuel called Treibstaff, a combination of gasoline and alcohol "of better quality than diesel fuel," would work well in the gas/kerosene-engined F-12s.

Improvements in tractor tires also affected manufacturing considerations. Growing acceptance of pneumatic rubber tires forced GPED to reconsider tractor speeds. Before this March 16 meeting, top

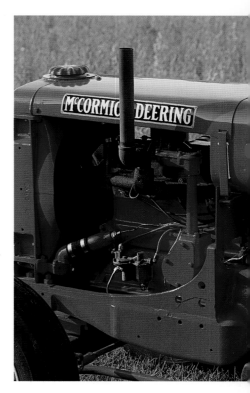

1938 Farmall F-20
Early in 1937, Gas Power Engineering experimented with high-test gasoline, using higher compression pistons. Ed Johnston, who was intimate with development of the tractor and drive train, protested. "It would be foolish," he said, "to put more power in the engine than the chassis or powertrain could take care of."

As with all the 14-series tractors, Farmall, Industrial, Orchard and W-models, the most significant difference from the previous 12-series was rated engine speed. The O, I and W-14 engines were allowed to run up to 2,000 rpm, providing them greater horsepower.

gear speeds had developed haphazardly. Now IHC needed continuity across product lines when each agricultural tractor got tested and catalogued at the Nebraska Tractor Tests. Every machine was fully described in sales brochures and service manuals produced by the advertising, sales or service departments. Numbers had to match and speeds had to increase with models of increased power.

Sperry, veteran of several Nebraska tests by this time, pointed out that the actual traveling speeds recorded in the tests varied due to lugs and ground conditions. David Baker revealed that IHC's engineers (and their competitors) selected lugs specifically for the day's conditions on the test track. He reminded his colleagues that the tractors' top speeds would have to be met with adequate brakes. "Such brakes," Sperry suggested, "would soon be made necessary by legislation."

In late March 1936, the first prototype rigid-track-frame TA-40 and TD-40 crawlers went into tests, fitted with side-mounted cranes for oil-pipeline construction. GPED interrupted the program for nearly six months when pipeline demand dropped. McCaffrey, spearheading this accelerated

development, expressed concern when he learned that material costs for rigid-frame modifications on IHC's crawlers would require a price increase of $131.50, whereas Caterpillar asked only $35 extra. Sperry explained that the difference in cost was due to "the structure of the two tractors, the Caterpillar having the pivot for the track on the rear axle and the TracTracTor having the pivot forward of the rear axle." This was necessary to avoid risk of further patent infringements, in the same way that Lift-All placement on the Farmall F-12 had been varied from that on the Deere Model A.

In early April, the first of five preproduction F-21s (the F-20X) reached Phoenix. Two remained in Chicago so Deering Works could design implements for its hydraulic lift mechanism. Early reports came back very favorably, encouraging NWC to built another 20 F-21 test tractors, completed by August 1, 1936. One F-21 in Phoenix ran 145 hours with a three-bottom plow working 10 inches deep. Sperry explained why this F-21 weighed 400 pounds more than production F-20s.

"The new 54-inch wheels required heavier-spoked rims," he said. "The extended axle brought

in additional weight. The larger diameter wheels effectively reduced the wheelbase by 7 inches, so the wheelbase grew 6 inches to accommodate front cultivators. Part of the added weight of the F-21 came from using cast-iron in lieu of more expensive material. Transmission weight came from extra gearing necessary to reach a 15-mile-per-hour high speed on pneumatic tires.

"Management insisted on carrying over the F-20 engine into the F-21. It could produce additional horsepower without much increase in weight, and up to 25 horsepower at the belt would be possible." Sperry said the new F-21 engine weighed 958.5 pounds (with new head, manifold and air cleaner), just 2 pounds more than the F-20 power plant, no penalty for nearly four more horsepower.

"If we are on the wrong track as to the type of tractor," Sperry said, "we must redesign it. There is nothing much we can do to reduce the weight of the tractor now proposed for the purposes for which it is designed." Field tests during design were disheartening. A John Deere Model A gained one round on the Farmall in every 10 rounds plowed.

By 1938, the F-20 successors, variously known as F-21, F-22, the New F-20 and the Intermediate F-20, the F-15 and the 2-F, were in and out of engineering, design and development. When the final version rolled out of the factory on July 3, 1939, it was called the Farmall H.

1938 W-30 Orchard California Special

The New Work Committee and the Naming Committee jointly created the W-30 during February 1931, as each made plans to replace aging 10–20 Gear Drive models. With its larger four-cylinder engine, the W-30 Orchard models developed nearly one-third more power than the O-14.

California Special Orchard models provided buyers with full fenders, a foot clutch, no belt pulley (to hang up on young trees or low branches) and a heavily shielded exhaust and intake manifold. Grousers were shorter, to lessen risk of damaging roots.

While the F-21, the F-20 replacement, was nearly 900 pounds heavier than the Deere, Sperry argued that its higher speed, quick implement-mounting system, now referred to as Quick Attach or "QA," and its improved plowing power brought it past the competition.

If they could keep too many new ideas from infecting their designs and slowing development, Johnston and Sperry both believed 1937 would be a strong product year. They had a new Farmall and two new crawlers, the T-35 and T-60, as well as yet another revision of the T-20 TracTracTor.

By early August, sales pressed GPED to adapt adjustable rear treads to the F-30 as well as the F-21, now referred to as the New F-20. Sales interfered again with engineering, proposing in mid-October that, instead of just adopting adjustable rear track-width mechanisms to the F-30, GPED should redo the big Farmall along the lines of the Intermediate New F-20, or F-22. Engineering also began work on a new tractor to replace the W-40. From the beginning, sales considered the W-40 a temporary tractor, even referring to it as the "converted 22–36 tractor."

By this time, field tests had begun at Hinsdale of the first F-22. NWC had approved the increased horsepower Farmall F-21 engine, but then backed off from the four horsepower jump. Now sales wanted less development time, lower costs, only two horsepower more, and an almost immediate introduction. The changed demands put additional pressure on Johnston, Sperry and their engineers to begin, develop and perfect yet another version. Work continued to pour out of GPED.

In April 1935, A. W. Seacord had suggested that changing from gray varnish to synthetic enamel paint would preserve tractor color longer when the machines were stored outside. This observation led shortly to discussion about changing tractor colors. As the experimental department worked with sprayed paint techniques, it tested various colors in May and June. There were already enough green tractors between Deere, Oliver-Hart Parr, and some of IHC's own lines. Case and Ford seemed devoted to gray as IHC had been, so a desire for differentiation led to tests at Hinsdale farm.

Of primary concern was how to make the tractors more visible, especially on roads. Red continually emerged as the answer. By summer of 1936, tests showed the new red synthetic enamel held up to steady exposure to sun and elements better than the previous gray had done. Red it was.

The Executive Council circulated decision papers, GPED issued change decisions, and manufacturing released specification change orders. On November 1, 1936, the first 1937 model tractors rolled out of Tractor Works and Farmall Works wearing "Harvester No. 50 motor red synthetic enamel paint." Wheels remained dipped in Harvester red color varnish.

Early in 1937, R. M. McCroskey experimented with high-test gasoline in F-20 tractors, using high-compression pistons. Johnston pointed out "that our tractors, including the F-20 Farmall, were designed with an 'engineering balance' as to power and strength throughout their various parts, and it would be foolish to put more power in the engine than the chassis or power [train] could take care of." (This concern would reappear through the rest of IHC's life.) McCroskey also stressed the importance of preparing to use the higher performance fuel.

"The propaganda of the Ethyl Gas Corporation and of the agricultural colleges," he said, "would create a sizable demand for tractors adapted to use high test gasoline," especially the benefits of improved fuel economy. Both McCaffrey and McAllister agreed that, while there may be benefits, it would involve developing a complete new line of engines.

"Farmers want low cost of operation," McCaffrey argued, "which we have shown is accomplished by our tractors using low-cost fuels. High test is not low cost." (Yet, within 18 months, GPED, which loved challenges, found an easy solution by replacing standard pistons with those acquired from outside sources, meant for altitudes above 5,000 and 8,000 feet. At sea level, this provided higher compression.)

The performance pendulum swung back in February when Sperry told NWC members that nearly all tractor manufacturers who submitted machines to the Nebraska Tractor Tests ran on distillate.

"With the proper compression, this [fuel] gave in the neighborhood of 4 percent better horsepower than a similar tractor designed for kerosene and 15 percent better results in fuel economy," he explained. Distillate was low-cost fuel, available throughout the United States and Canada.

1938 Farmall F-12
By 1938 the F-12 was on borrowed time. The last one was produced on January 27, the same day the first F-14 engine was assembled. Despite F-12 engine problems, it was a popular machine; during its six-year actual production life, IHC built more than 120,000 of the 12 series tractors.

Winter F-22 field tests at Hinsdale continued until snows got too deep. Results satisfied NWC members enough to authorize GPED to build five more prototypes. While GPED reduced the weight, the F-22 still was 156 pounds heavier than the F-20. The wheelbase, first stretched 6 inches, was trimmed finally to an increase of 1.375 inches.

W. E. Payton, service manager at the St. Louis Branch, sent Leonard Sperry a telegraph on April 8, telling him that two prototype Allis-Chalmers Model B tractors worked fields nearby. Sperry dispatched McCroskey. He and Frank Bonnes, from domestic tractor sales, were impressed with the semiunitized-frame and torque-tube construction. Bonnes was equally affected by the area and the scale of farming there. J. M. Strasser, assistant branch manager, told Bonnes that around St. Louis, there were more than 1,200 farms of between 5 and 40 acres, farms too small to use any tractor other than a one-row machine.

"We have, I believe, just missed this market with our 12 series tractor," Bonnes wrote to the NWC. "The price of our F-12 has gone steadily upward until at the present time these small garden farmers will not make the investment required. If this Allis-Chalmers tractor, with its main frame construction or torque-tube main frame, can stand up, this little tractor is certainly the greatest threat to our F-12 business today." Those observations would have a long-lasting impact on IHC's tractor planning strategies.

Through a stringent weight loss program, GPED cut F-22 weight to less than the F-20. This had developed an unwelcome side effect during IHC's Phoenix Tractor conference earlier that year, on February 22, 1938. Under certain farming and implement use conditions, the tractor front end was too light. Following the Phoenix demonstrations, Johnston added 400 pounds to the front of the F-22.

The updated F-14, also known as the F-15, now had 20 horsepower compared to 18 from F-14s and 16 from the F-12. The F-14 suffered from front-end weight and balance problems as well. Halohan and McCaffrey, apologizing again to GPED for telling them how to design tractors, proposed they lengthen the F-15's wheelbase by 6 inches to 85 inches, matching the F-22. Johnston argued this

It wasn't until 1939, however, that electric start arrived for any of IHC's tractors. It required little engineering, a few mounting points for the starter, a revised casting for a gear-toothed flywheel, a storage box for the battery, and a generator. Mostly it required customer demand.

1939 W-30 Electric Start

The serial number WB32038 ends with PTS, the P for pneumatic tires, the T for 10-mile-per-hour four-speed transmission, and the S for Special Equipment, in this case, battery, generator, and electric starter. This setup was more popular on industrial models.

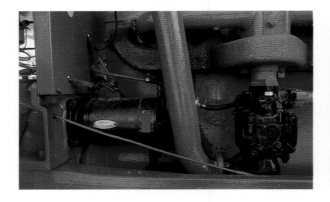

would make little difference; an additional 350 pounds might still be necessary. On March 17, McCaffrey urged quick decisions so F-22 production might begin on schedule on November 1, because manufacturing had promised him 4,000 copies available by January 15. Tooling and raw materials costs were rising, but sales was confident. Then on April 13, revised manufacturing cost estimates made McCaffrey reverse himself.

"The F-20 is one of the best tractors in the Harvester line," he proclaimed. "The F-20 is still salable if certain improvements are put into it. It will cost $2.5 million to put the F-22 into production and it will have to sell for $1,025 as against $985 for the F-20, both on steel. This higher price will put us out of the market. And this 'dressing up' of the tractor! A farmer puts a tractor out into the field to work. This dressing up does not mean anything. A tractor is built to do a job quickly and cheaply. Too much has been done on the appearance factor."

GPED design engineer A. W. Scarratt was incredulous.

"The F-22 is the result of unfavorable comments from sales on the F-20 when compared to competitive machines," he said. "As a result, features were developed which were incorporated into what is now the F-22. This machine has all the things that sales has asked for: clearance under the machine, adjustable tread, new transmission to offer speeds from 2 1/2 to 21 miles per hour, provision for pneumatic tires, variable speed governor, good brakes, better steering wheel, water pump, foot accelerator, and a standing platform, and it has the increased power everyone asked for.

"All these things were being developed," Scarratt continued, "and the effect of style consciousness crept in and we dressed up the job. The fact

of our having styled this job has caused no penalty in the tractor mechanically and this sheet metal can be taken off."

"But our competitors do not have all the improvements in one machine that we have in the F-22," McCaffrey replied, reflecting his sales department's insecurity about being first with new features. "If the F-15 turns out to be an honest two-plow tractor, I am not so sure that the F-22 should not be a bigger tractor to eliminate the F-30. After all, the F-14 is now taking F-20 sales. We need a one-plow, a two-plow and a three-plow tractor, but I question if the F-10, F-15 and F-22 will meet these requirements? How many of these things could be put on the F-20?"

David Baker suggested: "This would depend entirely on how far the management wanted to go with redevelopment. Some tooling cost might be saved, but it would be an expensive construction."

Charles Morrison, now vice president of sales for IHC and president of IH Company of America, asked R. C. Archer, manager of tractor sales, for his opinion.

"Last year," Archer said, "we sold all the F-20s that could be made. This year they are not selling so well. Dealers find them increasingly difficult to move. We must give the dealer organizations something soon." But McCaffrey wasn't swayed.

"The adjustable axle tractor business is less than 20 percent of the whole," McCaffrey announced. "We now have the F-14, which will supply the demands of part of the 20 percent. About 70 percent of the tractors in the field never adjust their axles."

Archer wasn't satisfied with that analysis, arguing instead that "Deere and Oliver are selling tractors because it is possible to adjust their wheels."

When Ed Johnston arrived, he found himself joining a meeting that threatened, unexpectedly, to undermine three years work, much of it done at McCaffrey's request.

"The question of revamping the F-20," Johnston said, "is whether or not sales can get along without the adjustable tread. If we start to remodel the F-20, it will mean we have to change the whole thing, and when we are finished we will still have a tractor which will not be considered new by the trade."

Johnston's clear thinking had no impact. The NWC met at Tractor Works on April 27 and killed the F-22, so far as its power or size was concerned. It created instead a three-plow tractor, the F-32.

"The term F-32 has a different meaning as to power and size than previously," Ed Kimbark reported in meeting minutes, "when it was tentatively assigned to a redesigned F-30 with an engine having horsepower of about 40."

Fowler McCormick sat in on this session. By the end, the NWC endorsed one-, two- and three-plow tractors, but with new designations. The one-plow F-10, authorized in September 1937, was renamed the 1-F by GPED, to avoid growing confusions with Farmall F-number designations. The two-plow F-15 with a new 22-horsepower engine became the 2-F. The F-32, its name actually used for a short while on a proposed "22–36 Increased Power Farmall" (authorized back in April 1936), had become the 33-horsepower F-32 three-plow Farmall. GPED renamed it the 3-F. Prototypes already under way with older numbering were hurried along. The F-10/1-F was due within weeks, the 22-horsepower F15/2-F was expected in June 1938, and NWC wanted the F-32/3-F by July. Johnston said he would have manufacture-ready prototypes in July 1939, adding, "this date being dependent on sales not changing their minds again, as to what they want in sizes and powers."

For the F-10/1-F, Johnston proposed an L-head engine and also a new overhead-valve version. The F-15/2-F provided drawbar performance to match Allis-Chalmers' WC. McCaffrey, yet again apologizing for designing tractors, said that the F-22, at 29 gross horsepower, was not enough to call it a three-plow tractor. "A three-plow tractor," he explained," should have at least 31 and better, 32 horsepower."

Johnston reminded him that the 33-drawbar horsepower F-32/3-F would weigh perhaps 200 pounds more than the F-20. However, few parts of the F-22 could be used on the now-proposed F-32/3-F. Charles Morrison asked what would become of the current F-30. "Under the present plan, then," he wondered, "does the F-30 just fade out of the picture? And what about a four-plow model?" Ed Johnston described to them two tractors known in GPED as the F-40 and the W-42.

"The engine proposed [a new 5x6.125 four-cylinder with dry liners] was in two forms, one with the engine base as part of the tractor frame and one with the engine to be mounted on a more conventional chassis structure. The W-42 would be a real four-plow tractor."

"We must have a four-plow tractor," McCaffrey urged, never one to let a new product pass in silence. His vision of the marketplace energized an engineering department still hungry for opportunity and approval.

As little demand as there was for an electric start W-40, there appeared to be even less for the W-30. Perhaps only a handful of these W-30s were produced in 1939. Its installation was slightly more complex; engineering had to snake a new air-intake breather tube around the starter.

1939 Farmall F-14

During New Work Committee meetings, John McCaffrey argued with R. C. Archer over adjustable front ends. McCaffrey said only 20 percent of the market wanted them; he felt they were too costly. Archer replied that Deere and Oliver were selling tractors specifically because farmers could adjust their axles.

As farmers demanded larger implements and Bert Benjamin's implement makers responded, Ed Johnston's tractor engineers encountered problems with the power lift mechanisms. A. C. Lindren, Scarratt and Benjamin used 5-inch-diameter hydraulic cylinders (replacing previous 3-inch sizes), mostly to accommodate heavier F-30 equipment. Carl Mott designed a system of lifts that raised left or right gangs or front or rear sets independently. A double-acting cylinder-valve and spring mechanism lifted and lowered front and rear equipment in sequence.

Meanwhile, GPED discarded the overhead-valve engines in F-10/1-F prototypes. Sperry cited large tooling expenditures as the primary reason. NWC authorized two more prototypes in late June 1938, one using an L-head engine and the other with a redesigned F-12 powerplant for comparison purposes. Sales kept pressure on Sperry to complete testing in time to start production on March 1, 1939. But H. D. MacDonald, from sales, confused things. While pushing an accelerated testing program, he also insisted on adjustable front and rear axles to straddle two rows.

Arguing for an accelerated testing program, McCroskey calculated that if GPED followed customary preproduction programs, including several-month lag-times between testing, prototype costs and

design changes, "our competitors will have sold 40,000 tractors before we even enter the market. Allis-Chalmers is building and selling 75 and perhaps as many as 100 Model B tractors per day. When we lose tractor business we lose everything that goes with it, plows, cultivators, disk harrows, mowers, harvesters."

Tractor design-by-comparison resumed a week later, on June 20, when GPED reviewed crawlers with the NWC. Johnston told the group they reduced "the height of the TD-25 to that of the Caterpillar D-2." Sydney McAllister, asking the height of Caterpillar's drawbar, was relieved to know that IHC's was the same. R. C. Archer said sales was "satisfied with the Caterpillar clearance and the decision that our clearance will be no less than that." They set track width at 42 inches, as with the D-2, and Ed Johnston reported that "the weight of this tractor will be reduced to a point where it is comparable to the D-2." In August, they revised crawler model numbers, changing the TD-25 to TD-6.

The New Work Committee and Executive Council met at Hinsdale on August 2, 1938, to watch several demonstrations, including a mocked-up 2-F tractor plowing against an Allis-Chalmers WC, both using two-bottom 14-inch Little Genius plows. Immediately afterward, the participants began to dissect and scrutinize the prototype.

Sydney McAllister asked, "Are we on the ragged edge as to horsepower? We must consider having ample power for two plows and also we must consider cost!"

Ed Johnston, frustrated by company management that wanted heroic efforts in development, and miracles in meeting deadlines while juggling too many projects, snapped. "If more horsepower is wanted," Johnston exclaimed, "we must start all over. IHC's outside industrial designer [Raymond Loewy] has approved the proposed styling of the tractor . . . though not what he would like to have, which, we've determined, would be too expensive."

The group soon approved accelerated preproduction runs of seven 2-Fs in addition to the mocked-up prototype demonstrated that day. McAllister wanted these samples sent into challenging conditions, as they had to accomplish trials normally given to many more prototypes. They moved on to 3-F models and signed off on seven of these as well, which would dovetail with existing programs in progress on the 1-F tractors. Johnston updated the group on the other GPED experimental projects, including 3-W and 3-WD tractors, 4-Ws, T-3 (formerly the development T-10 models), T-6 and TD-6 (previously the T-25), T-9 and TD-9 (formerly the T-36 series), TD-14 (formerly the T-45,) and the TD-18, which grew out of the T-60/T-65 projects.

"It would be very desirable," McCaffrey mentioned at the end of that meeting, "to announce all three Farmall tractors to the trade at the same time." McAllister and Morrison settled on phase-out plans for F-30, F-20 and F-14 models; new Farmalls would require factory production space, and markets for older tractors would surely disappear after new model introductions in September 1939. On October 3, they agreed to drop the W-30 and 10/20 tractors before May 1939, to meet demands on factory capacity.

Then, on November 9, during a conference at Hinsdale farm, another old issue returned to haunt the NWC members. The previous March, they argued that adjustable-tread tractors made up only 20 percent of the market, and adjustable treads were not needed on 1-F tractors. That was before they saw the Allis-Chalmers Model B with track widths adjustable from 40 to 52 inches. Allis-Chalmers sold nearly 11,000 of these tractors by year-end.

Fortunately, David Baker already had an adjustable front and rear axle ready. McCroskey reasoned that perhaps 90 percent of the 1-Fs would be sold with these axles. When Ed Johnston showed a prototype row-crop 1-F, with a single front wheel to accommodate two-row planters or cultivators, McCroskey urged his colleagues to move forward cautiously.

"When purchasers had in this size tractor the ability to cultivate two rows," McCroskey said, "they would want it capable of using larger implements. There would be an insistent demand for more power, followed by our need to provide more strength and weight." McAllister and Morrison agreed, telling Johnston that they could protect themselves by perfecting a three-wheel type 1-F, but not offering it to the trade unless some other circumstance—such as a competitor's comparable offering—forced their hand.

During a June 13, 1938, conference on "Development of New Machines," McCaffrey set out six guidelines for information he required before sales would consider new development or major redesign projects. These six items were: 1. Competitor's

weights; 2. Competitor's list prices; 3. Our weights required; 4. Our required list price; 5. Our product cost necessary to establish this list price; and 6. Estimated sales. Sales was much more likely to endorse a project if someone else already made it at a price IHC could meet or beat. Fowler McCormick had become an important player here. After five years as head of foreign sales, the board named him vice president of manufacturing in 1938. His staff determined costs that influenced IHC's retail prices.

Throughout that winter, GPED continued development work, and then IHC launched a number of new tractors. On May 23, 1939, Baker signed off on production orders to start assembly of 1-F tractors, now called the Farmall A. The first machine rolled out on June 21, 1939. On June 6, Baker approved the new 2-F as a Farmall H, and the 3-F as the Farmall M. Model H and M assembly began July 3. Implements designed for the three lines went on sale July 20. Baker released the Farmall B on August 8 and the first one emerged on September 5.

The next August 12, in 1940, Baker signed off on a Narrow Tread Farmall B, providing rear tread widths adjustable from 56 to 84 inches, in 4-inch increments. Manufacture began October 15. Nine days later, he launched production of a High Clearance Model A, the AV. The first one was manufactured on January 10, 1941. Sales, for the time being, was satisfied.

Gas Power Engineering always felt the front end of the F-14 models was a little light. Its 77-inch wheelbase was short enough that the extra power and torque it got from the higher engine speed made it twitchy under a heavy pull. By late in 1939, the F-14 replacement had resolved all questions.

1940–1944

Seven

WORK CONTINUES, THE PACE ACCELERATES

The New Work Committee pushed along one large engineering project after another throughout 1941, releasing them almost every other month. Most involved diesel engines. During a Farm Tractor and Implement Committee meeting February 27, Leonard Sperry, Sydney Morrison, John McCaffrey (just named vice president of worldwide sales), and soon-to-be-elected IHC President Fowler McCormick (succeeding his father, Harold) all agreed to build a sample Model H high-clearance tractor with a diesel engine.

1939 Farmall M with Elwood Four Wheel Drive

Final testing of the F-32/3-F preproduction prototypes took place in Phoenix, Atlanta, San Antonio, and Los Angeles during the Christmas season of 1938. Gas Power Engineering was extremely satisfied, and on January 16, 1939, it signed off on production start.

However, while the NWC kept busy and IHC was productive, its work force was not happy. The day after the diesel high crop approval, organized labor, battling since the 1920s to represent IHC's tractor assemblers, struck McCormick Works. Some 6,500 workers went out. By March 3, nearly 15,000 employees were outside, seeking representation by the Farm Equipment Workers Organizing Committee (FEW). Strikers returned to work March 23, content for the time being.

In mid-May, Leonard Sperry presented to the Executive Council proposals for a larger Trac-TracTor, a TD-24, to compete with Caterpillar's D-8 and Allis-Chalmers HD-14. Allis' crawler, with its lighter weight two-cycle engine and running gear, produced 132 drawbar horsepower. Yet field reports of failed transmissions, rear ends, and frames on HD-14s, directed GPED toward Caterpillar's 113 horsepower D-8 in structure, while matching the A-C in power.

A small group gathered in GPED in late September to discuss the Farmall B straight-axle

A growing need for more power and more efficient ways of getting that power to the ground prompted Elwood Manufacturing to produce these four-wheel-drive kits in the mid-1950s. Elwood made front-wheel-drive modifications for Farmall Ms and tractors from other manufacturers.

1940 Farmall H with Beet Harvester
H prototypes, the 2-F tractors, completed testing at the same time and in the same places as the Ms, or 3-F machines. Regular production began July 3, 1939. It was instantly popular. IHC produced more than 10,000 in 1939 and more than 41,000 in 1940.

tractor and a new Farmall E model, incorporating live hydraulic implement lift and independent PTO. Because of the B's older technology and difficulties with updating it, (necessary two years later when Hs and Ms would be revised,) the NWC chose the E instead, incorporating the Model B's straight axle for this new prototype. Throughout this project, Tractor Division Experimental Engineering continued mostly doing peacetime developments, even as IHC devoted more factory space to armament production.

On December 7, 1941, the Japanese bombed Pearl Harbor, forcing President Franklin D. Roosevelt to declare war the next day. World War II became an American reality; the semiannual Tractor Conference discussed shipping new tractors on steel wheels because the government curtailed rubber deliveries. IHC had a five-week supply of pneumatics remaining. Sperry and David Baker worried that steel-wheel technology no longer was adequate for more powerful peacetime tractors. GPED devised stronger steel wheels and recommended five-mile-per-hour transport speed limits.

On January 2, 1942, A. W. Scarratt showed a wooden full-scale model V-8 engine developed at Fort Wayne. "It seems sensible," he explained, "to be consistent in both carbureted and diesel types of engines, and standardize in basic designs for both trucks and tractors. The desirability of compactness in tractor applications is nearly as vital as in truck usage." GPED designed the V-8 in two displacement sizes, one of a maximum of 460 cubic inches and a larger one of 655.

"We can either try to work out an engine program that we know is going to cost a lot to put into manufacture," Scarratt said, "but which will be an accomplishment worth the effort and cost, (and give us a quality line of modern engines to offer our trade, both in truck and tractor lines,) or we can continue the rather futile effort of merely revising the old lines."

To Scarratt, products developed from the sales department dictates stifled innovation: GPED was perfecting competitors' machines so IHC could put its label on them. McCaffrey's six rules codified this, even as he apologized repeatedly for "appearing to design the tractors." With this engine project, engineering tried to take back engineering.

Because of the wartime need for raw materials and GPED's development program on the Farmall E (which they saw as a pilot model for future tractors,) GPED shelved the Farmall B Straight Axle tractor

IHC produced its first beet harvesters in 1946, immensely complex machines that dug up the beets and loaded them into wagons towed behind. Within a year, these HM-1 machines were scattered across the United States., mounted on and towed behind H and M models.

August.) The straight-axle B eventually would reappear after the war, introduced in 1947 as the Model C.

Fowler McCormick wrote to A. W. Scarratt on March 7, 1942, reflecting on GPED's proposed V-8s.

"Instead of setting out to design a V-8 motor which will be suitable for both trucks and tractors, the GPED should set as its goal the best V-8 motor which can be designed for trucks only. When it is nearly perfect, they will then test it in tractors, with whatever changes are necessary." The benefit to both applications was the lower center of gravity, improved handling of the trucks and cornering and balance of the tractors. If the only way these engines would work for tractors required extensive modification, he preferred GPED design a dedicated tractor engine afterward.

"Our experience in the past," McCormick continued, "has not been fortunate using tractor engines in trucks, or vice versa. If we set out from the start to design an engine suitable for both, we will so compromise the design to make it adaptable that it will be less desirable for either."

1940 T-9 with Trackson Crane

F. P. Smith Equipment Co., a supplier of new and used parts and equipment for IHC ag and construction crawlers and wheel tractors, uses this Trackson Swing Crane mounted on a T-9 to retrieve parts heavy forklifts can't reach. Here it hoists a grader front axle.

T-9s were in production from 1940 through 1956, using a four-cylinder 4.4x5.5-inch gas engine to develop 46.46 brake horsepower. Weighing 10,655 pounds (without the Trackson crane), they could pull more than 7,000 pounds.

on January 16, 1942. The war also sidetracked QA quick-attach hitch development for the A, AV, B and BN tractors. (This had been the QD Quick Detach system, but it was revised the previous

Seizing Fowler's "no compromise" rule, Arnold E. W. Johnson offered GPED's next invention on March 25:

"New machines must be designed to fit the crops and farming practice of numerous individual localities. The implement industry will always be encumbered with varieties. This may be improved by direct-mounted implements on basic front and rear frames. To each we can attach a variety of working tools that can be removed intact with the adjustments preserved, saving the operator time required for resetting shovels, disks, etc." Johnson dimmed the lights and flashed Kodachrome slides on the screen.

"Hydraulic fingertip depth control and power-lift eliminates varieties of hand lever assemblies. Fingertips regulate the depth of working tools. The power-lift is enclosed and located in the middle of the tractor. Two double-acting hydraulic cylinders lift, or apply pressure to the tools." Pictures showed several modified Farmall H tractors working Hinsdale Farm fields.

"The individual tools and frames detach from the tractor without the removal of a single bolt. Only one wrench is necessary. The tools are more flexible and adaptable to changing methods of farming." Close-up slides revealed the direct-mounted implement assembly.

"The system has tentatively been called the 'Frame-All' by the Engineering Department. We realize, however, that 'Frame-All' sounds very much like Farmall and no doubt a more appropriate name and one less likely to cause confusion can be found."

Johnson pointed out that, unlike the Ford-Ferguson three-point rear hitch, this Frame-All system used implements in front of the tractor as well as at the rear. Ford had one cylinder and one control lever; Frame-Alls used two double-acting cylinders and two levers, allowing adjustments on one side of the tractor or the other, front or rear. The Frame-All could accomplish delayed lift and drop of front and rear implements. While GPED showed a "Frame-All" Model H, they had already started work on Frame-All Model A, B and M tractors. "If Farmalls A and B are to be superseded by the proposed Model E, our development will work for that model," Johnson concluded.

Two days after the Frame-All introduction, Fowler McCormick clamped tight security on it and the QA system with hydraulic controls.

1941 Farmall AV

AV tractors originally were delivered on 8-36 rear tires. Sales heard of demand for wider tires, and GPED approved a 9-36 in late October, 1941. These would be standard equipment, at a factory cost of $7.14. They estimated 1942 AV production at 75 tractors.

Gas Power Engineering created the Combine Caravan program in the early 1940s. This was a research and development mobile workshop that started in Texas and worked north during harvest seasons. While caravan personnel handled minor repairs, they spent more time listening to farmers and devising new products and ideas on the spot. *State Historical Society of Wisconsin*

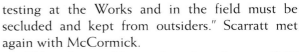

"Discussions on these subjects," he wrote, "must be confined only to those directly concerned with this new setup. Exhibits, experimenting and testing at the Works and in the field must be secluded and kept from outsiders." Scarratt met again with McCormick.

"After the war," he explained to the new IHC president, "farmers would have used up equipment and would need something new. Sales would want something new to sell." He suggested planning immediately to replace A and B models with this "E" straight-axle tractor.

"Adaptations of the 'QA-Frame-All' and hydraulic fingertip lift control should be confined to Farmall E," Scarratt argued, "because the basic principles of this scheme of tools and attachments lends itself readily to this tractor, which is more similar to the H and M in general outline than either the A or B tractors."

"This system looks like it has been made from the ground up," Fowler McCormick enthused.

War production consumed most of IHC's factory capacity. But once tooling was set up, GPED experimental engineers were not rushed to develop new machines every other month. The war offered them the benefit of time to perfect the Frame-All and the "E." Meanwhile, the Milwaukee Works produced torpedoes for the navy,

1941 Farmall A

Sales announced that the Farmall A tractor was the one-row tractor with Culti-Vision. This offset engine-versus-operator placement allowed excellent operator visibility during crop cultivation. To make the A more versatile, an adjustable front and rear axle were optional.

Gas Power Engineering specified that IHC's Model A tractor was the correct size machine for farms between 40 and 70 acres. Because the A's road speed was slower than an AV, in September 1941, GPED began testing a 20-mile per hour road gear.

and other plants made half-tracks and tanks, 20-millimeter and 40-millimeter cartridges. From IHC's refrigeration technology came blood coolers to aid field hospitals. (Government production would provide two-thirds of IHC's sales revenue by 1943.)

By late fall 1942, Scarratt's first Farmall E was completed and construction of a "Reverse Direction Super Farmall E" began. Half a world away, in mid-November, a former Kansas farm boy led American forces into North Africa. Within four days, Lieutenant General Dwight David Eisenhower liberated land previously held by governments sympathetic to Nazi Germany.

On New Year's Eve 1942, David Baker gained approval from Fowler McCormick to begin assembly of 11 "Intermediate H" and six "Intermediate M" models. "The purpose of this preproduction program," Baker explained, "is to provide tractors upon which 'Frame-All' implements or mounted implements can be field tested during 1943." Four of each were sent to Hinsdale, while one H, one M and one M diesel remained at GPED for further development.

1941 TD-14

The TD-14 frustrated the Industrial Sales Division. Customers complained they were underpowered, but IHC maintained it could not offer additional power output from these engines as they were designed, and the existing frames would not fit new engines that engineering had in development.

These were powered by IHC's in-line four, 461-cubic inch diesel, which developed 61.6 brake horsepower. During their 1939–1949 production life, IHC manufactured 26,259 of these crawlers. Despite registering dissatisfaction, sales sold every one they could get.

It took five years for the impact of Frank Bonnes' April 1938 visit to St. Louis to coalesce into a product plan for tractors for small farms. J. M Strasser from sales put the idea to dealers in Dallas on March 23, 1943:

"There ought to be a complete line of machines," he said, "for each principal classification of farms. Surrounding large cities, it is possible that part-time farming on small areas beside factory works may become a definite trend after the war." Another planner, J .R. Orelind, theorized that, "By making use of the so-called Frame-All system, which avoids duplication of frame work, it ought to be possible to sell the farmer a full line of good tillage tools for complete mechanism of the farm at a very reasonable cost." T. B. Hale, in regional tractor and implement sales, admitted that, "For years we have introduced new equipment without knowing what the actual market was and what the farm's income was."

David Baker joined Neal Higgins of sales, along with H. J. Kicherer and A. C. Richmond of manufacturing, for meetings from New York City to Los Angeles in late March 1943. These Chicago-based managers questioned 124 regional branch managers and dealers about IHC's current equipment and its uses, the competition and its advantages, field service and factory changes, mistakes of the past and rumors about the future.

"The consensus was that many wartime developments might well be carried over into the design, production and uses in commercial industrial power

industry after the war," Baker told Johnston and McCormick. "Dealers leaned toward expanding the line upward in power, to 120 horsepower-or-greater TracTracTors; the 60-, 90- and 120-or-more horsepower wheel industrials; and they expressed need for diesel power units as high as 200 horsepower." Baker and his colleagues developed several conclusions from these sessions that would steer IHC toward a new direction that Fowler McCormick only hesitantly endorsed:

1. Produce a full line of industrial power equipment comparable to competition

2. Speed up preparation to meet stiff postwar competition

3. Consider industrial powered equipment as important and major line of production

4. Develop separate industrial power organization

After reading the report, John McCaffrey wrote on his copy, "I approve and think every item should be brought to conclusion as soon as possible."

McCormick waited until the end of an Executive Council meeting on April 26, 1943, to offer his perspective.

"Before any large programs are inaugurated, there should be an approximation of investment required, volume of business anticipated and possible return to the company. A TracTracTor larger than the TD-18 might be necessary to round out the line, but equipment, manufacturing space and new buildings would be important items to consider." Council Chairman Sydney McAllister seconded McCormick's wariness:

"Road machinery and equipment for contract work are questionable for us because of the varieties and peculiarities for that kind of business. Management is hardly in favor of big industrial equipment at this time." Yet management favor was not rigid. On May 21, managers told David Baker to outline specifications for Sperry's TD-24, proposed two years earlier as a 37,500-pound diesel TracTracTor with a 165-horsepower engine. Industrial operators had asked for "A large crawler tractor with the weight, traction, durability and convenience of the Caterpillar D-8 with the flexible power like the Allis-Chalmers HD-14." Back in May 1941, no one had faith in the market for IHC construction equipment, and so no funds were forthcoming. Now McCaffrey prevailed and got money released.

The Farm Tractor and Implement Committee (FTIC) updated management on the Intermediate H and M tractors. David Baker lead the July 12th meeting.

"The second, or 'revised Intermediate' jobs are laid out to increase capacity in the hydraulic control system. Theoretical lifting capacity of one cylinder for each rockshaft would be stepped up from 1,720 pounds to 4,000 pounds. The probable cost of the hydraulic 'Touch Control' system is proving cheaper than the original (Lift-All) system," because Baker eliminated some cylinders, hoses, and springs. An experimental program to fit Frame-All hydraulics and 'Touch Control' systems onto prototype A and B tractors had begun testing at Hinsdale. R. P. Messenger, Carl Mott and Arnold Johnson now felt strongly that the A- and B-size Frame-All tractors offered IHC's best threat against the Ford-Ferguson three-point hitch and hydraulic control system, although R. M. McCroskey maintained the Farmall E had greater potential.

Then, because they felt the Executive Council still had ignored the significance of Bonnes' message, on July 9, 1943, Leonard Sperry, with McCroskey and Strasser, distributed an eight-page "Survey of Potential Demand for Farmall 'X' Tractors (smaller than the Farmall A)."

1942 Farmall H with Ronning Ensillage Harvester
Ronning produced ensillage harvesters under license to International from 1927 through 1945, bedecked with IHC and McCormick Deering logos and badges. Ronning manufactured more than 1,065 of these as feed crop technology and practices improved.

1942 Farmall M with Tobacco rack
Even with the widespread use of tractors in every kind of agricultural harvesting, tobacco harvest is still back-breaking human toil. On this small Wisconsin farm, the owner devotes just 4.8 acres to mostly chewing tobacco, while the rest of the operation is a dairy farm.

They acknowledged the Farmall A as appropriate for farms from 40 to 70 acres. However, the 1940 U.S. Census revealed that of 5.7 million farms reporting crop acreage, 3.3 million, or 58 percent, were smaller than 40 crop acres. Of those, 2.2 million had an annual gross farm income of $400 or more.

Sperry wrote that "In the 15 years of Farmall tractor type selling, IHC has sold 733,000 Farmalls." The potential, therefore, was "to reach the untouched market demanding smaller equipment." The Farmall "X" would "do the work of two or three horses or mules, be a four-wheel tractor, row-crop type, with eight horsepower on drawbar. It would be designed 'CultiVision-style' (engine offset to the operator for better crop visibility) for QA Quick Attach machines for truck garden and field work, whose retail price is not to exceed $400." They proposed a complete line of implements, tools and attachments.

To keep manufacturing costs at around $213, necessary to make a $400 list price, Baker and Sperry, while preferring a four-cylinder engine for torque and running smoothness, suggested a new two-cylinder, parallel, upright engine for the "X." Both believed cost reductions to existing Farmall As (at $575 list), by deleting some standard features, could bring it to the Farmall "X" price. The "X," but using a four-cylinder engine, got McAllister's

approval and a single sample was started.

New Work Committee members watched the latest Frame-All demonstrations at the Hinsdale Farm on August 11, 1943, seeing a new rear tool mounting system that embodied a preloaded cushion spring, connected to its draft control system. This relieved the tractor and attached tools of excessive shocks from working across rows.

Later that day, NWC members also saw an 8-foot harvester-thresher mounted on a prototype Super Farmall M with the reversed transmission, extended rear (now front) axle and hydraulic control. The efficiency of this "narrow-cut self-propelled" machine led the group to interrupt development on "reverse-going Super Farmall H and E models, concentrating instead on the higher-priced and higher-powered 'M,' providing a reverse-going tractor of advance design for early Post-War production."

Farm Tractor and Implement Group (FTIG) released specifications for the Model E. It ran the basic Model B engine at 1,650 rpm, with pump circulation-engine cooling. The E-chassis used a straight-axle with 36-inch rear tires, 15-inch fronts, 21-inch ground clearance, and tread adjustable from 48 to 84 inches on an 86-inch wheelbase. The transmission provided five forward and five reverse speeds. The E offered continuous running PTO and hydraulic lift pump with Touch Control; it added the simplified and improved QA-Quick Attach implement mount system, and had "styled and nonvibrating sheet metal enclosures," over the engine and rear fenders with cutouts for implement movement.

On September 1, 1943, while development continued on V-8 diesel and gas engines for trucks and tractors, GPED resurrected another previously put on hold, the large six-cylinder D-501 diesel. The effects of that discussion were far-reaching.

"The principal demand," McCroskey reported to Fowler McCormick, "comes from manufacturers who use IHC engines to power their equipment, motor graders, scrapers, and others who point out they cannot remain in a competitive position with our present engine line. If these customers must go to other manufacturers for their increased power requirements, they will place orders for other engines with that same manufacturer." In accepting McCroskey's presentation, IHC gave birth to its construction division during that September 1 meeting.

1942 Farmall H on steel
The onset of World War II removed rubber and other crucial manufacturing raw materials from domestic industry. Farm tractor makers, concerned that they could even remain in business during the war, willingly returned to crank starts and steel wheels.

Farmall H tractors weighed 3,300 pounds on steel wheels, without electric starter, generator, battery or any of the wiring and switches. IHC began mounting H and M radiators on rubber in 1942, and changed the fuel tank support from a stamping to cast iron, both changes done to reduce breakage.

As McCormick dispersed his engineers over a full-range of tractor products for agriculture, industry and construction, he grew concerned. He saw stressed managers pulled taut by the work load and variety of projects they had to manage. Fowler, like his grandfather, recognized people's strengths and weaknesses. IHC had strengths, too, but its tendency to force division general managers to do too much, he feared, could harm the company. In meetings he had heard lapses, errors. With millions of dollars at risk in development and tooling costs, mistakes were lethal.

McCormick conceived a plan of reorganization in which areas of expertise and interest influenced managers' job selection. Throughout 1944, he effected changes, giving autonomy to division vice presidents. He separated IHC's farm tractor, farm implement, industrial power, motor truck division, and the general line, including refrigeration and other products, from the tightly centralized rule his grandfather had established. His first goal was to reduce the executive workload.

His second goal was to diversify his own Executive Council, which by this time counted eight

1943 TD-18A with crane
IHC produced several hundred tractors for U.S. military uses. The U.S. Air Force mounted a Hughes-Keenan Roustabout crane Model MC8, on a number of TD-18a crawlers. This crane used a 30-foot boom and provided a 12-foot lift radius, up to 12,000 pounds.

When the boom was horizontal, the entire crawler was nearly 40 feet long and 12 feet tall. With the boom and its ballast over the operator's head, the machine weighed 45,075 pounds. It incorporated a magneto-electric start.

former sales managers among its number but only one engineer and one manufacturer. He suggested company officers accept board positions outside IHC when offered, not to spy but so the experiences would broaden the vision of too many senior staffers with too small a world view.

At the new Tractor Division, testing the Intermediate H and M tractors with Frame-All hydraulic controls revealed that the larger double hydraulic cylinders were inadequate for middle busters or four-row cultivators. Operators found control levers poorly placed and discovered they needed to hold onto them until the lift or drop was complete. Baker and Carl Mott devised automatic stops that enabled hands-off task completion.

Tractor Division and the council reconvened at Hinsdale farm to see bigger hydraulic cylinders and pumps, and better-placed controls work on revised Intermediate Farmall H's and M's. They also saw a BN (with front and rear Frame-All mounts) demonstrated with a two-row corn cultivator and a two-bottom moldboard plow. As the October 19 show wore on, E. F. Schneider from sales grew impatient with discussions of further testing.

"In recent years, competitors have put new machines into production after a test with only one experimental machine. We should release our new machines, whenever possible, without the usual pre-production lots, in order to be in the lead rather than to follow others." Industrywide, manufacturers were beginning to rely on customers to do their final development programs.

Just before Christmas, on December 20, in the motor truck sales room on the southwest side of Chicago, Tractor and Implement Divisions showed off the Farmall "X" prototypes to nearly four-dozen members from engineering, sales, manufacture, service and executive committees. A. W. Scarratt played master of ceremonies, introducing the Farmall-X. Nothing on the X came from Farmall A or B tractors, because those parts could not meet weight, size and cost specifications for the X, which sometimes they referred to as the "Baby Farmall."

The industrial tractor unit completed the first prototype TD-24 TracTracTor with 130 drawbar horsepower on December 28, using one of the first experimental turbocharged V-8 diesel engines. Two days later, Baker and Mott met in McCaffrey's office with implement group engineers to discuss another

run of Frame-All hydraulics-equipped A and B tractors for testing through 1944. McCaffrey approved 12 As, one AV, eight Bs and four BNs, to be in the fields by May 1. These would resolve final design specifications and operating characteristics of hydraulic controls, Frame-All implement mounts and QA-Quick Attach hitch system.

The pace of creative development increased in the first weeks of 1944, paralleling U.S. participation in the war in Europe and IHC's growing involvement in supply manufacture. It took its toll on departments and programs. (It was a mixed hardship; IHC sales reached $640.5 million in 1944; profits funded every engineering project.) McCaffrey's Frame-All program to add 25 A and B tractors to the tests nearly brought manufacturing to a halt on January 2. A and B assembly line production was under way; manufacturing had orders for 5,000 of them through 1944. Interrupting this to hand-build 12 tractors was impossible.

David Baker told the Executive Council that the Farm Tractor and Implement Group (FTIG) already was producing 16 prototypes and it was overburdened with major programs on cottonpickers, intermediate and postwar programs on other tractors, power units, refrigeration and other things. Baker understood the need to complete Frame-All hydraulic control system tests, but felt manufacturing should cooperate fully to become familiar with this important new development.

McCaffrey, just elected to the Board of Directors as an IHC second vice president, had aimed at July 1, 1944, as the production approval date, based on Frame-All models testing nonstop through May and June. Now, it appeared he would have to reset this to July 1, 1945, unless major effort moved the program.

Manufacturing was adamant. It would not interrupt two assembly lines for a single A highcrop and four BNs. Fowler McCormick agreed to slip introduction back to 1945 but he reminded Manufacturing Vice President H. K. Kicherer that Canton Works had a variety of 25 Frame-All implements in A- and B-tractor sizes that needed thorough testing. McCormick ordered Kicherer to "make an immediate, intensive study of the hydraulic system and gain the necessary knowledge of and experience with this unit preparatory to its production."

The Farmall E program was in jeopardy in early January 1944. Created in September 1939, FTIG had converted a standard "drop-axle" Farmall B into a straight axle tractor. But this required costly revisions when testing revealed strength problems and implement mounting constraints. As a result, in late September 1941, FTIG had created the new straight-axle Farmall E prototype it demonstrated in mid-August, 1943. Now, getting cold feet, the Executive Council ordered FTIG to greatly reduce cost and weight, and eliminate "certain features it felt it could not afford to incorporate in a tractor of this size and capacity."

At this point, the council doubted it could "achieve the desired results, and is now considering dropping the Farmall E and reinstating the Straight Axle B." With each innovation eliminated from the Farmall E, it came closer to GPED's Straight Axle B. "A more favorable cost can be obtained, and the hydraulic touch control system now being developed for the Farmall B can be used on the Straight Axle B. Frame-All implements can be converted with small modifications," McCaffrey said.

"However," Baker countered, "if the Straight Axle B is adopted, such features as a full-reverse five-speed transmission and continuous-running PTO cannot be included. These were originally designed into the Model E.

1943 Frame-All A
The Frame-All power lift system operated from the middle of the tractor, attaching double-acting hydraulic cylinders to bolts still visible on the bell housing of this prototype. Attachments were driven by the sides of the tractor, a drive system embodying both a throw-out and a slip clutch.

"The Farmall E," he reminded FTIG members, "was the pilot model for a complete line, because it would be restyled and incorporate features which it was felt were essential for an up-to-date future line of tractors." Accepting defeat, he urged they use the experience and knowledge they gained from this project in developing the Model M to create an ultimate line of tractors.

"Such tractor," he proposed, "would become the fore-runner of a new line instead of the Model E. The M size has sufficient horsepower to satisfy power requirements for a complete line of attaching tools, which are considered in new implement developments, including mounted harvester threshers." The last coffin nail, however, came from R. C. Archer in sales.

"Because the Farmall E was larger than the A and B but smaller than the H and M, it would render both larger and smaller tractors obsolete prematurely, thus interfering with the sale of these tractors pending new developments." This was crystal ball gazing, similar to what sales had done worrying about McCormick-Deering's 10–20 after introducing the Farmall.

McCormick's note to H. K. Kicherer got manufacturing's attention. By late January, 13 Farmall A and 12 B tractors appeared, ready for modification

with Frame-All systems. While five would remain at the Hinsdale farm, at the Canton and Hamilton, Ontario, implement works, 20 would be offered for sale, because, as McCroskey put it, "By selling the tractors and implements, we derive more information by reactions from the customers than by loaning these outfits for tests."

After the Farmall E died, Sperry assigned Carl Mott and William O. Bechman to revise the hydraulics to produce two Improved Farmall M prototypes. These would incorporate side-mounted PTO, cultivator shift levers, a second battery for diesel start, QA Frame-All mounts, QA rear axle (hexagonal) housings, provisions for "Harvest-All" implements requiring heavier axle carriers, larger diameter axles and reinforced transmission case. Even as the fully equipped MDs were being designed, Mott and Bechman converted two gas-engine Ms and an H to these changes. FTIG added a single-cylinder hydraulic installation for Farmall A tractors and a revised double-cylinder system for the Farmall B and a new C tractor (as the production version of the five-year-old Straight Axle Model B idea.). This was a four-rockshaft arm system, identical to H and M versions, with two arms for independent action of the front section and two for the rear. These would be standard equipment on the latest B, H and M versions and the new C.

The war continued to strain time and energy; existing programs soldiered on, sometimes with unanticipated results. Just as during World War I, while the male population fought, wives and daughters ran the farm to feed and clothe the world. IHC's branches, organizing tractor operation and repair schools for women, told Chicago it needed to adapt current production hydraulic Lift-Alls to existing F-20 and F-30 tractors.

This was not easy. FTIG built one and found it required 42 separate pieces including fabricating an angle steel frame. The chance for leaks was great and GPED did not encourage the idea. However, because it would aid farmers at home, primarily women, GPED agreed to make it work cleanly and quickly.

FTIG had Farmall A and B Frame-All-equipped prototypes to the fields by the end of April 1944, but IHC's Executive Council decided instead to lease or loan the tractors "for test purposes only" and not sell them outright, fearing another farmer falling

On March 25, 1942, Gas Power Engineering showed the Executive Council this invention: hydraulic fingertip depth control power-lift. It eliminated multiple levers and let fingers regulate precisely the depth of working tools. GPE called it the Frame-All system.

in love with a unique prototype, as happened with the 8–16 four-wheel drive two decades earlier.

"Branches will be requested to locate these units at points where they will not be conspicuous, to prevent any possibility of these coming to the attention of persons other than those to whom they have been leased." Leasing was preferred because it placed a financial impact on the farmer who was more likely to use the tractor fully and report honestly any complaints and failures as it directly affected normal farm finances.

In IHC's plants, workers busy making half-tracks and torpedoes found it difficult to remember farming-as-usual. Throughout Europe and the Pacific, soldiers and sailors used IHC products and those from other U.S. manufacturers in the fight for the return to living-as-usual. On June 6, 1944, tens of thousands of Allied troops landed on the northern coast of France. Within two weeks, Allied soldiers captured more than 30,000 Germans occupying areas near the coast. The war was not over, but progress now was measurable.

On July 11, tests confirmed success of Farmall A single-cylinder hydraulic touch-control, and B, C, H and M double-cylinder systems. Questions of manufacturing cost and retail sale price rose against manufacturing's production schedule. The start date slipped back from July 1, 1945, to September 1, when FTIG learned it should not use, advertise or list the term "Touch Control" relating to its hydraulic system, until IHC had it trademark-protected.

R. C. Archer from sales met with R. M. McCroskey and Leonard Sperry from engineering to schedule tests for both Farmall Model C and the Model X tractors. Complete Farmall A Frame-All tractors weighed 1,856 pounds, the Model C weighed 2,150, and the Model Xs were only 1,058 pounds. Calculating sales and cost benefits of the Frame-All tractors compared to standards, McCroskey reported that creating the Frame-All removed $44.13 in parts, which were replaced with parts costing $47.01, a total of $3.12 difference in production costs. While this represented a nearly negligible amount, IHC at this point was envisioning a production run between 70,000 and 100,000 A, C and X tractors.

This required a staggering investment, more than 5 percent of its previous year sales: $30.4 mil-

lion in tooling, labor (two shifts, five days a week, 50 weeks a year), materials, sales and distribution costs, not including those expenses incurred in design, development and testing. Based on this and Manufacturing Manager R. M. Watkins' statement that this equipment represented "the last word as to efficiency, quality and production at a minimum cost," Fowler McCormick and the Executive Committee launched the two lines with a run of 20 pre-production models each.

On Thursday, September 14, FTIG engineers staged a massive Show-and-Tell for the Executive Council, division general managers, and others of the Tractor and Implement Divisions. Starting at 8:30 a.m., FTIG demonstrated what it believed were "sign-off" versions of Frame-All equipped-hydraulic touch control-operated Farmall A, B, C, H and M tractors. There were no failures, no miscues, no disappointments.

When Implement Group engineers parked the last demonstrator ensilage harvester at 4:30 p.m., company cars and busses loaded and rolled out of the Hinsdale Farm yard. IHC management knew it had seen its future working that day. Once the war ended, IHC would have innovations, techniques, products and tools to sell the farmers who came home from Europe and the Pacific.

The Frame-All system used implements in front and back of the tractor. Its two double-acting hydraulic cylinders, with two levers, allowed adjustments on either side, and delayed lift and drop of implements.

1945–1954

Eight

BUILDING THE HOUSE OF CARDS

World War II engaged Fowler McCormick's imagination. Through the diversity of wartime products IHC manufactured, Fowler came to believe his corporation no longer needed to be strictly a farm equipment and truck maker. With nearly 100,000 workers in 17 plants, sales increased more than $100 million each year during the war. Fowler had money to expand product lines and to buy new factories to build them.

The Tractor Division staked its share of development money on a tractor meant for the small two-or-three horse farm. For this machine, the Naming Committee broke form. The letter series Farmalls, beginning in 1939 with the

1945 Farmall BN

The BN provides narrower rear wheel tread, varying in 4-inch increments from 56 to 84 inches, while the Farmall B would stretch from 64 out to 92 inches. The BN was designed to work row crops, such as beets and potatoes.

Model M, reached Model Es in the early 1940s (with jumps to H and A). This new prototype was referred to either as the Farmall X or the F. Now, in September 1945, public relations man Art Seyfarth, patent attorney Paul Pippel, engineer Leonard Sperry and the five other committee members named it the "Cub." IHC's sales department aimed 45 percent of total Cub production at the East and Southeast.

Production began in Louisville, Kentucky, late in 1947. Nearly 135,000 rolled out over the next four years. Half the purchasers were first-time tractor buyers replacing horses or mules on farms where the Cub was to be the only tractor. (In 1945, 30 percent of the United States, about 1.6 million farms, still used only draft animals.) Cotton, tobacco, poultry and vegetable truck farms favored the Cubs, as did people who farmed part-time or maintained large gardens. Most Cubs sold went to farms of 10 to 19 acres.

At the other end of the spectrum, Fowler's perceptive but forceful friend, John "Mac" McCaffrey, IHC's vice president, found a growth

1946 Farmall B

The Farmall B offered the same extremely tight turning as the BN, but it was more useful for crops planted in 34- to 42-inch rows. IHC suggested it was a suitable machine for a single-bottom plow but two-row cultivation, plowing five-to-seven acres per day, but cultivating 25 to 30.

1946 McCormick-Deering O-4

IHC began producing the O-4 in October 1940, eight months after the first W-4 appeared. Standing a full 20 inches lower than the W-4, the orchard model weighed 420 pounds more, due to its full fenders and engine cover panels.

industry in construction. To reward his work and ideas, IHC's board elected McCaffrey president and chief operating officer in 1946.

In the construction business, IHC faced formidable competition. Caterpillar sold $230 million in equipment in 1945, compared to IHC's $35 million. Cat had a postwar advantage from G.I. heavy equipment operators, who had learned on Cat's machines and now told their peacetime bosses what to order. To McCaffrey, Cat made a big target. (Cat's legal threats over the 10–20 TracTracTor ended May 5, 1946. IHC, tired of 15 years of trials and appeals over patent infringements on its 1922 crawler, settled with Cat for $6 million. The payment actually eased IHC's corporate taxes, bringing the company down below a level where "Excess Profits" were heavily charged.)

IHC's attack on Cat came through a $30 million investment that included acquiring a former government plant in Melrose Park, Illinois. In 1947 IHC's Industrial Power Division introduced the TD-24. It weighed 36,000 pounds and developed 148 drawbar horsepower. Invented by Leonard Sperry and designed by David Baker, it was manu-

factured by Fowler's 30-year-old cousin Brooks McCormick, who became Melrose Park works superintendent in 1947.

The big crawler, TD-24, introduced "two-speed steering," fingertip-controlled planetary power steering, using three big disks encased in hydraulic oil. The first disk handled direct drive, the second disk provided a 33 percent reduction (similar to the Torque Amplifier but actuated hydraulically, not mechanically), and the third disk was the brake rotor. This improved on differential steering of earlier models. Pulling one steering lever back dropped that track to 67 percent speed while retaining full power to the inside track. If the operator needed a tighter turn, pulling the lever all the way back wrapped a band around the inside disk, stopping the track altogether. With a power-shift high-low range, the crawler effectively offered operators eight speeds forward and reverse. The TD-24, promoted by McCaffrey and supported by McCormick, was 10 horsepower more powerful than Cat's D-8, and it was more sophisticated than Cat's track clutch/brake steering. While development of the crawler, plant purchase, tooling and related costs had been high, initial reaction was good. The sales department, which had hurried the crawler along, was pleased.

McCaffrey's trucking background—he'd sold them in Ohio before moving to Chicago headquarters—hadn't prepared him for agricultural equipment. Through his career, he had little understanding of farm equipment markets. But he did understand equipment needs for construction. As with trucks, bigger was better, and more powerful was more useful.

McCormick wasn't done expanding, however. IHC's line of 1907 cream separators led to coolers when 1930s laws required farmers to refrigerate fresh milk within an hour of milking. From wartime field hospital blood-coolers, McCormick envisioned a full line of refrigeration equipment. In 1946 he bought a plant in Evansville, Indiana, and within a year, IHC turned out 200 freezers a day, then adding humidifiers and air conditioners. By the early 1950s, IHC was the market leader in freezer sales, and refrigeration sales more than doubled from 1950 through 1953.

Alfred P. Sloan, General Motors' brilliant chairman, had outlined his mission to provide "a car for every purse and pocketbook," during a 1921 interview. He inspired generations of businessmen. During Cyrus McCormick Jr.'s time, IHC produced tractors for every farm and function. In the mid-1940s, McCormick paid more attention to GM and saw a separation of divisions that made sense to him as president of the "general motors of farm equipment." Fowler strengthened Farm Tractor, Industrial Equipment (encompassing portable power units, industrial and construction machinery), Motor Truck, and Refrigeration divisions, as well as a Steel Division and Fiber & Twine (which supplied his har-

For beet planting in central Montana in the mid-1940s, this W-4 operator used a No. 41 four-row planter with fertilizer attachments and irrigation shovels. It was designed to drill segmented or whole burr beet seeds at high speeds. *State Historical Society of Wisconsin*

1948 Farmall HV

High-clearance Farmall H tractors were born May 2, 1940, in a Farm Tractor Committee meeting discussing agricultural needs in California, Louisiana and overseas. The first one tested nonstop for 988 hours outside New Orleans in September 1940.

1948 Model M Industrial

Marion County, Kansas, (between Salina and Wichita) purchased two electric-start M tractors equipped with W-6-type splined, non-adjustable rear axles. They ordered IHC cast wheels fitted with 32-inch tires. Front axles, as delivered, were adjustable agriculture-types.

1948 H Grader

Unlike Galion, which used an industrial I-30 as the foundation for its leaning wheel graders, American Grader Company used an ag-tractor, a Farmall H as the basis for its No. 6 leaning wheel road maintainer. This one worked in Omaha, Nebraska.

vesters). He gave each its own experimental and research departments, sales organizations, and personnel and administrative departments.

Sloan's decentralization required one central leader to make course corrections among the scattered divisions. Chairman McCormick, by several accounts, created a different version. Sloan was a director who trusted vice presidents and managers to make all but the most critical decisions or long-term plans. For these he was always and immediately available. McCormick's system required they put more trust in their subordinates because the chairman often was unreachable and far away.

All the McCormicks traveled. Cyrus Sr. sold harvesters; Cyrus Jr. set up factories in Europe. Harold checked on the plants worldwide. Fowler, as head of foreign sales, visited Europe and Russia, but not all his travels were business. Overworked during war years, he continued afterward to enlarge IHC's vision. To manage stress, he spent months in Switzerland with Dr. Carl Jung, the psychologist who was his mother's favorite.

Fowler caught pneumonia in late 1947, which for reasons never explained, he kept secret from his executives and directors. Even after nearly dying, he let only McCaffrey and few others know that, in relocating to Phoenix, he was following doctor's advice. It was something that was "not discussed." As a still-active board chairman, he took work with

him—boxes of it. He communicated with McCaffrey by phone or mail. He looked into a dedicated telephone line to McCaffrey, an early attempt at telecommuting. But McCaffrey felt the $1,020 monthly charge was too extravagant. Without instantaneous communications, McCaffrey followed his inclinations more easily.

McCormick's extended absence confused his directors. They concluded he didn't care about IHC. When projects flew out of control, few people knew to alert him. McCaffrey's job grew without McCormick there handling future planning and budgets. Problems required quick decisions. Complications arose in cleaning and retooling Louisville Works from wartime production. Extra labor and facilities costs in 1946 and 1947 tapped budgets of raw materials for tractor manufacture. Tooling had to be stored, delaying Cub production, and later the Farmall C. Labor costs remained but there was no offsetting income from tractor sales. (In 1940 IHC had owned 39 percent of the farm tractor market; by 1949 its market share had slipped to 31 percent, despite the fact that its factories worked to capacity and the overall market grew.)

1949 TD-14A

After protesting it couldn't find any more power in the TD-14 crawler, engineering revised the injection pumps, redesigned the cylinder heads and increased engine speed from 1,350 to 1,400 rpm, to create the 14A. This developed 71.79 brake horsepower, compared to the TD-14's 61.56.

A report to Farm Tractor Division on June 12, 1952, spelled out the damage clearly:

"From 1946 up to the end of 1949, Louisville Works had a cumulative operating loss of $21,594,000. To the end of 1952, the average investment at Louisville during most of this time has been approximately $50,000,000. As pointed out, we have not only had no return on this investment, but have very high fixed costs, depreciation alone being in excess of $3,000,000 per year."

The figures were grim; reality was no better. Delays in tooling up Cub and Model C production threw off outside parts suppliers. Looking for income, they bid other projects that came through more quickly. When IHC was ready to assemble the Louisville tractors, suppliers often couldn't comply. A huge labor force, supported by union contracts limiting IHC's flexibility, was not always available when parts arrived. If certain portions of assembly slowed or stopped waiting for parts, Louisville Works managers could ask union members to work another job. The contract gave workers the right to refuse. They could go home. Then other portions of assembly backed up, waiting for workers.

One other labor problem confronted the Tractor Division, at this point run by Ted Hale, another sales vice president without manufacturing experience who was named a division manager. Between 1950 and 1954, resignations and layoffs from production slowdowns or assembly line changeovers wreaked havoc with the employment forces at the Farmall and Louisville plants. During this period, the annual turnover rate was two out of three employees.

Fowler McCormick blamed McCaffrey for the company's failings, even among unions with whom Fowler had exercised a typical McCormick family animosity. But other faults did lie with McCaffrey, including an almost insatiable hunger for power. In

1950 Farmall C Demonstrator

Once the Louisville, Kentucky, Works was up and running and early teething problems with IHC's new Farmall C were cleaned up, sales and the Executive Council agreed it was time to do something dramatic to promote its small tractors including the Cub, the Farmall C and the Super A. This pristine reproduction of a C demonstrator was created by referring to old photographs.

early 1951, McCormick, concerned for the future, tried to boot out his former friend. He hoped to force a showdown: McCaffrey or McCormick. But the board, especially the older outside directors, resented his intrusion. They chose McCaffrey, granting him Fowler's chief executive officer title as well. Fowler was forced into an inactive Executive Council and board position. That July, the board promoted Fowler's cousin, Brooks. He had moved from Melrose Park manufacturing to truck sales in Kansas City and then to district manager for general sales in Dallas in 1950. Before coming to World Headquarters, his job was joint managing director of IHC's British operations at Doncaster.

As the McCormicks journeyed through the world, they put distance between themselves and daily corporate responsibilities in a hereditary repetition of styles. Almost from the first, from Cyrus Sr., there was a kind of noblesse oblige, a behavior that gave the message to directors that "we have others to do this work with us. We trust their abilities as much as our own." With Senior, it was his younger brothers Leander and William who ran things; with Junior it was Funk and then Legge. For Fowler it would be John McCaffrey. It was as if,

even though machines and buildings were named after them, the McCormicks adhered to a genetic family blueprint that told them to leave others to manage some portions of the business in the McCormicks' best interest. They behaved as though programmed to give others the responsibilities to bring in other perspectives, to seek diversity in management, often letting others take the credit, even when the McCormicks believed they could do it

1950 Farmall Cub Demonstrator
Just before Christmas 1943, Tractor and Implement Division showed off its newest idea, the Farmall X, or Baby Farmall. Sales Division had concluded that a huge market existed in the Southeast for a sub-Farmall A-size tractor, for use among small-acreage tobacco and cotton growers.

1950 Farmall M-8-speed prototype
A larger rear-axle diameter, longer axles, larger disc brakes, and shorter rear axle housings distinguish this 1950 M prototype from production versions. The most significant difference, however, is the transmission, a four-speed dual-range unit that wouldn't appear on production models until 1963, on the 706/806 series. The belt pulley casting, steering wheel support, brake and clutch pedals, and lightbar are also prototype parts. The prototype also features live PTO. The hydraulic pump is housed within the rear end case, another improvement that didn't make production until 1963.

135

1951 Farmall M LPG conversion

Howard Weaver, co-owner of Weaver & Lingg in Sturgis, Michigan, did more than 140 of these conversions, taking gas-engined Farmall M tractors and replacing parts to run them on liquefied petroleum gas, LPG.

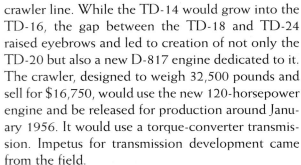

1952 TD-24

In 1947 IHC's Industrial Power Division introduced its biggest crawler, equipped with planetary power steering and power-shift high-low range final drive. This gave operators eight speeds in forward and reverse. The blade is a 12-foot Bucyrus-Erie. Everything about the crawler was massive. It weighed 38,740 pounds, used a 1,091-cubic inch six-cylinder diesel that developed 142 drawbar horsepower, capable of pulling 21,873 pounds. Between 1947 and 1955, IHC's Melrose Park plant produced about 7,500 of these.

better than those they'd hand-picked. This shared responsibility style of directorship built the company but ultimately hastened the end as well.

Tom Hales' Tractor Division suffered its highest labor turnover at Louisville, 72.4 percent annually. Production and labor conditions there led McCaffrey and the Executive Committee in 1953 to consider moving the entire production line of the new Farmall 300 to Kentucky from Farmall Works before regular production began to stabilize the work force. A study indicated that such a move also would save IHC $400,000 a year in tractor shipping costs, but the relocation itself would cost $5 million.

McCaffrey's enthusiasm for construction equipment fueled expansion and improvements in IHC's

crawler line. While the TD-14 would grow into the TD-16, the gap between the TD-18 and TD-24 raised eyebrows and led to creation of not only the TD-20 but also a new D-817 engine dedicated to it. The crawler, designed to weigh 32,500 pounds and sell for $16,750, would use the new 120-horsepower engine and be released for production around January 1956. It would use a torque-converter transmission. Impetus for transmission development came from the field.

"There has been an insistent demand from the field for a hydraulic drive for the TD-24. In response, the Engineering Department has developed, in cooperation with the Allison Division of General Motors, a combination torque converter and power shift transmission which can be introduced into the basic TD-24." Throughout late 1947, the big crawler's insufficient development time began to show. The powerful DT-1091 engine coupled to a sliding gear transmission put too much force too abruptly on final drives before the steering planetaries. With a clutch, either the tracks moved or the engine died. Gears overheated, failed, and in some instances, shattered inside the cases. A torque converter reduced the shock from the engine to the drive train. More than that, when an operator stalled the tracks, it could keep the engine running and hydraulic controls functioning. The first torque converter prototype went to the U.S. Navy in April 1953 for testing. However, increasing financial constraints meant the engineering department built fewer prototypes and had shorter testing periods than necessary on new projects.

Rather than slowing new product approval, McCaffrey encouraged more construction equipment into life. In January 1954, Engineering Manager Arnold Johnson reported on his cooperative effort with Bill Schumacher's Truck Division "to manufacture an off-highway construct, four-wheel, rubber-tired tractor unit to be developed through the utilization of presently available component units." Two would be built quickly with production planned a year later. The meeting minutes report that "Mr. McCaffrey commended the program and urged that it be developed as soon as possible."

Gross sales from Tractor Division for 1953 were $257.6 million, but that dropped by $100 million in 1954, to $156.6 million. Shipments to dealers decreased by almost half, from 14,601 in 1953

to 7,952 in 1954, taking division net income down steeply from $18.9 million to $5.4 million. (Truck sales beat farm equipment for the first time in 1954, and would exceed it by half-again in 1956.) Fowler's reorganization made each division responsible for itself; money needed to prove products before manufacture dried up. Some of this budget tightening resulted from price cuts on Farmall Hs and Louisville tractors, because IHC began slicing inventories before releasing the hundred series.

In mid-1954, as introduction of the new Farmalls approached, IHC began to feel more painfully the cash flow slowdown. The company responded by shipping tractors rapidly and randomly. In August, McCaffrey received letters from several branches complaining because "a sizable quantity of tractors had been shipped to territories for which they were not suited." He learned from general sales that "errors had been made in this distribution, but many of the tractors originally shipped had been sold and they were confident that the remaining units would be moved in due time." (Thirty years before this, as inventory of soon-to-be obsolete tractors grew, Alex Legge had the luxury of Henry Ford's price war to move out Titans and Moguls before the 10–20 and 15–30 gear drives arrived. Legge also had a much more solid financial footing from which to survive the losses.)

By October 1, 1954, McCaffrey recognized that IHC's sales projections of $1 billion for the year

were too optimistic. Peter V. Moulder, executive vice president for Tractor and Implements Division, summed up the bad news.

"Results were very poor in spite of drastic economy measures taken, particularly at Louisville Works. As you know, this was because estimated production for 1955 represents only 31 percent of the tractor capacity of that works." Unfortunately, even though Louisville could produce more, there were no customers. In 1953, 42 percent of IHC's farm tractor sales were in Farmall A, C, and Cub ranges of 9- to 24-horsepower tractors; 30 percent went to Super M sales, the 40-horsepower-and-up class tractor. The remaining 28 percent was split between H (25-to 29-horsepower) and Super H (30-to-34) models. The new Farmall 300, replacing the Super H, would move a tractor into the previously vacant 35- to 39-horsepower bracket.

A sales memo decreed that this move "opens up for consideration increased horsepower for the 200 model, which replaces the C and will probably be in the 25- to 29-horsepower category. By increasing the horsepower even further it could be moved up into the vacated 30- to 34-horsepower category, where there is a big market." Nature was not alone in abhorring a vacuum; thus did IHC's sales department formulate its product planning and marketing decisions. The proliferation of IHC models was self-perpetuating.

1953 Super HV

High-clearance Farmall Super H tractors provided 30.25 inches of space below the standard tread front axle. It was slightly adjustable, at 60, 63 or 66 inches. Rear tread width was fixed at 69 inches but working width was adjustable through a wheel rim kit. Just 70 of these high-clearance Super H models were manufactured during 1953 and 1954.

1953 Super AM

International Harvester of Australia produced the Super AM at North Shore, Geelong, Victoria, from 1953 into 1957. The Australian Super series picked up many of the improvements of the U.S.-manufactured tractors, such as live power take-off, but retained band brakes over the discs. These narrow fronts were uncommon in Australia, which made better use of AW-6s and Super AW-6s because of its wheatland-type farming.

When IHC first introduced the MV, sales agreed with manufacturing to keep the new tractors out of Louisiana and Florida until the last of the F-30HVs were sold, because the modern M offered so many improvements. Sales got the same message with the Super MV.

Yet this broadening product line-up missed the mark. Industrial growth during and after World War II pulled 1.5 million families off farms. Many who remained bought their neighbors' land and needed bigger equipment to work holdings that encompassed a half-section (half a square mile) or more. By 1954, some 130,000 farmers or ranchers worked 1,000 acres or more. While these were fewer than 3 percent of the farms, their owners bought 9 percent of the tractors in the United States.

Taking cues from the auto industry, IHC, like Ford and Deere & Co., introduced a new, improved tractor model every other year. As engine developments raised output, some horsepower categories filled and others emptied. In some instances, farmer demands for tractors sent IHC scrambling, as happened in mid-1955. Certain territories sold high volumes of diesel M and M-TA (Torque-Amplifier)-equipped tractors but IHC ended production of those in October 1954. While engineering completed preproduction development of the new Farmall 350 diesel (using a direct-start Continental engine) to introduce in 1956, McCaffrey authorized the Tractor Division to look into acquiring outside-built engines. R. M. Sheppard, Cummins, and Detroit Diesel eventually provided repower engines for larger 450 series models.

McCaffrey's models' proliferation occasionally blurred lines between McCormick-Deering Farmall farm tractor lines and the International utility models. Through the history of the Cub, Super C and Super M tractors, IHC became aware of utility buyers using the solid axle tractors for farming purposes. This continued with 300 Utility models, the W-4 replacements, to such extent that 87 percent of first year sales went onto farms. R. W. Dibble, general sales manager, likening these to Ford-Ferguson N series tractors, encouraged this application and set up dealer strategies to further promote it. Tractor Division added diesel-engine and high-clearance versions to the International 350 lineup. These duplications began to resemble the overlap of Titans and Moguls.

Steadily decreasing income strained budgets and made new development even more difficult. Debt increased from building and equipping factories and acquiring outside resources. These obligations, coupled with a sales force-driven corporate strategy, forced management to tighten development schedules further. By the late 1950s, this issue arose regularly in Executive Council meetings. Referring to cylinder head difficulties with diesel engines used in tractors, combines, trucks and power units, R. M. Buzard from national sales challenged McCaffrey over "the possible impairment of new product development as a result of the demands made on the time of company personnel to assist in the correction of current problems. Such practices serve to extend current product difficulties to the future, and the realization of future sales [is] dependent upon the early introduction of new equipment."

This was the conundrum facing McCaffrey: Diminishing resources forced him to cut corners. His sales background gave him sympathy for IHC personnel who moved product. He had little understanding of those who invented or manufactured it. To McCaffrey, when a prototype or two worked, especially when they incorporated proven technology, there was no reason to delay production. Sales, to justify accelerated development requests, began exaggerating sales potential. Manufacturing designed the assembly line and ordered raw materials to meet sales projections and it "priced" the tractor (or truck, combine, crawler or refrigerator) accordingly. Labor needs were organized prior to assembly.

In February 1956, Mercer Lee from finance gave McCaffrey some sobering figures. "The present production program is in excess of the revised sales estimates by 17,000 trucks and exceeds current retail sales experience by 15,000 tractors," he said. "Current material stocks were estimated at $26,000,000 in excess of the budget." From a financial perspective, IHC was nearly out of control. Eventually sales' reports would come in two forms: projected and estimated. The former was the number hoped for, the latter was the realistic expectation.

Another manufacturing company, run by an aggressive salesman, approached IHC in March. Two distinguished auto makers, Studebaker and Packard, had merged in October 1954, to keep each other alive. But that wasn't enough, and S-P chairman James Nance, a former refrigerator salesman, needed a stronger, wealthier manufacturing company to see benefit in helping them turn around their economic disasters. IHC saw no value in the ailing car makers. Studebaker's trucks competed with IHC's lightweights and no one in Farm Equipment or Construction Division was interested in taking on unexciting economy cars or faded luxury models. Declined by Ford and Chrysler, Nance and his board thought about Kaiser and Massey-Harris as well, before following IHC's path of going back to bankers and insurance companies for additional financing.

(Fearing an end over which they had no control, Packard's Nance and many of his exec-

utives quit in May 1956. Packards continued on Studebaker chassis in 1957 but the directors never mentioned the Packard name during the 1958 annual meeting. S-P sold only 1,745 Packards all year. On July 13, Packard quietly went out of business.)

IHC's sales slipped where it made its largest investments. Refrigeration products never reached mainstream urban retail outlets such as Sears, Wards and Penney's. Company stores were in the country; once farms had refrigerators and freezers, that market, barely 2 percent of the nation, was saturated. McCaffrey faced becoming a "white goods" maker, offering stoves, sinks, washing machines and dryers, another huge capital investment. A merger of big manufacturers into a conglomerate owned by Sears (much as IHC was in 1902) claimed most of the business and McCaffrey unloaded the ailing Refrigeration Division for $19 million in 1955.

1954 Super C Hi-Hi-Crop
Hajime Kayano farms 10 acres in suburban Orange County, California, catering to local shoppers and restaurants. In the late 1980s, needing a rig to spray corn and strawberries, he fabricated this Hi-hi-crop onto one of his Super C tractors. Kayano had seen a commercially built Farmall C on stilts, but couldn't purchase it. He welded his own together, providing nearly 70-inch ground clearance. With sprayer arms out, he covers six rows, fed by the two 75-gallon tanks. One benefit of the Super C was its Hydra Creeper, a 1/4 mile-per-hour gear particularly beneficial to vegetable farmers.

1950–1965

Nine

ENGINEERING GAINS GROUND

While McCaffrey loved construction equipment, agricultural implements, one of IHC's two "core" industries, were a mystery. His engineers, always rushed to finish and release new products, were reassigned once he authorized manufacture. If customer products failed, the same engineers split their time. They had new work but also had to create repairs.

W. F. Hebard of Chicago, Illinois, had been producing industrial tugs since 1918. This 1948 Hebard A14V, one of eight models available in 1945, used International's U4, four-cylinder, 30.5-brake horsepower engine, transmission, drive train, brakes, and steering in its own chassis to produce these 3,000-pound 80-inch long mules. This tug was purchased new in 1948 by Douglas Aviation, Santa Monica, California. In the background here is a 1952 Piper Tri-Pacer. In 1950, Buda Company acquired Hebard.

McCaffrey acknowledged need for a "proper balance between advance engineering (experimentation and development) and product engineering (preparing it for production, then doing revisions and redesign afterward). "When a decision has to be made on a product engineering program," he wrote to Farm Equipment Division, "it should be expected that enough work will have already been done by advanced engineering to provide a sound basis for judging the feasibility of proposed product engineering work." (For 1956, the ratio was $600,000 for advanced and $2.5 million for product. All advanced engineering was canceled for 1957.) By the late 1950s, due to rapidly expanded product lines and burgeoning problems, IHC was tilting off balance.

On May 4, 1951, the Board of Directors had elected McCaffrey its chairman and chief executive officer, repudiating Fowler McCormick, and Paul Moulder became IHC president. In fiscal 1954, gross sales fell from $254 million to $166.

experiment costs. Despite this austerity, nothing appeared promising to the finance people.

In April 1956, the Industrial Power Division was renamed Construction Equipment Division. The flagship of its fleet, McCaffrey's cherished TD-24, sold 1,136 in 1953 (at 90 percent factory capacity) and produced $1.8 million gross income. For 1955, it reached only 60 percent capacity and 1957 looked no better. Proposals to combine construction and farm tractor factories quickly fell apart. Tooling was different and retooling was time consuming and costly, so much so there was no benefit to shuttering one factory and combining reduced output in another. The only way to achieve real savings was to cut product lines, something McCaffrey could not yet do.

Engineering let outside manufacturers do development. Arnold Johnson, by now vice president of engineering, worked with Frank G. Hough Company of Libertyville, Illinois, on a prototype four-wheel drive farm tractor in late 1956.

Shortened advance engineering cycles continued to play havoc with IHC's production schedules and reputation. The large turbo-charged diesel 817 engine, in development for five years, still scuffed

1956 Farmall 100

Introduced on December 15, 1954, with the boast that "The all new Farmall Fleet is the greatest line of farm tractors ever built," IHC brought out its 100 series with the Farmall 100 replacing, and improving on, the Farmall A. The Fast-Hitch was now available for the small models.

1954 Farmall 200

The new 200 (replacing the B) shared the C-123 engine with the 100 but ran at 1,650 rpm, while the 100 was rated at 1,400. Where the 100 developed 19.5 drawbar horsepower, the 200 produced 22. It brought along the Hydra-Creeper Drive from the Super C, a system providing 1/4-mile-per-hour "transplant" speeds for vegetable and tobacco growers.

Net income plummeted from $10 million to $2.5 million; the estimate for 1955 was only $1.7 million. Every division cut expenses, labor, inventory, and

pistons. Tractor Division was ready to shut down the 650 series Farmall and International production line, possibly replacing the tractor with the new 660 series six-cylinder machine. And Construction Division's ongoing request for a smaller crawler was beyond budget until tractor engineering created savings by modifying its proposed Model 340 to utilize 70 percent of existing components, as Ed Johnston's TracTracTor 10–20 and 15–30s had done 30 years before.

Farm tractors faired no better. Daily production at Farmall and Louisville was cut by 66 percent over two years. By mid-1957, these regular reductions in staffing needs had affected employee morale. Build quality deteriorated. The lack of future product engineering disheartened not only engineers, but it allowed IHC's competitors, running second and third behind them in sales—and reputation—to close the gap. Paul Moulder, with no funds available to him, felt the threats to IHC's position.

The Construction Division, diversified to include a "pay" line of scrapers, haulers (dumping trucks) and loaders, had begun to hemorrhage. By mid-1957, sales were 17 percent below the previous year and IHC had 2,011 crawlers and more

than 260 payscrapers and payhaulers in unsold plant inventory. At year end, with Construction Division sales 54 percent below the forecast while

1956 Farmall 400 with 120A Cotton Picker

The new version of the Super M-TA provided 45 drawbar horsepower and the torque amplifier, making it an ideal platform for mounted cotton pickers such as this Model 120A. Some of the additional power output came from increasing engine compression from 5.9:1 to 6.3:1.

1956 Farmall 300 LPG

IHC promoted LPG as a tractor fuel by reminding farmers it also could be used to heat and cook within their homes. For tractors, IHC used high-altitude pistons, increasing compression from 5.9:1 up to 6.75:1. It changed carburetors, used a stronger starter motor with a lower gear and added a regulator-vaporizer, as well as the 20-gallon LPG tank. All this added about $500 to the base tractor price.

Produced jointly with General Electric, Electralls could be mounted on the frame, towed behind or lifted with the Fast-Hitch. This version produced 12.5 kilowatts at generator speed of 3,600 rpm. Only 103 were sold in 1955 and 1956. Frame mounts were available only for F-400 and I-400 models, for Super M-TAs and for W-6-MTA models. Two-thirds of the owners bought them to continue dairy operations in case of a power failure.

1955 Farmall 400 with Mounted Electrall

Engine designers worked most of the real changes that came about bringing the 400-series out of the Super M-TA. They revised intake manifolds to bring in colder air, and reshaped the camshaft for better breathing. One interesting option was dealer installed, the tractor-mounted Electrall generator.

published Deere and Caterpillar sales were steady, Moulder knew the problems with IHC Tractor and Construction Divisions were not economic. Then two things happened, and neither was good for IHC.

First, William Hewitt was named chairman of Deere & Co. in 1955. Soon after he assumed his new job, a new product announcement from IHC's Farm Equipment Division crossed his desk. The product was not important to Hewitt but the motto across the bottom got him thinking. In red print it said "Not Content To Be Runner-Up." It started him thinking about why Deere was content being second to IHC.

The second event was the rapid failure of Farmall 560s lining up outside dealer's repair doors during and after the fall harvest season of 1958. The final-drives were inadequate to handle increased power and torque of the new 60 horsepower, six-cylinder gas and diesel engines, which were jammed into what was basically still a 34-horsepower Model M tractor.

By the end of 1958, the year IHC introduced 40 series and 60 series tractors in every power range farmers might need, the company sold $391 million in farm equipment. Deere sold $464 million. IHC was runner-up.

IHC's board elected Frank Jenks, a former accountant, as company president in 1957 and then to board chairmanship in May 1958, when McCaffrey retired. According to Barbara Marsh in A Corporate Tragedy, one of Jenks' first acts was to fire the chief engineer of the 460 and 560 project. This was misplaced retribution. Those deserving discipline were decision makers who cut development budgets and rushed product introductions.

After about 350 hours, Farmall 460, 560, and International 660 tractors (for which production started May 19, 1958) began to fail as final drive gears shattered. This became an epidemic in early 1959, when nearly 4 percent of big 60 series tractors sold were inoperable. Bull gear and pinion sets showed "the tendency toward galling, excessive scoring, and welding," according to engineering reports. Galling, defined by automotive engineer John Edwards, was the "tearing apart of metals due to overexposure to extremely high temperatures as can occur in inadequately lubricated systems."

Farm Tractor Engineering Department (FTED) wasted no time investigating the problem. It revised bull gears, pinions and brake shafts for every tractor still in production. Then on April 24, it expanded revisions to include the differential bevel gears wherein "the oil holes are eliminated and oil grooves on back face of gears are revised to ensure lubrication to outer face of gears." On June 12, they began revising tapered bearings and redesigning the entire differential case.

IHC was hampered by tight cash. Engineering reported it could have new gears manufactured for the 460s by late September 1959 and for 560 and 660 models a month later. Until then, it had no replacements either for tractors in production or for the 3,000 already sold. It had to replace failed sets with identical sets.

To resolve these problems and restore farmers' faith in IHC tractors, the board doubled the warranty on those three lines, out to 12 months and 1,500 hours on differential and rear end assemblies. Then, in a report meant to remain confidential, it authorized full replacement costs and the 19-hour labor charge for the 594 affected 460 models and 428 of the 560 models. When the project was completed (FTED replaced the parts July 20), IHC had spent more than $113,000 on customer 460 and 560 tractors alone. But the report leaked out, especially a paragraph revealing that "the marginal status of the final drive components on the Farmall 300, 350, 400 and 450 series tractors was also becoming apparent in the field after one, two and three years of service." A recall, even one similar to early TracTracTors and F-12s, could not save the company's reputation.

"It is known," Tractor Product Review Committee secretary A. J. Butler wrote, "that final drive failures, particularly bull gears and pinions, are caused

1956 Farmall 350V

The next "new" line of IHC tractors arrived in 1956, with this Farmall 350 in the middle as the third generation Farmall H. New, however, was a power-adjustable rear wheel system. The High Clearance gas engine model sold for about $4,575.

1956 International 340 with Chisolm-Ryder Bean harvester

Chisolm-Ryder Company of Niagara Falls, New York, purchased nearly 100 Farmall 340 High Clearance models per year beginning in 1956 to convert to bean pickers, such as this, or to their pea pickers. The bean picker machinery more than doubled the weight of the 340.

by failure of the present ball-type inner rear axle bearing." Engineering tested the new replacement bearing "on maximum rear wheel tread at maximum drawbar pull with added side load to simulate extreme field conditions. The new bearing has sustained loads that caused failure of the current bearings, without perceptible evidence of wear or stress."

However, engineering was not nearly done with these tractors. Almost two years into the production run of 560 and 660 diesels, crankshafts began breaking (42 had failed by July 1960). The much higher compression of the increased horsepower diesels made weaknesses more apparent; it did not occur in gas engines.

But it hadn't ended yet. Hundreds of customers reported they loved their tractor "if you can keep it running." Many returned to dealers for the

same repair a second and third time. The legacy of 1957's unbudgeted advance engineering cost a fortune. In mid-July IHC interrupted I-660 production for two weeks to revise all tractors still there. They installed treated crankshafts, semimetallic-faced clutches, and rear end bearing and gear set replacement kits on every tractor. Then in late October, IHC called back all unsold I-660 models to the factory for disassembly. They replaced serial numbers and every suspect piece. For each customer tractor, 19 mandatory and 10-as-inspection-indicated pieces were replaced at no cost. Each tractor required 70 hours labor, for which IHC paid nearly $376,000, not including parts for 1,829 chassis and 1,667 diesel engines.

To provide a diesel for small tractor customers, the board approved on May 3, 1959, importing the

Doncaster-built B-275 tractor to U.S. markets. Already available to Canadians, the Standard McCormick International diesel headed to the United States on May 4, 1959.

Nine months later, February 4, 1960, the Farm Equipment Division approved "Federal Yellow, No. 483-21 or No. 483-23 oven dry or No. 483-22 air dry" paint as standard equipment on all International 340 and 460 industrial tractors and optional on International 240, 340 and 460 utility models. While yellow was an accepted standard color, IHC felt it was more visible at night and "yellow coloring appears to create the illusion of a more massive appearance, which is beneficial in the sale of industrial equipment."

On March 31, the committee extended that decision to include the Cub (optional), Cub Lo-Boy (standard), International 140 (standard), and International 460, 560 and 660 series industrials (all optional). On standard yellow tractors, "The current red and white color combination will be available optionally when so ordered." (This set of rulings would create havoc among collectors and restorers for decades to follow.)

The Executive Council under Frank Jenks pressed ahead with the "Improved or Increased Power" 240X (35 horsepower) and 340X (45 horsepower) line of tractors scheduled for production in July 1961. Part

of the improvement was final settlement of the three-point hitch dilemma:

"One of the reasons why our tractors in the horsepower category of these models have been losing ground to competition is the lack of an adequate three-point hitch. In order to regain our former position in the tractor sales in this particular category, it will be necessary to have a three-point hitch and hydraulic system equal to or better than

1956 International 600 Diesel

As successor to the W-9 series, the 600s introduced 12-volt electrics, and Hydra-Touch power steering as part of the on-board live hydraulic system. The 6,500-pound tractor ran on IHC's 350-cubic-inch four-cylinder diesel, rated at 60 horsepower.

1956 International 650 LPG

IHC's biggest liquefied propane gas tractor turned out 60.7 drawbar horsepower. The actual number manufactured is uncertain; serial numbers were included in all IH-650-build totals of 4,933 from 1956 through 1958. Only a small percentage would have been LPG-powered.

the Ferguson system." These were included on Improved 240X and 340X tractors tentatively set for July 1961, and on the 460X and 560X models for 1962. The new models, designated the 404 and 504, retained 240- and 340 series styling until introduction in 1962 of the 706 and 806. All four lines appeared in the new bodywork of the large tractors.

Even though budgets were tight, Jenks, no stranger to cost considerations but no friend to sales pressure, sought to improve the products. The oldest factories in the company, the McCormick, Milwaukee and Rock Falls Works, were inefficient. Because of their construction and layout, they could not be made into facilities IHC needed to build tractors rapidly and economically. Jenks shut down the McCormick and Rock Falls plants, leaving his successors to deal with Milwaukee Works.

At the same time, he quietly enlarged the engineering staff. He approved experimental projects and demanded more complete testing. After the 60 series disasters, Jenks pushed all new line introductions back a year, because "there would have been an insufficient length of time to do an adequate job of testing."

1957 Farmall 450 with Auger

While 1957 production continued with 6-volt electrical systems, steady improvements over the long life of the 450 models included updating to 12-volt electrical systems, authorized in late April 1957 for 1958 production.

1956 Farmall Cub with Factory Hi-Clear Attachment

One of the marvels of the Cub was that it provided small-scale farmers with every option and implement available to someone running 1,000 acres or more. One uncommon "attachment" was this high-clearance modification, which added a mere 3 inches by changing front king pins and rear drop axles.

148

With engineering's contributions acknowledged at last, projects began. Wild experiments and those with practical futures mixed, reinvigorating a department that had taken hard criticism for errors forced on them.

International Harvester Experimental Research (IHER) completed its first regenerative gas turbine engines in early 1960. Running at 36,000 rpm, IHER No.1 developed 425 horsepower and at the actual output to a reduction gearbox, produced 160 horsepower at 25,000 rpm. While the first one remained in the test lab, engineering installed a second version in a TD-24 to evaluate durability at the Phoenix test farm.

Between January 24, 1958, and May 15, 1961, IHC operated a Boeing 502-10C gas turbine in a TD-24 at the Huntsville Proving Grounds. The engine developed 149.7 drawbar horsepower and while there were two major engine failures and several minor problems during the months of testing, IHC learned a great deal from the tests, operating a standard turbo-charged similarly rated diesel TD-24 alongside. The turbine had no engine brake on downhill slopes and its 15-inch-diameter exhaust pipe obstructed forward visibility. If it were cut down to improve vision, the engine noise deafened operators. In real-world-type scraper and bulldozer tests, the torque-converter turbo-diesel out performed the gas turbine by a small margin, but one large enough to convince IHC that gas turbines might not be efficient power sources for large crawlers or some Hough products such as scrapers, loaders and haulers.

IHER tried another technology, the free-piston engine, in which two pistons not connected to a crankshaft bounce off each other to compress fuel for combustion. The engine output is the exhaust, which, similar to the gas turbine, rushes past a vaned-turbine wheel connected via a reduction gearbox to ground wheels. Each system offered benefits: the free-piston engine showed extremely low fuel usage, but was difficult to start and to cool, while the gas turbine started easily and was almost insensitive to dust, but drank fuel.

IHER's third energy technology project used commercially available electric motors to propel a fuel cell-powered vehicle. The most effective variation involved gas turbines running direct current (DC) electric generators. The motors drove

through purpose-built electric transmissions, using a system derived from diesel-electric locomotives.

IHER went back to the gas turbine engine for another test in a prototype TD-50 crawler late in 1960. IHC had acquired Solar Aircraft Company of San Diego, California, to dovetail into new research in gas turbine engines for construction, trucks and tractors. Using a 600-horsepower Solar regenerator, IHER worked with several varieties of powertrain, including gear-reduction into the torque converter, a main hydromechanical transmission with a hydrostatic auxiliary drive to control steering, and a third that used separate hydromechanical transmissions

This 1959 4-WD-1 prototype grew out of the original Payloader construction tractors from 1948. Subsidiary Frank G. Hough Company collaborated with Farm Equipment and Construction Equipment Divisions, and in early 1957 Hough had a running prototype. This prototype provided two- and four-wheel steering or crabbing. *State Historical Society of Wisconsin*

1957 Farmall Cub Lo-Boy

When the Cub Lo-Boy first appeared in 1955, IHC offered both a Farmall and an International model. Farmalls offered an adjustable front axle. On January 24, 1957, affecting 1958 production, the Lo-Boy was made an International tractor only. Beginning March 31, 1960, International Cub Lo-Boys were painted yellow unless buyers ordered red.

1959 International 240 Utility

This was a very efficient mechanical package. While the tractor weighed 3,440 pounds with fuel, water and 175-pound operator, in first gear, it was capable of pulling 4,384 pounds on concrete with 12-24 rear tires. Its C-123 engine produced 28.9 drawbar horsepower at 1,200 rpm.

for each track and hydrostatic auxiliary drives for main power. A fourth model, built as a benchmark for comparison, ran IHC's DVT-1089 diesel, producing 450 horsepower, through a torque converter.

IHER ran these experiments in a tractor just 18 inches longer than the TD-25 but with more than twice the horsepower. Their goal was to transfer increasing amounts of torque to the ground without incurring the catastrophic failures, the "shock load," that they experienced with the 460, 560 and 660 models.

The TD-50 development prototype was a little-known research platform. Months earlier, in mid-March 1960, however, IHER began a "full hydrostatic drive research tractor using commercial pump and motor units with I-340 tractor components." This became a well-known experimental.

Ed Jedrzykowski, staff engineer with IHER, wrote several memorandum reports and outside papers during and after development work on this machine, beginning as early as March 15, 1960. "Full hydrostatic drive replaced clutches, spline shafts, axles, gears, etc., used for propelling conventional tractors. The research hydrostatic tractor proved the feasibility of using a single hand control for infinitely variable ground speed regulation in either direction at constant engine speed with the ability to brake with the same control lever on deceleration."

The continuously variable ground speed at steady engine speed allowed PTO-driven attachments full independence. Another advantage, for plowing, rototilling or snow blowing, was that with engine speed set for maximum torque, full engine power was available from zero miles-per-hour up to maximum ground speed.

IHER devised the systems in January 1959 and tractor design began in June. Jedrzykowski led the group that installed matching motors for each rear wheel, "used in parallel, which eliminates the need for a differential." Jedrzykowski specified 188-cubic-inch radial motors built in England and fed by a variable displacement pump. Main power for the hydrostatic pump came from an 80-horsepower Solar Industries Titan T62T single-shaft gas regenerator turbine. The tractor, designated the HT-340 (hydrostatic turbine), first ran December 7, 1959.

The hydrostatic drive eliminated the shock upon engaging forward drive under heavy implement load, minimizing strain on drive train components. By mid-March 1960, Jedrzykowski and his colleagues found an opposite problem: Under no load and at high speeds (road travel), pressure dropped in the pumps. This affected hand control response. Hydrostatic braking was nonexistent. IHER added separate brakes purchased from Truck Division. After its development life concluded, IHER repainted the prototype, whose sleek fiberglass body was created by IHC's chief industrial designer, Ted Koeber.

Following brief tests at the Farm Equipment Research Engineering Center (FEREC), its first public showing was at University of Nebraska's 10th Annual Tractor Day, July 20, 1961, on the campus at Lincoln. It was meant to go on tour to fairs and displays throughout the Midwest to offer audiences a glimpse of the future. Returning from Lincoln, however, the HT-340 was severely damaged when the transporter carrying it rolled over in Missouri on July 21. It was hastily repaired and shown throughout the rest of the summer, including an AeroSpace Show in Philadelphia, Pennsylvania.

During the winter, extensive repairs and parts replacements for the show circuit during 1962 transformed the prototype into the HT-341. For 1962 IHER added a three-point hitch, stabilized steering, larger tires, rear lights, slightly desensitized controls and an improved fuel-filtering system. (After years of alternating static displays with active field tests at public events, IHER retired the HT-341 to storage until September 1, 1967, when IHC donated it to the Smithsonian Institution in Washington.)

Gas turbine research led to conclusions that the technology sometimes created greater expenses than it saved. An IHER project completed in early 1962 produced a dual regenerator solar engine that developed 600 horsepower, but it was the size of an office desk. To fit it into any existing construction or farm tractor, crawler, or loader required near total redesign from chassis through bodywork.

Falling under rules of Fowler McCormick's reorganization, Solar had to support itself while developing turbines. Solar's internal transfer costs, the price it charged IHER, or Farm Equipment, Truck or Construction Divisions (cost-plus-60 percent to cover engineering, planning and tooling expenses) made the engines too expensive. Even at a 30-percent mark-up, Simon Chen, an IHER cost analyst, concluded in February 1962, that "Due to the higher cost and substantial mark-up, the economic advantage of gas turbine-powered equipment is greatly reduced or becomes insignificant."

IHC unveiled the "Turbo Star," a "Turbine Truck of the Future" in 1968 but then ended turbine research, yielding the business to Ford and General Motors, who had deeper research pockets. Solar continued as a highly profitable outside supplier. While the gas turbine held little future for farm or industrial tractors, the hydrostatic transmission showed great potential. At shows and demonstrations, farmers who were put off by the turbine's howling noise, always asked about the tractor's continuously variable speeds.

FEREC also concluded that Ted Koeber's ability to produce a startlingly attractive fiberglass package for the technological showpiece had succeeded because design happened alongside engineering. As the HT-341 final report said, "When future vehicles are to be restyled extensively, the styling design and vehicle design should be done simultaneously."

While FEREC directed experiments and development efforts toward larger tractors, it also looked into garden tractors. Tentatively priced at around $500, their concept would develop just seven horsepower, primarily for gardening and estate maintenance. It should resemble the large tractor and clearly be a derivative of the Cub. FEREC proposed three names, the Cubette (or Cub-Ette,) Cub-Urban and Ranch-All. The first 100 production models were completed by November, manufactured at Louisville Works. IHC predicted first year sales at 5,000 units. When it counted the first year (1961) sales figures for its new Cub Cadet, 46 percent of the 11,509 total went to urban and suburban areas, serving a market that had never before needed an IHC tractor.

In mid-1961, FEREC also designed a hydromechanical transmission as an option for its proposed I-660X tractors. In this system, input power was split into a mechanical and a hydraulic power flow path. The mechanical path allowed a high level of efficiency while the hydraulics made possible a stepless speed change. IHC (and other farm equipment makers) used the same oil for hydraulics, power steering and brakes, and for transmission and final drive lubrication. This new drive system took advantage of the common lubricant/transmission fluid.

Frank Jenks' efforts at cost controls were widely known, reported in local papers and national financial and farm journals. To the business community, these were sound, if belated, steps taken toward getting IHC back on track. To farmers, it caused concern. Rumors flew that IHC was for sale, that Massey-Harris tried to buy the farm equipment business. Jenks and C. C. Brannan, president of IHC of Canada Ltd., sent out letters to branches and district managers in May, 1963, to calm anxious employees.

Because of the crankshaft failures on the International 660 tractors, when Farm Equipment Division (FED) revised specifications for the I-660X (the replacement designated the I-806), they asked Construction Equipment Engineering Department (CEED) in late February 1961, to produce the new D-361. The 101 horsepower in-line six-cylinder engine was a nonturbocharged diesel, already proven in trucks as the Red Diamond Series engine.

At the same time, the Executive Council approved manufacture of an industrial line of Farmall 404 and 504 tractors, the International 2404 and 2504, in Federal Yellow, with a heavy-duty, fixed-tread front axle with the one-piece cast-iron

1958 International 330 Utility

On March 13, 1957, FTED released to manufacturing final specifications for this tractor. It used a new four-cylinder C-135 engine but carried over many mechanical parts from the previous I-350 utilities. These would also be carried forward into the planned International 340.

1959 Farmall 140 with Loader

Introduced in 1958, the 140 was offered as Farmall and International models with a wide range of implements carried up from the 100 and 130 models. This well-equipped Farmall carries the Model 1000 side-arm loader and a Model 100 one-point rear blade.

1959 International 660 Diesel

Farm Tractor Engineering Department (FTED) released to manufacturing the final specifications for the 660 D on May 19, 1958. The pages described full floating (rear) stub axles splined to wheel driving members. The lubricating oil supply in each rear axle planetary unit was separate from the transmission oil. Sadly, this proved inadequate for the 64.4-drawbar horsepower, 9,875-pound machine.

radiator-guard/grille with inset headlights. This heavier piece provided "an 'industrial-tractor' look and, at the same time, adequate protection for the radiator and additional front end weight for better balance when the tractor is used with backhoe-loader combinations." In mid-September, the Executive Council signed off on manufacture of International 606, and Farmall and International 706 and 806 models, running on gas, diesel or liquid propane gas (LPG) for introduction in late 1962. The International 504 and 606 and the Industrial 2504 and 2606 had the new hydrostatic power steering as standard equipment.

A surge in sales of Elwood Four-Wheel Drive conversion kits for later-production Farmall M, and 460 and 560 tractors pushed new chairman Harry O. Bercher (who replaced the retiring Jenks in May 1962) to reinstate the Frank G. Hough Company development programs on an IHC-produced true four-wheel drive. IHER tested the Elwood and other kits and found them weaker in durability and performance than a comparable horsepower true four-wheel drive.

During this period, small farm operators continued to sell out to larger neighbors, and the U.S. Census projected that the number of farms of 500 to 1,000 acres and those of 1,000 acres and more increased by 5 percent from 1954 through 1959. On February 1, 1962, the Executive Council launched a two tractor program, with 105-drawbar-horsepower diesel engines driving through sliding gear transmissions, to be designated the International 4100 Four-Wheel Drive tractor. Co-developed with its Frank G. Hough subsidiary, prototypes began testing in August 1962. Before that happened, however, IHC's worst nightmare reappeared.

"Field reports are being received to the effect that, after a year or more of service, failures are occurring in some of the vital areas on 460 and 560 series tractors which have been rebuilt. Failure in one of the parts in question frequently results in extensive damage to other transmission and/or final drive parts, requiring an extensive overhaul of the entire drive assembly. Most of the components are bearings."

For the Executive Council, the 706 and 806 models could not arrive soon enough. Between April 20, 1961, and May 15, 1962, IHC had ordered, authorized and paid for 38 running changes on 460, 560 and 660 models.

In late August 1962, FED authorized development and production of high-clearance versions of the new 504 Farmall, following requests from cane farmers in Mississippi and vegetable farmers in Florida. In October, after introduction of the 404 models, dealers let IHC know their disappointment "that the tractor did not have a constant running, or independent type of power take-off, such as is available on Ford, Massey-Harris and Deere models in the 35-horsepower category." While the 504 model had it, and the 404 had a transmission-driven PTO, "live" take-off was eliminated from 404 design specifications to save money. Cost analysts determined that IHC needed to sell 636 of the 404s with live-PTO to pay back belated development and tooling costs. Sales estimated the company would sell 1,500 tractors with live PTO that would go to other companies if the new tractors didn't have it. Board

Chairman Harry Bercher, who shared Frank Jenks' support for and belief in IHC's complete revitalization, approved it.

But this was barely six months into Bercher's job, in late October 1962. FEREC was at work on the Hough-based 4100 four-wheel drive prototype. FED began to plan the next generation of large two-wheel drive tractors, diesel-engine only, producing 120 PTO horsepower with 12,000 pounds of drawbar pull.

This four-wheel, non-Farmall-type tractor had a three-point hitch, Torque-Amplifier from the 806, and a hydraulically actuated 1,000-rpm PTO. Engineering layout began January 1, 1963; three proto-

Throughout 1962, its last season on the road, the International HT-341 performed demonstrations and static displays at nearly two dozen county and state fairs, general tractor exhibitions, and several industrial expositions before IHC retired it to storage. Those who saw it remember its noise but were more impressed by how the operators never shifted gears. First run in December 1959, it was donated to the Smithsonian Institution in 1967. *State Historical Society of Wisconsin*

1961 Farmall 560 with Auger

Tractor Committee Report No. 12, September 15, 1959, approved a no-charge warranty program "covering parts and labor on Farmall and International 460 and 560 differential and bull gear assemblies on which failures occur within 12 months after first use." The failures of over-stressed rear ends ultimately cost IHC millions of dollars and the support of longtime owners.

Division's turbocharger spun the diesel engine to full power, tire sidewalls began buckling. Prototypes peeled lugs off treads. Wheels spun on the tire beads. Project engineers from Firestone and Goodyear redesigned belts throughout the casings and reoriented lugs to grip as well as unload mud. They developed an 18.4x38 heavy-duty tire specifically for the 1206. Once FEREC had tires that would stay underneath its prototypes, development continued. Production as both a Farmall and International 1206 Turbo began in July 1965.

Early in 1964, the Executive Council agreed with FED that there would be benefits in standardizing tractor designs for all of its markets. The concept of World Wheel Tractors was born and its first committee meeting, July 9, 1964, set up development programs for a 40- and 50-PTO horsepower tractor through joint production in U.S. plants and at Doncaster. FEREC, at its Hinsdale facility, designed the tractors and by the second meeting, April 15, 1965, the large tractor had increased to 52 horsepower. FED decided soon after to manufacture complete tractors for IHC's overseas markets at the Doncaster Works, while 17 varieties of partially completed tractors, delivered on skids, would be completed at Louisville Works. Badged "International," these became the 454 (40-horsepower farm-utility), 2454 (industrial-utility); 574 (52-horsepower farm-utility), 2574 (industrial utility) and 574 (row crop).

In a blurring of the lines, Doncaster supplied diesel 454s to Canada, while Louisville provided all other models to Canada. Gas engines came from Louisville, while IHC's Neuss Works in Germany produced diesel engines. Tractors were offered with either mechanical or hydrostatic transmissions. FEREC designed bodywork for the series to create a "family styling" silhouette and appearance. The Executive Council funded assembly of six prototypes of each for extensive testing.

1961 International 4300 4WD

Restyled and enlarged, this 4300 was the result of earlier experiments with Frank G. Hough creating the 4-WD-1. But this machine awaited arrival of IHC's turbocharged six-cylinder D-817 engine. Another delay was waiting for 23.1-26 tires. The 4300 weighed in at 29,815 pounds.

1961 Farmall 340 Diesel

By October 1959, the D-166 diesel was near to production as a planned engine for the 340 crawlers starting January 1960. Farmall and International models got the new diesel beginning in July 1960, for 1961 model year production. Most went into the crawlers.

types were ready in September. The budget for design, prototype assembly and testing was $800,000. Originally this Model 1206 was to be released to production in January 1964; instead the first three prototypes weren't completed until June 1964. Tight finances were not what delayed the project. One went to the Engineering Center for 2,000-hour endurance track testing (where it showed 98.2 drawbar horsepower) while the other two went to Pecos, Texas, for customers' use. In Texas, one 1206 did heavy-duty deep plowing; the other, equipped with four-wheel drive, did ripper and land leveling work.

What held up the 1206 was tires. Once Solar

The trend toward larger farms, needing more powerful tractors, became clear to farm equipment product planners when they got responses in early 1963 from 615 farmers about their future tractor wants and needs. Fifty percent of the respondents ran farms larger than 500 acres and 30 percent claimed gross sales beyond $40,000 the previous year. They averaged four tractors per farm (although a few collectors admitted to having more than 20 by then.) Only 11 percent owned tractors with more than 70 horsepower in early 1963, but 29 percent felt they would need that power in five years. On farms larger than 1,000 acres, 58 percent needed four-wheel drive, either below 65 horsepower or with 95 horsepower or more. Gasoline still was the fuel of choice up to 50 horsepower; between 30 and 70 horsepower, owners preferred LPG, while users above 60 horsepower wanted diesels. Sixty percent of the farmers mounted plows rather than pulling them.

The survey also told IHC that owners of tractors with less than 40 horsepower were more satisfied with their machines than those with more power. "This may suggest," the unidentified researchers concluded, "that the demand of tractors is dividing into two classes: small tractors and large tractors." For IHC, whose sales had jumped thanks to 1964 and 1965 tax cuts, this was not bad news.

Bercher moved the company from its longtime world headquarters at 180 N. Michigan Avenue across the Chicago River into the brand new Equitable Building, built at 401 N. Michigan on the site of Cyrus McCormick's first reaper factory.

Bercher invested in his business, pouring money like molten ore into Wisconsin Steel, IHC's boutique mill, and even more into McCaffrey's favorite, the Construction Equipment Division (CED). After valvetrain and transmission problems stopped TD-24s on construction sites in the early 1950s, engineering worked at the problems for several years, before introducing the TD-25 in 1960. Then Caterpillar introduced its D-9 and IHC felt obligated to compete again, this time with the TD-30. But this crawler, with its power-shift transmission and something like 320 horsepower out of the DT-817 engine, stretched components too far. As Joe Nehl, a product service engineer with Hough at the time, recently put it, "it was an ill-prepared warrior against Cat's D-9."

After the frustration of the TD-24 and the Farm Equipment Division's 460/560 Farmalls, CED dealt with repairs and frustrated owners for just two years, then pulled the TD-30s off the market in 1965.

IHC, with all its interests—Solar, steel, construction, trucks and agricultural equipment—impressed customers and Wall Street investors as a corporation gone to greed: if it could do well now in this, maybe it should try that too. Still, with more

successes than TD-30s and 560s, their customers and the stock market remained loyal. (Stockholder loyalty worked both ways; IHC reliably paid dividends, even when it needed money for plant modernization or engineering.)

IHC's resources, grown fat in the wealthy mid-1960s, were not limitless. It soon found itself laying too thin a financial blanket over its core industries. Some of this impetus to spread out came from Brooks McCormick, the latest in the family line to

1961 International 140 with Mower

The 140 models carried on the Culti-Vision offset engine-to-operator position that farmers found beneficial cultivating on small acreages. The optional front bumper, an obvious industrial product, hides an adjustable front axle.

1961 International 460 Grove

In February 1959, IHC introduced orchard fenders as a factory option or an after-delivery installation for International 340 and 460 Utility models. IHC offered a side cowling or fairing as well for further protection of vines or low hanging branches. When the improved version, the Grove tractor, appeared about a year later, it included engine panels and a protective screen for the operator. The sheet metal and support brackets added about 500 pounds to the weight of the Utility 460.

1961 Farmall AMD-7
The diesel version of the Australian M was in production there from 1957 through 1961. While otherwise similar to the U.S.-produced MDs, this used a CAV diesel injection pump, and it retained band brakes.

exercise influence. As Barbara Marsh wrote in A Corporate Tragedy, "Brooks was a great brainstormer. He could sit down and in five minutes rattle off more expansion and development programs than you could accomplish in five years!"

To give small tractor sales a shot in the arm, Bercher agreed to restyle Farmall and International 140 models and the Farmall Cub and International Cub Lo-Boy in January 1963. Now matching 706 and 806 tractors, they resembled the new Cub Cadet. Soon after, FED proposed an International 606 model to replace the long-troubled 460 that was going out of production in April. After testing three prototypes, production began March 1964.

Responding to increasing four-wheel drive requests and rejecting the Elwood system, FED produced its own, using a front axle developed by American Coleman Company with a differential from current production at Fort Wayne, Indiana, truck works. Because of its size, Farmall Works completed assembly on 706 and 806 four-wheel drive models in its Special Feature Department, set up to accommodate small series production requests. The four-wheel drive option was intro-

duced when regular production went public in August 1963.

Two years after approving development of a 120-horsepower four-wheel drive, known as the 4300, FED shelved plans for the smaller 4100 four-wheel drive co-developed with Hough. While everyone agreed the tractor had potential, Deere introduced its 5010 with 109 horsepower and others had four-wheel drives closer in power to IHC's 4300, introduced back in 1961. FED concluded in mid-September 1963 that the Hough-developed 4100 prototypes no longer could be produced profitably.

To finish 1963, FED proposed blending the best of its International 404 with the British B-414 models to make the 424. It used the B-414's diesel engine with an independent PTO, while absorbing the I-404's swept-back front axle and its better looks. This Anglo-American hybrid accepted the full range of accessories industrial customers wanted, taken from domestic parts bins without need to import the modifications. FED reasoned this model could be production-ready within nine months, around May 1964, whereas engineering from scratch required three to four years from proposal to first sale.

The International 606, approved in February 1963, was released for preproduction on May 12, 1964, as the Model 656, and as both an International and a Farmall. Economic constraints, combined with new product teething difficulties, delayed development. It was originally planned with either gas (or as LPG) or diesel, Torque-Amplifier, "Power Shift" PTO for either 540- or 1,000-rpm use, two- or three-point hitch. The 656 used the hydrostatic transmission and prototypes tested a new "cab-forward configuration," known internally as XCF-65, experimental cab-forward. Ten tractors for "acceptance tests" were completed March 1965, but the tests were slipped back six months.

"Cab-forward" addressed complaints IHC market researchers heard about operator seat comfort and access, and inadequate standing position. The XCF-65 was a "low silhouette, deluxe agricultural and industrial vehicle." To provide a tractor with optimum operator's comfort, the cab-forward model improved the controls, placed the cab ahead of the rear wheels with amidship "walk-in" accessibility. The fuel tank went behind the operator's seat, which was moved forward 14 inches from regular I-606 position to provide for easier entry and an improved ride. The cab was insulated, with opening windows, heater/defroster, and air conditioning.

Two weeks after releasing the 656, FED discontinued production of the Farmall Cub on May 25, 1964, citing "the trend toward consolidation of small farms into larger acreages and the fact that less human labor is available to operate these larger farms." As a result, FED concluded, "agricultural use of this size tractor has declined." The company continued production of the International Cub, in yellow-and-white only.

IHER, continuing research and experiments, constantly sought additional uses for new technology. In mid-June 1964, it suggested replacing the existing gear transmission of the Cub Cadet. While other tractors in this market used belt drives, IHER suggested IHC leap ahead with a hydrostatic transaxle to eliminate the clutch, transmission, axle, differential and brake, and reduce tractor weight by 55 pounds in the bargain. It completed a prototype June 7, 1963, and tested it intermittently through the end of the year, concluding that "the Cub Cadet hydrostatic transaxle should be only the first of an expanding family of hydraulic components for use in vehicle transmissions or as hydraulic power

sources for power steering, front end loaders, bulldozers, etc."

They followed it up immediately, with development plans for hydrostatic transmissions for 504, 606, 656, 706, 806, 1206, 3514 and 3616 agricultural and industrial tractors. In the interim, the Industrial Equipment Division began installing torque-converter transmissions in the 3414 and 3616 models, produced by Funk Manufacturing in Coffeyville, Kansas. It was meant for "shuttle-type operations, such as loading and dozing."

Economic conditions forced a hiatus on continued development of some tractor projects during late 1962 and 1963. Some testing was postponed, some was canceled. The Hough-designed International 4100, shelved in September 1963 due to costs and inadequate power output, had been popular in engineering. Testing and development funds materialized and by November 1964, preliminary structural and durability tests had only reinforced engineering's belief in the tractor. Only a 2,000-hour endurance test remained and manufacture was scheduled to begin after that test, with sales beginning in August 1965.

For engineering, once again, there seemed reason to have hope.

1962 Farmall 806
This was IHC's monster, a six-plow rated, 86-drawbar horsepower row-crop tractor that, at the time, was the world's most powerful. The 24 prototypes accumulated 33,000 hours of testing, so Farmall Works geared up in August 1961 to produce nearly 100 more for 41 simultaneous dealer shows. This was the first, serial number 501.

Ten

GROWTH AND EXPANSION RESUMES

During the 1960s, Farm Equipment Division began asking questions about itself. A new department for market research anonymously questioned recent IHC equipment buyers and also registered owners of competing makes. Conscious of problems in the past, IHC hoped to learn where it stood against the competition. What it found was not music to its ears.

Surveys expressed dissatisfaction with "the personality of the dealer." FED's chief market researcher, M. J. Steitz, took this criticism to mean the dealer's overall attitude of professionalism, including helpfulness to past, current and future customers. Frequent equipment problems also drove some longtime customers away. The problems with the Model 560 were severe enough to turn away families who had been customers since the early 1920s. The completed surveys, which addressed specific departments, urged engineering to improve quality and manufacturing to eliminate production defects. Most important, the people polled stressed the need for sales to pay better attention to farmers' needs and situations.

Other surveys allowed FEREC to glimpse the future from the farmer's point of view. These asked the retailers to describe the qualities future tractors should have to best serve their local markets. Most of them saw a trend for higher speed plowing, reporting that farmers preferred plowing at five miles per hour with five bottoms, instead of four miles per hour with six bottoms. Some dealers passed on farmer requests for tractors with 140 to 150 PTO horsepower. They wanted dual rear tires, partly to get power to the

This 1965 International Industrial-2806 is the industrial version of the Farmall 806. IHC quoted power output of its 301-cubic inch in-line six-cylinder engine at 90 brake horsepower at 2,400 rpm. The industrial used a nonadjustable tubular front axle and weighed 8,115 pounds.

ground without slippage and partly to decrease soil compaction caused by single tires. Hearing the demands of the marketplace, dealers were ready for the next Farmall and International. They hoped that IHC was ready to start leading again.

Part of IHC's efforts to lead involved assimilating Frank G. Hough Company into IHC's mainstream. Hough's engineers worked with Construction Equipment Division (CED) to design and develop a replacement for the TD-340, which was discontinued at this time, and one for the expensive-to-produce-but-still-in-production TD-6.

FEREC fitted its first experimental hydromechanical transmission (designed in mid-1961, built by hand, and bench-tested) to a regular production Farmall 806 early in 1965. By February 1966, it approved production, incorporating an "exhaust gas ejector/heat exchanger" to cool the hydrome-

1956 International TD-6 Series 61

This model was produced between 1956 and 1959, and only about 2,500 were manufactured. A powerful compact tractor, it developed 39.6 drawbar horsepower at 1,550 rpm in Nebraska tests. The Series 61 was devised especially for agricultural uses. Besides its serial number and some badge differentiation, the only obvious change is that IHC enlarged the foot wells on the series 61.

1958 International T-340 #501

On July 3, 1957, the Construction Equipment Division (CED) slotted into its future planning a small crawler that it would call the T-4, based on the I-340 farm tractor, with about 30 drawbar horsepower. Those attending the meeting agreed to contact Farm Equipment Division to see if they had any need for a similar crawler. Obviously they did.

chanical transmission oil. This worked similarly to the heat pump concept and offered the added benefit of quieting the exhaust noise without need for a muffler. FED canceled production plans and IHC never manufactured the 806 Hydro.

On March 10, the Executive Council released the F-656 and I-2656 models to production beginning October 1, with public announcement two weeks later, followed almost immediately by the F-656 Hi-Clear. By May, plans to start November 1 production of the restyled 706, 806 and 1206 tractors with increased-power were pushed back to June 1967. IHC was selling all the 706s it could produce and could ill-afford to shut down the line to retool for its replacement. Pilot models of the new 756, 856 and 1256 were completed September 1, 1967, and production started in October.

In May 1966, CED looked at the engines used in its machines, compared to those used in tractors in FED. They found that CED's engines from 282 to 429 cubic inches had few interchangeable parts and no family resemblance to each other. While FED used engines by the hundreds or thousands, CED had runs of 250 or 300 scrapers or crawlers. CED's limited sales did not justify manufacturing unique engines for its machines.

CED knew the Neuss Works in Germany, despite its modern assembly facilities, made no engines for CED into the 1970s. To reduce engine costs, CED minimized the number of engine blocks and maximized the parts common to each engine to provide the greatest benefits to cost, design, engineering, testing and maintenance.

Two engine "families" grew out of this research, a 300 series, with two engines of 312 and 360 cubic inches, and the 400 series, with three blocks of 414, 436 and 466 cubic inches. To further reduce costs, CED proposed to Motor Truck, Farm Equipment and to its Power Unit engineers that they design future products to use these five displacements. CED configured the large 360 and all the 400 series engines for production with and without turbochargers, in this way achieving a power range from 94 to 231 gross horsepower.

In February 1967, FED completed a product plan reacting to dealer and farmer comments and inquiries. Each tractor, from current production Cub Cadets up the line to 1206 and 4100 (introduced in 1966), gained horsepower. FED also planned two new big tractors, a 1556 (with 140 PTO horsepower) and a 4256 (160 PTO horsepower) for production in late 1970. FED enlarged

On April 9, 1958, Farm Tractor Engineering Department (FTED), in collaboration with CED, released to the Melrose Park Works specifications for the new C-135 engine to use in the T-340. Production started on November 14, 1958, and this crawler, No. 501, was the first one off the assembly line.

1966 International of Australia A-554 Diesel

This was a one-year production model from International of Australia, introduced in late 1966. Australian diesel tractors used IHC's AD-264 engine. This is the same one that Doncaster's British International factory installed in its B-450.

1969 International of Australia A-564

This model is another Australian model, the replacement for the A-554 that remained in production through 1970. The A-564 Series B followed this one and continued until IHC suspended all tractor manufacture at Geelong in 1973. Australian and British diesel tractors used glow plug start. Both 554 and 564 models offered live PTO, but they never adopted U.S. disc brakes.

1969 International 1256 Turbo Loader

Introduced in late 1967, these tractors used the six-cylinder turbocharged D-407 engine to produce 116.1 power take-off horsepower at the University of Nebraska. The 16-speed sliding gear transmission was offered with the torque amplifier.

fuel tanks to allow longer working hours common on larger farms and configured more mounting positions to fit tanks onto tractors for those who sprayed chemicals during tillage operations.

A. O. Smith Corporation, an Ionia, Michigan-based company that made fiberglass car bodies and IHC's Scout tops, contracted with IHC in March 1967 to manufacture tractor fiberglass cabs. This too was a response to survey information. Smith's cabs, on FED designs, insulated against weather, dust and noise, provided air conditioning, heat and defrosting, tinted glass, opening side and rear windows, windshield wipers, turn signals, coat hooks, storage areas for tool box, lunch box and thermos, and a provision for a radio. The first prototype reached FED on February 1, 1968, and regular production delivery began October 15, for Farmall and International 656, 756, 856 and 1256 models.

As an interim measure responding to growing safety concerns over tractor roll-over accidents, IHC developed a protective frame attached to the rear axle carrier, with a fiberglass canopy and seat

belt for factory application to 656, 756, 856 and 1256 models beginning in December 1967. FEREC modified fenders and exhaust pipes to be compatible with the new roll-over protection system (ROPS).

The 806-856 and 1206-1256 models, as well as the 4100, also benefited from the introduction of a new Category II and III Quick-Hitch coupler for use with the three-point hitches. As with IHC's previous Quick-Attach and other rapid implement mounting systems, the goal was to make implement attachment possible without requiring the operator to leave the cab (except for PTO-attachment). Another objective was to allow compatibility with other makers' quick-couple implements.

In late March 1967, FED solidified plans for its World Wheel Tractor series. The first, a 40-horsepower medium-duty utility-type model for farm or industrial uses, was coded TX-19 for internal documents, and became the International 454. Plans also included the TX-36 in International and Farmall 574 model designations, produced in Louisville for the United States and Canada, for introduction in 1970. To test features and marketability, FED released the

International 444 series in the fall of 1967 and launched the 544 series with a conventional five-speed manual transmission (coupled to the torque amplifier to provide 10 forward and 2 reverse speeds), or the hydrostatic transmission introduced on the 656s. Production began in August 1968.

Earlier attempts with a 7-horsepower Cub Cadet and hydrostatic drive proved the engine was not strong enough. By late 1966, IHC introduced International 123 Cub Cadets with 12 horsepower that performed better. First year sales were nearly 6,000 tractors by July 1967, prompting FED to offer the 12-horsepower 125 and a new 10-horsepower version 105, four months later.

Beginning in 1967, FEREC used computers for experimentation and testing systems, cutting development time greatly. (Tractor Engineering had made its first serious attempt to program a digital computer for farm equipment engineering problems in 1954.) With the experiences gained during the redesigns of 460/560 rear ends, transmissions and TD-24 engine failures, the department created a base of knowledge. Everything from compression spring design to V-belt life to rockshaft arm stress analysis to gear design and axle bearing load analysis now was possible, as the science of metallurgy merged with the body of field experience in the computer.

1970 International Farmall 826 Demonstrator

Recalling the attention-getting success of its white-painted demonstrators 20 years before, IHC painted hoods, fenders and side panels gold on special demonstrator models. The 826 introduced IHC's new D-358 90-power take-off horsepower diesel coupled to a sliding gear transmission that could be ordered with the torque amplifier to double the number of speeds available.

1970 International 756

On September 19, 1966, Farm Equipment Division dropped the 706 model and replaced it with the 756. FED planned only to revise styling and improve operator comfort, but an opportunity came to utilize IHC's Neuss Works-built D-310 diesels to match the 76 power take-off horsepower of the gasoline and LPG C-291 engines.

1970 International 1456

Hydraulics took on an interesting new roll with the 56-series, introduced in 1967, especially in this new top-of-the-line 1456 model, with its hydraulically adjustable—and suspended—operator's seat. IHC's D-407, producing 114.7 drawbar horsepower, easily handled the Model 720 automatic reset six-bottom plows.

By February 1968, 12 prototype World Wheel tractors, 6 each of 40- and 52-PTO horsepower units, completed thousands of hours of testing. One 454 (40-horsepower model) ran 1,550 hours at 125 percent of rated load; one hydrostatic transmission-equipped prototype endured a like-amount of endurance testing on a tractor dynamometer. One powertrain alone had 2,100 hours on it. FEREC released designs to Doncaster and the British plant produced another 6 prototypes to begin its own testing.

A small problem arose with hydrostatic transmissions affecting forward and reverse control. It involved few 656 models and FED "had mixed emotions about initiating a mandatory improvement of the recently introduced hydrostatic transmissions." FED quickly moved to install a small spring to secure the pump servo cylinder control valve, about an hour's work, at company expense. FED installed the spring on all tractors on the production line and the Executive Council agreed "it would be in the company's best interest, in order to promote the sale of the hydrostatic drive tractors, to fix all tractors built" before the production change (2,657 of them by early February). Harry Bercher told FED that supporting engineering was "in the company's best interest."

In early March 1968, FED released the International Cub 154 Lo-Boy, a Cadet-styled tractor with a 15-horsepower C-60 water-cooled engine and companion 60-inch rotary mower, to replace the nearly 20-year-old original Cub Lo-Boy farm trac-

tor. FEREC continued testing a hydrostatic drive system for the new tractor as well. Gear-drive 154s began production in October 1968, selling for $1,975 with the mower.

The visual appearance of the 154 paralleled styling updates to the entire Cadet line. FED saw that suburban owners traded in very useful two- and three-year-old Cadets "on the basis of wanting the newest models. To maintain high levels of customer acceptance, it is the committee's plan to provide model changes every two years." Auto-industry styling had reached the garden tractor market by May 1968, as IHC elected the fourth McCormick, Brooks, as president and chief operating officer.

Brooks, 51, was a great-grandson of William McCormick, Cyrus Sr.'s business manager and youngest brother. He majored in Victorian literature at Yale, but upon graduating in 1940, his uncle Fowler hired him into the training program. He started at McCormick Works, sold farm equipment in Indiana in 1941, learned manufacturing at Tractor Works and became superintendent at Melrose Park in 1947, as they tooled up McCaffrey's first TD-24s. He sold trucks in Kansas City, then in 1951 became joint managing director at Doncaster, where he conceived the World Tractor.

Brooks observed that IHC derived most of its profits from farm equipment, most of its sales from trucks, and most of its costs and losses from construction equipment. He championed the World tractor concept, though not as a crowd-pleaser. He saw it as a way to cut costs by reducing tractor lines, by collaborating on international designs and universal parts.

To supplement 656 hydrostatic drive tractors, in mid-June 1968, FED proposed new 826 and 1026 models at 84 and 112 PTO horsepower for introduction November 1969. In July they released the 4156 with 140 PTO and 125 drawbar horsepower, to replace the 4100 four-wheel drive model. To ensure no future problems with this power/workload increase, FEREC revised rear end gears to specifications that worked with the 460 and 560 models.

Hydraulics technology had not kept pace with drawbar power, leading to tractors that could pull more than they could lift. This imbalance did not affect field work too badly, but led to great difficulties when farmers sought to drive tractors on roads with the implements raised. Adding hydraulically actuated implement-mounted wheels helped, but this also encouraged farmers to use even larger implements. To resolve the imbalance, FEREC introduced IHC's latest weight-transfer hitch in November 1968. This hitch advanced Harry Ferguson's geometric A-frame structure to transfer load off the rear of the tractor to the steering and drive wheels. In this way, the hydraulics could raise heavier implements without lifting the front of the tractor. Production units of the new hitch, for tractors up to the 1256 models, were available in December 1969.

The 1256 was not upgraded because it was set for replacement to keep up with the newest marketing war in farm equipment, the battle over superior horsepower. Deere's new Model 4520, with 120 PTO horsepower, forced FED to raise the ante with a 125 PTO-horsepower model, the 1456, and a later 155-horsepower model to follow. Just months before, industrial 3800 and 3850 models had experienced frame failures. To accommodate the additional power in the 1456, FEREC revised virtually every dimension and element of the model for increased size and strength. Engineering widened gear faces from the transmission through the rear end, and enlarged the radiator and moved it forward to fit a bigger fan and give it greater clearance. The brake disc diameter was increased from 8 inches to 11.375 inches, and every brake component was enhanced; rear axle diameter was increased from 3.25 to 3.5 inches.

On February 28, Neuss Works related to the Executive Council Europe's need for larger tractors, as occurred in North America. With no 80-horsepower tractor in their line-up, IHC's French and German distributors sold Deutz, Hanomag, Renault or Fiat tractors in that range. Under agreement with FED, Neuss Works imported D-310 engines that it linked to partially synchronized transmissions to produce a prototype X-47, 80-horsepower tractor by November 1969. Regular production, as Model 846, started March 1971.

In the lawn tractor market, Fuji Heavy Industries approached IHC, indicating it could beat the prices Kohler charged the company for engines. Fuji offered to provide single-cylinder air-cooled engines for Cub Cadets. IHC tested these for six months but decided against production using the Japanese engines.

Existing tooling, factory production lines and parts inventories challenged Brooks McCormick's dream of a World Tractor line. So, too, did demand. While 400 series and 500 series tractors performed well and were successful, machines larger than the 756 were in little demand outside of North America, where they sold well. "Horsepower wars" drove FEREC, and sales fed IHC's treasury. Responding to the market, the company invested $24 million in tooling at the Melrose Park plant to expand production to 40,000 of the DT-466 diesel engines. Late in March 1969, FED authorized the two-phase replacement plan for its large tractors. With production beginning November 1, 1970, FED released the 60 series upgrades, amounting to small increases in power but a new grille, hood, side panels and overall appearance. It more closely resembled World Wheel series, yet many major components were in current production. Cost estimates to turn IHC's entire line into World Wheel machines approached $100 million, far beyond what was available.

The World Tractor philosophy created a model for U.S. markets only. Louisville Works product committee took requests from eastern and southeastern farmers for a 32-horsepower tractor, larger than Cub 14s and 154s, but smaller than 444 and 454 models. Doncaster provided running gear from its B-276 tractor with front axle, grille, hood, instrument and steering mechanism from the World TX-19 and TX-36 tractors. Louisville had a 32 PTO-horsepower trac-

1970 International 4156

IHC's original Frank G. Hough-derived Model 4100 four-wheel drive added nine drawbar horsepower, bringing output of the D-429 up to 125 (and 140 horsepower on power take-off.) Designed for balance under load, the 4156 carried two-thirds of its weight on the front axle when it was unburdened.

tor configured with few modifications for regional U.S. markets as an International 354. Doncaster did all testing and development work. FED approved it on April 24, 1969, and began production in November 1970.

In late June, 1969, FED released for Louisville production a new 14-horsepower hydrostatic drive Cub Cadet as the 147 model, to compete against the Case 444, Deere 140 and Ford 140 models, each with 14 horsepower, all with hydrostatic drive.

FED discontinued the 756 diesel from U.S. production in mid-July, replacing it with the 826, using IHC's own D-358 diesel, produced at Melrose Park. Yet it continued to ship partially assembled 756 models on skids to its plants in France, Mexico and Australia, where they installed Neuss Works D-310 engines sent directly from Germany.

R. W. Johnson, a design engineer with the Crawler Tractor Group of CED, outlined to the S.A.E. in mid-September, 1970, a history of CED's three new crawlers, the TD-7C, TD-8C, 100C and 125C. Johnson pointed out that the crawlers were made by CED for the Farm Equipment Division. These were

designed by Hough and CED engineers, with unit construction and rigid suspensions to work effectively also as loaders or bulldozers. CED designed all four tractors with a high percentage of parts compatibility. Engineers at CED and Hough fitted torque converters to full powershift transmissions to decrease drive train shock. CED put eight prototypes through a combined 24,000 hours of testing.

Cub Cadets also got major attention during 1970. FEREC developed new transmissions for both gear-driven and hydrostatic drive versions, which reduced cost and simplified manufacture and maintenance. FED then gave them substantial exterior restyling and minor power increases for model year 1972. New tapered frames allowed wider outside vendor engines when cost advantages were available. The seven-horsepower Model 73 became the 86 with eight horsepower. The grille and hood sheet metal resembled the new 66 series farm tractors. Louisville began production July 1, 1971.

Yet the Louisville plant had problems with the International Cub 154 Lo-Boy. Assembly difficulties at the plant caused about one of every four to suffer driveline failure. Tolerances designed too tight for assembly-line manufacture caused clutch shafts and drive coupler hub assemblies to wear through. The problem never occurred in hand-fabricated proto-types but production-line tooling and fixtures made proper installation very difficult. IHC authorized repair for all affected tractors in mid-February 1970. FED revised the Louisville assembly lines building the Lo-Boys, just as it approved creation of an industrial 25-horsepower companion to the Lo-Boy that used the hydrostatic transmission and a four-cylinder water-cooled Renault engine from France. It was called the International 254. Production started November 1972.

In late 1970, Mississippi Road Supply (MRS), of Flora, Mississippi, began a cooperative program with FED. MRS had been manufacturing construction equipment and some farm implements since 1943. The cooperative combined MRS's specialized knowledge and manufacturing facilities and IHC's prestige, financial position and dealer organization. MRS developed and manufactured for IHC two four-wheel drive articulated tractors of 130 and 155 PTO horsepower, and took over production of the 4156 four-wheel drive, four-wheel steering tractor. In addition, MRS licensed its three current-production four-wheel drive tractors (up to 236 PTO horsepower) to IHC. MRS also gained access to IHC's engines, using CED's D-466 six-cylinder and Truck's DV-550 V-8, for 130- and 155-horsepower four-wheel drive models. IHC handled worldwide distribution.

IHC signed a three-year contract to distribute the MRS A-60 as the International 4166, the A-75 as the I-4168, A-80 (with IHC's DT-436) as the I-4266, A-100 (using a GMC6-71 diesel) as the 4366 and A-105 (with the GMC8-71) as IHC's 4468. Production was supposed to begin in February 1971 after a $12,000 tooling expense was approved to adapt IHC engines to MRS chassis mounts. But the program collapsed. IHC then went to Steiger, acquiring some of the Fargo, North Dakota, firm, after proposing Steiger use IHC engines in some of Steiger's four-wheel drives. Several model designations disappeared, while other numbers were recycled for the IHC-Steiger models.

During this time, big power drove product development, sometimes from outside. FEREC engineers knew that tractor owners modified or replaced

IHC's engines to get more power. V-8 engines began to appear not only for power and smooth operation but to give farmers bragging rights, as occurred when Ford tractor owners 10 years earlier installed flat-head V-8s for power and prestige.

In June 1970, FED approved production starting in mid-October 1971 of its DV-550 tractor, with 130 PTO horsepower at 2,400 rpm. The V-8 appeared as the 1468 model while the 1466 (DT-436) was kept in production. A year later, a higher speed, 2,600-rpm, version increased output to 145 horsepower. Development budgets spread thin over a multitude of projects delayed this until November 1973.

Weeks before McCormick became IHC chairman in May 1971, his grand plan for simplifying product lines suffered two quick hits. Farm Equipment Division, and its Hinsdale engineering research center in particular, had an inspired burst of invention and creativity when Frank Jenks and Harry Bercher tried to get IHC back on balance.

Engineering and manufacturing, neglected during McCaffrey's years, always were rushed by sales. Jenks and Bercher diminished sales influence, giving engineers time to get caught up and to think ahead.

The 4156's optional insulated cab offered a heater and an air conditioner. Even without optional climate control, a positive air pressure ventilation system kept dust out, as long as doors and windows were not latched open.

1970 International TD-20C Special Agricultural Crawler

They had no PTO, but Special Agricultural Crawlers came with a swing drawbar and additional hydraulic attachment points for towed implements. These crawlers used IHC's turbocharged D-691, which IHC rated at 128 brake horsepower. This 33,000 crawler could pull two-thirds of its own weight.

1972 International 1468 V-8

On June 12, 1970, FED answered a request from recently appointed Agricultural Equipment Group president Ben Warren. FED created a V-8-engined tractor using Truck Division's long awaited diesel DV-550, detuned to produce 130 power take-off horsepower at 2,400 rpm. FED modified the engine to fit within the 25-inch-wide frame of the 1466 tractor.

Then IHC's profitability from a growing economy reinvigorated sales. During Bercher's last year, May 1970 to 1971, even as the economy contracted, sales resumed its old habits: If any competitor introduced something IHC did not have, it created a vacuum in IHC's line that product planners abhorred.

Describing the International 644, FED's tractor planners proposed fitting the Neuss D-239 diesel engine into a combination of International 544 and 656 components. "The resultant tractor," it said on May 11, "would be targeted to compete with the utility type Ford 5000 and Massey-Ferguson 175 diesel tractors in this size and price range." It would be renamed the International 654. Two days later FED argued that "The Tractor Product Committee for Louisville products has been aware of the need for a general purpose utility type tractor in the 20- to 30-horsepower range to fill the gap between the present 154 Lowboy and the forthcoming 354 tractor." FED proposed importing the Kimco 242 tractor as the International 242. Kimco, Komatsu-International-Manufacturing Co., was a joint venture between Komatsu and IHC created in the late 1960s to manufacture Frank G. Hough-Libertyville-designed rubber-tired products for the Far East. (Komatsu produced its own steel-track crawlers.)

"Importation of tractors from abroad has steadily increased in recent years. Figures show 3,220 Japanese tractors imported into the United States in 1970," FED said. "This [I-242] will place IHC in a competitive position to enter that segment of the market now enjoyed by these imported Japanese tractors." Sales chased a market for 3,000 tractors to provide products for dealers who wanted to carry Japanese imports. Soon after FED approved these programs, Brooks McCormick took over.

Warren felt challenged by Massey Ferguson's Model 1150 V-8 diesel that produced 135 power take-off horsepower. Just before releasing the 1468 V-8, he pushed FED. While IHC manufactured its first 500 1468s, FED continued working, increasing engine output to 145 power take-off horsepower at 2,600 rpm.

This 15-horsepower increase required powertrain and final drive modifications, including a new planetary gearset integral with brakes outside the bull gears, a new 4-inch-diameter rear axle, new rear wheels and tires, and revisions to the brake valve.

The company he inherited was in trouble. The corporation's entire profits, $45.2 million, just paid the shareholders dividends. He had no reserve funds. Budgets set for 1972 and beyond had no flexibility. While his predecessors closed plants that could not manufacture his products profitably, he inherited employee wage and benefits packages that were more generous and costly than either Deere or Caterpillar.

Brooks obsessed over costs and making IHC "well managed." He hired outside executives, hoping to bring in new ideas. Senior managers felt betrayed because they didn't get promotions that, before Brooks, were part of their job description.

McCormick demanded new thinking. He developed a five-year plan that gave IHC a direction to follow, rather than chasing competitors' sales catalogs. Some issues, of course, demanded attention. As author Barbara Marsh pointed out, the Vietnam war produced inflation that raised the consumer price index 60 percent from 1967 to 1975. Part of that came in February 1971, when the six-country Organization of Petroleum Exporting Countries (O.P.E.C.) agreed with 23 of the world's oil companies to a settlement nearly tripling fuel prices in the United States.

Oil producing countries, wealthy from sales of their natural resources, purchased U.S. produce.

The Soviet Union bought grain. Famines starved millions in Asia and Africa, frightening the rest of the world about adequate supplies of food. Farmers expanded their holdings and bought equipment.

Arriving just in time, IHC introduced its 66 series, as successors to the 756-through-4156 four-wheel drive model. Because demand for big four-wheel drive tractors spread nationwide, the new 4166 was painted red and white, like the other 66 series tractors. The 4100 and later 4156 were sold only in yellow and white.

IHC engineers James D. Wilkins and Richard N. Coleman spoke to the S.A.E. in mid-September, 1971, to discuss high field-speed tractors.

"As the American farmer continues to substitute capital and technology for labor, his need for more powerful tractors will increase. Utilization of this increased power can be achieved by the use of tools of greater working widths, performance of several combined operations in one pass, and increasing the field speed at which various operations are performed."

Barely nine months after the 4166 went on sale and the first of the expected Steiger-four-wheel drive tractors was born, FED already had questions of maneuverability and soil compaction nagging at FEREC engineers. They joined two 1066 final drives with a 4166 transmission and transfer case to

create a prototype articulated four-wheel drive as a forerunner of the series later known as 2+2 tractors.

But the Steiger relationship proved "badge-engineering" was more cost efficient than millions spent developing their own tractors. (Badge-engineering involves one company purchasing already-engineered and developed products from another and then putting it own name—or badge—on the item. Not a new concept, McCormick Harvester Company did it in the 1890s when Robert Hall McCormick acquired outside-manufactured steam traction engines which he sold as McCormicks.) Steiger agreed to build a 175-gross horsepower unit (based on the twin 1066s) and a 275-horsepower version using the DT-466 engine. Steiger would design and manufacture the transfer case, buying transmissions from Fuller. The project was designated the TX-111.

On April 24, 1972, FEREC introduced its synchromesh transmission to replace the previous sliding gear type, especially for the 700, 900, 1000 and 1400 series tractors. This four-speed unit provided shift-on-the-go capability under unloaded conditions. It would not accomplish moving shifts under full load that the torque-amplifier could do, nor did

it provide the variable speed characteristics of the hydrostatic. Still, IHC was the only maker offering synchromesh with an optional torque-amplifier. Tests were performed on a 966, 1066 and three 1466 diesels. Production began October 1973 for the 1566 and 1568 models.

These, and all IHC farm tractors released in late 1973 as 1974 model year production, no longer bore the name Farmall. Over the previous two years, as part of a corporate strategy to eliminate duplicate product lines, the International name grew larger on FED tractors, while Farmall diminished. At the end of 1973, it disappeared altogether.

After six months of discussing consumer products among FED product planners, they were confident that IHC's name, because of the successful Cub Cadet garden tractors, was back in public awareness. That belief motivated new methods to reduce time and funding required for testing new products. Sales had regained much of its former stature and product development was again a catch-up role, in which engineers produced IHC's version of someone else's improvement. It was half a century from the time when Bert Benjamin could convince Alex Legge to build a few more prototypes to test another year. Now products were conceived one day and on sale 18 months later.

Still IHC's engineers continued to innovate. FED and CED encouraged them to promote their accomplishments to other professionals. In mid-September 1972, FEREC engineer George F. Boltz addressed colleagues at S.A.E.'s national convention, explaining how IHC accelerated tractor testing. During the 1950s, endurance testing went on at Hinsdale's 1.125-mile test track, towing tractors whose engines were replaced with water brakes. It took six operators per tractor to run tests all day. Boltz described days when six or seven prototypes ran at once. FED had devised a "tractor treadmill" during prototype testing for the 806 model that rested the 806 on the rear wheels of a water brake tractor set in a pit. The prototype's rubber tires ran against old IHC steel wheels onto which FEREC had welded a 24-inch-wide steel plate. The second technique involved a "tether test," in which a tractor was attached to a 110-foot cable and, with two load machines towed behind, it was set free to go in circles. By running operator-less tests, FEREC routinely accomplished 140-hour weeks

1973 International 1066 Turbo Rail Tug

Fred Eivens, the agronomist at the Clarion, Iowa, Farmers Cooperative elevator, was trained to deal with crops, not necessarily to deal with crops on trains. But harvests can't wait for switch engines to move hoppers. Eivens created two of these 1066 turbo hopper tugs to move rolling stock at the elevators.

on prototype tractors. A thousand hours of testing took just six weeks.

When FED introduced hydrostatic transmissions, it kept drawbar horsepower as close as possible to gear drive models. Buyers could compare work potential. Engine developments increased horsepower, but the gear drive's greater efficiency produced higher power readings. With the 66 series, the discrepancy was so great that 1,066 hydrostatic drawbar horsepower was nearer to 966 gear drive statistics. In March 1973, FED renamed the hydrostatic tractors to obscure direct comparisons. It eliminated both 966 and 1066 models, replacing them with the Hydro 100. The 666 became the Hydro 70.

In September, FEREC engineer John Horsch told S.A.E. members about design and development programs for Modular Power Trains on the new TD-20E 210 horsepower crawler.

"We set out," he said, "to design four powertrain subassemblies (torque converter, transmission, steering and final drive), connecting them with 'flexible' couplings to provide ease of manufacture, serviceability and reliability. The flexible couplings allow reasonable misalignments. Any of the four basic units would be removable and interchangeable as a complete assembly without disturbing the others."

Ronald J. Fanslow of Construction Equipment Engineering then spoke about the evolution of their projects from concept to tractors. Designs had to meet federal regulations. Months earlier, Congress passed the Occupational Safety and Health Act (OSHA), forcing employers to provide safe working environments for their employees and safe products for their customers.

After October 1973, when OPEC shut off its wells, Brooks McCormick faced confusing decisions. OSHA affected not only tractor operators in the field and engineers creating crawlers for them, but also it meant that IHC's foundries, manufacturing plants, its Wisconsin Steel Mill and its test facilities had to comply with strict regulations, no matter what it cost the owners. Three years earlier, Washington dealt an equally serious blow to heavy manufacturers with creation of the Environmental Protection Agency (EPA), formed to give teeth to the 1963 Clean Air and Water Act. McCormick saw IHC's aging plants and its dirty, inefficient and unprofitable

foundries and steel operations as future money pits, facing cleanup and modernization costs of hundreds of millions.

Despite the corporation's many concerns, IHC's profits increased in farm equipment. In 1975 sales topped $2.1 billion and for the first time in 10 years, farm equipment outsold trucks. That was a hollow distinction; it was near the height of the OPEC fuel crisis and the truck division experienced a huge loss. A year later, the Construction Equipment Division lost $4.7 million. IHC's credit rating, already marginal with important lenders, dropped to bad risk status. McCormick no longer trusted his judgment. He hired outside consultants but they made errors as well. He still had to face the nightmare of IHC's Wisconsin Steel Company (for which operating and improvement costs in the next two years could exceed a quarter-billion dollars). He discussed closing Construction Equipment Division. However, engine manufacture was tied to truck, tractor and construction needs. Shuttering construction meant layoffs in the foundries as well. Estimates to pay off creditors and employee settlements exceeded $300 million just to shut the doors. For Brooks, the outlook was bleak.

1973 International 1066 with blade

In 1973, the name Farmall appeared on IHC tractors for the last model year. Through previous years, the name had shrunk on the tractors, finally appearing only below the model number. This particular tractor is uncommon, because it has a factory-installed D-436 engine. Farmall Works ran short of 1066 engines near the time for model changeover and retooling, and installed a slightly more powerful engine to keep production moving.

1976–1985

Eleven

STRESS AND FRACTURE

The bicentennial put most of the United States in good cheer. The mood at 401 N. Michigan was glum, but in a patriotic flurry, FED released the 4568, its 300-horsepower tractor built on a Steiger chassis. IHC sold it only in 1976, renaming this big articulated four-wheel drive the 4586 for 1977.

IHC launched the 86 series in November 1976, with two hydro models, the 86 and 186, and a full range of small-to-large tractors, from International 886 up to 1586, 4186 and 4386. Along with more power, the 86 series bought

1985 International 7488 2+2

The Super 70 series also was meant to be home to IHC's new Synchrotorque and Vari-Range transmissions. Probably only 14 of these tractors were completed. These 195-power take-off horsepower 2+2s were fitted with "STS" Synchro-Tri-Six transmissions, variations of the TR-4 meant for the new 50-series.

farmers the "Control Center," the new weather-and-sound insulated cab derived from the owner surveys conducted in the 1970s. The Control Center provided the farmer with more instrumentation than earlier tractors because polyfoam and Iso-mount insulators, thick carpet and wraparound glass separated farmers from sounds that told them whether all was well. Dealers taught farmers to trust the gauges.

Steiger developed an even larger chassis for 1979, the 4786, with 350 horsepower. IHC then began to replace the 54- and the 74-series lines in 1980 with the full-diesel line of 84 series small and medium-sized tractors, reducing two lines to one. These tractors, while not carrying on the Control Center cab feature, did continue some features and introduced others. They offered hydrostatic power steering, hydraulic disc brakes, standard equipment differential lock, along with an optional German ZF-built mechanical front-wheel-drive (MFWD) attachment to make two-wheel drive tractors into

1976 Cub Cadet

For the U.S. bicentennial, IHC produced a Spirit of '76 Cadet 76. By this time, two notable things had happened to the Cadets. First, on May 1, 1974, IHC produced its 500,000 lawn tractor. Second, concerned over government attention to noise pollution, IHC introduced the Quiet Line of Cadets in 1975.

1978 International 1086 Hydro

The 86 series tractors were introduced in 1976, amidst a frenzy of new names for new products. The entire line of tractors was named the Pro-Ag line, after a successful agricultural management computer program IHC offered its customers. Most beneficial to farmers' comfort was the new two-door Control Center cab.

four-wheel drives. The 84 series also provided torsion-bar draft control, planetary final drives and the three-lever hydraulic hitch control. International 884s came with Torque Amplifier standard, while IHC offered it optionally on 584, 684 and 784 models.

Mitsubishi built IHC's smaller tractors. These small diesels provided between 15.2 and 21 PTO horsepower as Models 234, 244 and 254, manufactured in Japan with IHC specified features.

FEREC, which had mated rear ends of two 1066-production tractors to create a prototype articulated four-wheel drive, tried the same with 86 series prototypes in a continuing effort to develop mid-power range models. It designated these 2+2s, because they consisted of one two-wheel drive tractor plus another one, a 1970s version of the tandem tractors of the late 1950s and 1960s. FEREC carried over the Control Center cab system but was undecided about putting it in the middle as Steiger, Versatile, and others did. To take advantage of the cab and the 86 series final drive, IHC designed the 2+2 so the solid front axle steered by pivoting the front half of the tractor rather than turning individual tires. The long nose housed the engine-before-drive-axle configuration of 66 and 86 series tractors. This needed no engine redesign and very little drive train modification. It also increased the tractor's stability with heavy rear-mounted implements.

IHC introduced the new 3388 (130 PTO horsepower) and 3588 (150 horsepower) 2+2 tractor in

1978 International 86 Hydro

Following 14 years of experimentation and development, IHC introduced hydrostatic drive on its farm tractors with the Model 656 in 1967. Development of the sophisticated hydraulic fluid drive system continued, and it was offered in nearly every size machine from Cub Cadets up to this 69.5-drawbar horsepower Model 86 and a more powerful 79.8-horsepower 186.

When IHC submitted its 86 Hydro to the University of Nebraska for testing in the summer of 1980, the tractor produced 52.5 drawbar horsepower at four miles per hour speed setting. Power take-off output was impressive, at 70.9; these figures compared favorably with sliding gear models, while offering easier operation.

very late 1978. Then, a year later, it followed with the 170-horsepower 3788 2+2, using the latest DT-466B turbo diesel.

Several philosophies emerged from World Head-quarters as the Bicentennial came and went. In 1975 McCormick approached Booz, Allen & Hamilton (BAH), a management consultant firm that previously had helped IHC reorganize engine production into the 300 and 400 series. BAH proposed IHC incorporate its foreign plants within the divisional structure in the United States. McCormick embraced this philosophy. European and Asian tractor operations all fell under Agricultural Equipment Group. Construction became the Payline Group (including smaller industrial machines). Truck Group and Solar International Group remained separate divisions.

As the farm equipment market improved, Brooks McCormick, who felt more confident after this latest reorganization, envisioned overtaking Deere as the farm equipment industry's number-one manufacturer. The belief that AEG could again make IHC the number-one agricultural equipment

and expensive results. The 86 series was a perfect example: While its engine was original, powerful and efficient, and its cab was new, its frame, drive train and controls were updated pieces introduced in the 706/806 models in 1963.

IHC watched Deere and Caterpillar produce big technological jumps in the 1960s and early 1970s. Common sense told IHC engineers and board members that these two companies would need to leave these in production for 10 years to pay for them. This gave IHC room to introduce innovations in the 1980s that might allow them to move ahead and reclaim the title Deere wrested away 20 years earlier.

Two other new philosophies arrived at World Headquarters. One came with Archie McCardell. Archie was Brooks McCormick's hand-picked successor. He joined IHC in late August 1977, as president under McCormick. The other philosophy, one harder to swallow, came with McCardell's personally selected successor, Warren T. Hayford, who left the aluminum can industry in mid-1979, a year after McCormick stepped aside to make McCardell chairman.

1978 International 1586

This powerful model needed the dual rear wheels to take advantage of all it had to offer: as many as eight plows with its 134.9 drawbar horsepower. These 15,000-pound tractors used a planetary gearset final drive unlike other 86 series tractors that still used bullgears. These helped introduce radial tires to farming as well.

1978 International 1460 Axial Flow Combine

Full production began on IHC's axial-flow combines in 1978, following nearly 15 years of design, development and testing. IHC offered three sizes and capacities. When Tenneco began looking at IHC in 1984, it was because its J. I. Case subsidiary wanted the combines, not IHC's tractor lines.

manufacturer forced McCormick to see how, during the 1960s and 1970s, IHC had recycled 1940s and 1950s technology. Sometimes this had disastrous

McCardell came from Xerox where careful financial management and advance planning—5 and 10 years out—kept them in control of their market. However, strategic missteps left McCardell dissatisfied with Xerox and them disappointed in him. Long-term planning and economic controls (rather than short term reaction funded by whatever source was available) was what Fowler McCormick knew IHC needed.

Hayford had ideas for cutting costs by increasing plant efficiency. What Hayford's background had not prepared him for, however, was the cyclical nature of the farm equipment market.

Agricultural Equipment Group sales continued to climb, yet the Truck and the Payline Groups still suffered. Inefficiency made these two groups IHC's loss leaders. McCardell increased the corporation's investment and research budget 25 percent in 1978, and 35 percent in 1979. Some money went into modernizing or building new plants and the rest funded new products. He committed $150 million to expand DT-466 engine manufacture, and nearly $200 million to another AEG project, dubbed TR-4 and TR3-A. To finance this, other cost cutting was necessary and McCardell trimmed and clipped excesses and waste from everywhere within the corporation except the still profitable Solar Turbines

International Group. He managed to whittle $300 million out of overhead and costs in 1978 and 1979.

Hayford took over McCardell's cost-cutting chores and introduced his can industry work ethic. Principal among his contributions was the 8760 plan, representing the number of hours in the year during which all of IHC's plants would operate. When Hayford arrived, IHC worked 14 of the 21 shifts a week which, to his mind, meant one-third of its capital resources were wasted in those seven idle shifts. The number 8760 became a mantra to Hayford and a battle cry to IHC's labor force.

His aluminum can experience didn't prepare him for seasonal buying. There were three seasons and a buying cycle for farm equipment. According to author Barbara Marsh, first season was prior to spring planting (about a third of annual sales); second was fall harvest (half of annual totals because of combine and other high-price equipment sales) and last was in late December (for year-end tax planning). The cycle, as it had evolved since the 1950s, was one peak sales year in every seven. As Lee Klancher pointed out in his International Harvester Photographic History, 1966 had been a peak year and so was 1973. IHC was looking for 1980 but was pleasantly surprised to find it in 1979. That was the year that nearly every good thing in the short term turned out bad in the long run.

1980 Cub Cadet
The Quiet Line of Cub Cadets fully enclosed the engine to muffle the noise. With this 82-series, IHC returned to its big-tractor red-and-black color scheme. Models within the series also were available with hydrostatic drive.

1980 International 3588 2+2
Essentially one two-wheel drive mated to another was what made up the 2+2 concept, a solution to increasing problems in getting higher horsepower to the ground without excessively compacting the soil or slipping on it. IHC introduced this 150-power take-off horsepower version and a 130-horsepower 3388 in very late 1978.

1980 Hough 100C and 1981 International Payloader 560A

The 100C was Hough's largest front loader, weighing 46,843 pounds, with IHC's DT-817 diesel rated at 340 horsepower. It was capable of lifting its 9-cubic-yard bucket 14 feet in the air. At right, IHC's 560A was equipped with a 13-yard bucket, which it could raise more than 16 feet. The 560A weighed about 76,000 pounds and used the DT-817, rated up to 420 horsepower.

1981 International 7788 Four-Wheel Drive

Not a 2+2 but a true articulated four-wheel drive, this was the highest end of the Super 70 series. Approved by IHC's new president, Don Lennox, in August 1983, two of these prototype 265-power take-off horsepower machines were assembled in late 1981. The full line of Super 70s was scheduled for introduction and production through the mid-1980s.

On May 19, 1977, the newly named Agricultural Equipment Group approved an earlier FED "development & testing" request. This involved power-trains for a series of larger horsepower tractors, along with a new pressure-flow compensating hydraulic system, and a combined project originally referred to as "MATH," for Modular Axle, Transmissions, Hydraulics that first was used in CED's TD-20E crawler.

The Modular Axle, described in a 1978 "Engineering Data" report, was a "final drive housing with a new cast center housing containing an increased capacity differential with spiral bevel reduction and inboard-mounted planetary final drive. An integral differential lock electrically energized will be offered as an option.

"In addition to being the final drive on two-wheel drive tractors, this assembly in modular axle form will be used as a front and rear unit on large four-wheel drive articulated tractors, (TX-191)."

The pressure flow-compensated hydraulic pump provided low hydraulic pressure for steering, the transmission, hydraulic oil cooling system, independent PTO and wet multiple disc brakes. The high pressure side took care of lubrication, draft control and auxiliary valves. The fluid reservoir was inside the transmission housing sump. FEREC derived this PTO from the 1086/1586 plug-in system controlled by an oil-cooled hydraulic multiple disk clutch. While the highest proposed output for future engine versions of the TR-4 was 185 horsepower, AEG

rated the transmission at 200 horsepower, needing only to revise PTO clutches to accommodate even more power. FED planned to produce three models: the 135-PTO horsepower TX-146, using either the DT-436 or DT-466 engines; the 160-horsepower TX-147, powered by the DT-466; and the 185-horsepower TX-148, using Melrose Park's new DTI-466 turbocharged and intercooled diesel.

"The tractor front end will be restyled for model identification and to conform to new tractor family lines," the report continued. "Design emphasis will be toward smooth clean lines with minimum split lines, and free of external fasteners. The styling concept will complement the innovative reverse airflow engine cooling system." (Cooling air entered the top forward portion of the hood, passed the fan and was expelled forward through the front grille, blowing out any foreign material that stuck to the grille.)

The greatest technical advancements were in transmissions offered with the TR-4 and the lower-horsepower range TR-3A tractors. For the 3A series, FED had in mind the new P-3A Constant Mesh (synchromesh) transmission. For TR-4 models, either the Synchro-Torque or the Vari-Range transmissions were being completed. FED originally intended to introduce these transmissions in the 2+2 models. The Synchro-Torque transmission improved helical gear design technology and required a "white room" clean lab to assemble the internal parts. This incorporated a three-speed constant mesh speed box, a two-speed double-clutch pack Torque Amplifier unit and a three-range constant mesh set (3x2x3) providing 18 forward and 6 reverse speeds. FED also planned to produce a high-clearance version of the TR-3A.

In October 1976, FEREC research center delivered product specifications to AEG before it completed design work in August 1979. The tractors would be built at Louisville and Farmall Works with hydraulics coming from West Pullman. The preproduction timetable set engineering sign-off for design and prototypes in February 1983, with actual production to start in October 1984.

FEREC's report suggested that "The program proposed in this request is the basic building block for development of high-horsepower agricultural tractors well into the 1990s. The TR-4 tractor, in fiscal 1985, will be upgraded with hydromechanical transmissions capable of operating efficiencies near

gear-drive transmissions with infinitely variable speeds. The hydromechanical transmission becomes the foundation for further refinement of tractors through development of electronic monitoring/control of critical functions and, conceivably, fully automated tractor operation." AEG now had taken technology of the late 1970s and looked far ahead.

Early tests of the Vari-Range transmission demonstrated hard gearshift engagement common to sliding gear transmissions; in these prototypes, this was caused by hydrostatic drag on the range synchronizers not matching gear speed quickly enough. AEG devised a compound planetary gearset. Speed capability ranged from 0 up to 17.5 miles per hour transport speed, operated by a single T-bar control lever.

On April 5, 1979, an internal memo, written by R. J. Roman, the TR-4 project manager, to J. T. Tracy, director of product planning and development for AEG, alerted him to engineering and manufacturing delays with the Synchro-Torque-System and the Vari-Range transmissions. Engineering needed time to perfect the compound planetaries and manufacturing was moving slowly, due to the major tooling necessary. As a result, plans to incorporate these two new transmissions on 88 series 2+2s would be delayed until May 1982.

Clear evidence that the demand for more powerful tractors led to the giants of the 1980s and 1990s. Here Jay Graber's 7788 matches the height of his Farmall M with mounted cotton harvester.

1981 International 560A Payloader and 1982 International 350B Payhauler

Nearly filling its 11-cubic-yard bucket each time, this 560A took just four loads to fill the 42-cubic-yard, 50-ton Payhauler. IHC built these off-highway rear-dump haulers with either 16-cylinder 16-V71 Detroit diesels or 12-cylinder Cummins VT-1710Cs. Payhauler split off to become Payhauler Corporation when IHC sold Payline construction division in late 1981 to Dresser. Terex Corporation acquired Payhauler in 1998. The unloaded 350B weighed 71,800 pounds.

H. B. Simmons, from the Strategic Business Unit, the financial responsibility arm of AEG, blew up. He hand-wrote a note to H. C. Flanders, IHC vice president of marketing, wrapping his message around his copy of Roman's memo:

"H. Flanders: 2WDs with new transmissions will make 2+2s with old transmissions a 'dead duck.' Attached represents nearly a one-year delay!"

While internal squabbles in late-1979 dealt with the products designated to restore IHC to first place, other factors outside AEG conspired to make that much more difficult.

By year end, sales from all groups were at record levels. Because of McCardell's and Hayford's efforts at cost cutting, the corporation's profit margin was the highest in 10 years. This convinced McCardell to restructure some of IHC's debt into short-term financing, ending at the end of 1981, rather than the typical long-term arrangements used for such expenses as new factories and tooling.

Manufacturing in all groups increased production through the spring and summer before labor union contract negotiations and an expected strike by UAW workers. Barbara Marsh quoted one IHC executive as saying IHC added "$125 million of additional inventory to sell in case the strike went on any period of time."

Because of the higher profits, greater sales and raised production levels and several other favorable factors, a complex formula fell into place rewarding McCardell with a $1.8 million dollar "hiring bonus." This large bonus was not a good prelude to requests that workers and the union make sacrifices when talks began August 9, 1979.

The UAW walked out the door with 35,000 workers on November 2, the day after IHC published annual figures. As the strikers received their $50-per-week benefit, it hardened their resolve against Archie McCardell and his bonus. McCardell ultimately found a way to return the bonus, temporarily, but too much damage had been done. Worse, while neither he nor Brooks McCormick wanted a long strike despite high inventory preparations, neither would interfere in the negotiations, trusting a succession of ill-prepared but unyielding company representatives.

The strike lingered. IHC's debt remained. Sales in all three groups dwindled because inflation forced the Federal Reserve to raise the prime rate to 20 percent and consumer rates higher still. In March IHC realized that labor's demands were less threatening than its overall financial status. Working at the bargaining tables almost without a break, they settled on April 14, 1980—six months after the strike had begun.

The strike cost $579.4 million in losses during the first half of fiscal 1980 (November 1 to October 31). Viewed from the perspective of years later, it was, despite the losses, a mixed benefit: Sales gains in fiscal 1979 encouraged high production levels for 1980, continuing at the strike preparation pace.

No one at IHC could predict the future. Had the strike not occurred, IHC would have entered 1980 with an enormous inventory growing by the day, fueled by a man fixated by a number: 8760.

Hayford's 8760 philosophy came with very high overhead costs. With all plants supposedly working 21 shifts per week, there would be a lot of expensive assembly line workers standing around idle if major tooling broke down and could not be quickly fixed. Production would stop. What's more, in Hayford's perfect world, workers changed shifts just as their replacements came to pick up their tools during the few seconds between tasks. Real world shift changes don't have the precision of relay-team baton handoffs.

Hayford had proposed that critical plants—Farmall, Louisville, the converted diesel plant at

Indianapolis—duplicate some tooling and partially duplicate assembly lines. While one was in use, the other would be there "just in case." But lack of available funds made this impossible.

At Farmall Works, tooling breakdowns were handled expeditiously. Supervisors hauled out pieces that needed machining to friendly department heads at the Rock Island Arsenal, Caterpillar or even Deere. When the shoe was on the other foot and IHC's machinists had time, they returned the favors.

While the market for all the products that IHC manufactured had slowed, Hayford saw only inefficient, idled plants that, in his view, cost the company money when they weren't turning out products that made the company money. That nobody was buying didn't matter to him. Fiscal 1980 ended with tractor sales 14 percent lower than 1979. Overall sales dropped by 29 percent. McCardell reduced his ambitious capital investment plan for 1981 by one-third, cutting back on plant construction, acquisition and tooling, as well as new product development. McCardell urged managers to save money at all costs.

McCardell, despite his financial background, believed IHC's problems all could be solved if the company just had a couple of great selling seasons.

Hayford supported that vigorously. To both of them, there still was a future for IHC, and in that future the groups would need new products. Funding for the TR-4 and TR-3A programs continued.

In January 1980, Project Manager R. J. Roman went back to AEG President Bill Warren to ask him for more money. A Synchro-shift mechanism from Clark Equipment Company did not prove strong enough. A worldwide search for alternates found nothing useful, so FEREC went back inside and developed its own, for $8 million. Revisions to the reverse airflow cooling system and costs of relocating operating controls to the Control Center right side cost $1 million each. Other designs and component development took another $8 million while production success of the 2+2s from Farmall Works meant manufacturing facilities intended for TR-4 use were not available. Farmall Works started building a plant addition.

Development of the Synchro-Torque transmission resulted in improvement, simplification and standardization that benefited the Vari-Range. Another $4.2 million would apply these updates to this state-of-the-art transmission. Roman allocated $5.8 million to accommodate the effects of 1980s inflation, adding a total of $34.4 million to the $193 million project.

**1983 Dresser
International TD-25C**
Dresser Industries acquired IHC's Payline Division in late 1981 and continued for several years producing IHC's products in Dresser's name. This big crawler used the DTi-817 Series B intercooled turbo-diesel and was offered with Power Shift. It weighed nearly 54,000 pounds.

1984 International 6588 2+2

Agriculture Equipment Group updated the 2+2 models in 1982 with the 60-series models, this midsize using the DT-466 engine and a 16-speed forward, 8 speed reverse transmissions. While there was no rated power increase, the larger engine offered better fuel economy and greater torque.

The success of the 2+2s accelerated development of a 195-PTO horsepower version. The drive train was marginal above 180 horsepower, so engineering now considered the 195 model as a segment of the Synchro-Torque TR-4 program that became the 7288 and 7488 2+2 "Super 70" models. Complete sign-off engineering prototypes were not scheduled until August 1980. Even that extended date was delayed when problems appeared in late spring. F. A. O'Donnell from the Product Reliability and Support Center near Hinsdale alerted AEG in early June 1980.

Failures during final testing of the 3788 tractor with the old 86 series transmission suggested final drive reliability problems would occur in the second or third year of average operation, or just beyond the warranty period. The 3788 powertrain was a risk in terms of future farm tractor liability.

"Project Reliability," O'Donnell wrote, "recommends 3788 Tractor production held until the above engineering and production problems can be successfully resolved." These were not minor considerations. The next day, O'Donnell submitted a "projected failure cost" of the final drive of the 3788s.

"This type of failure most likely will require rebuild of both the range and speed transmission," he explained. Taking marketing's estimates of three-year sales at 1,695 units, he calculated 55.5 hours per repair at $18 per hour shop costs, or $1,000 labor plus $2,300 in parts at dealer net, or $3,300 per tractor. The total: $5.5 million.

"With the high load factor projected on the 3788 tractors, the failure cost is on the conservative side."

H. K. Arp, director of product liability for AEG, recommended on June 16 that production be delayed until O'Donnell's problems were solved. Four days later, J. W. Youle (Bud) got the word from Simmons and the agricultural tractors SBU: There would be no dead ducks.

"Production was to start August 13, 1980," Simmons said. A flurry of meetings followed in which marketing's Youle expressed concern over releasing a transmission that engineering knew would fail. Engineering fired back a detailed analysis of its revisions and fixes. Instead of delaying it, AEG advanced the start of production to August 5.

Two months later, on October 7, Youle again wrote to Simmons at World Headquarters, concerned now about large four-wheel drive sales. IHC's percentage of the business had fallen steadily since 1976, when it was 14.4 percent of the total market. By 1979 it was only 10.8, and Youle projected it at 8 percent for 1980. He was concerned that even with 1981 improvements to the Steiger articulated four-wheel drives, IHC still had no powershift or PTO option for those tractors, although they had been proposed. Simmons agreed, penning across the top of Youle's memo:

"If we don't get the changes for '81 we must have—we will be out of this business." While Simmons meant the articulated four-wheel drive business, his words were prophetic.

Through 1980 and 1981, TR-4 project manager R. J. Roman authored a stream of "Market Rationale and Product Description" papers to World Headquarters and around AEG, much as Bert Benjamin had done 60 years earlier in his battle for the Farmall.

"The TR-4 models will have a synchronized transmission and planetary final drive," Roman wrote. "The concept will allow lower vehicle noise levels, due to constant mesh helical transmission gears and a fully enclosed engine compartment." He released a budget proposal of $2.3 million to launch the first of the new transmission 2+2s and the TR-4 with the Synchro-Torque transmission on September 17, 1981, including a $1,000,000 dealer show in Kansas City, Missouri.

In late October 1980, the TR-4/TR-3A (and now TR-2) programs asked for another $9.4 million. Of this, $6.5 million was to make up engineering time lost during the UAW strike, which occurred during peak development and testing for these tractors. Now, more than 100 design engineers and managers who had shop skills were reassigned to move the project forward. The remaining $2.9 million was for design, assembly and testing of additional prototypes, since some elements done during the strike failed and needed redesign. Assembly of the TR-4 involved 220 new major machine tools requiring new automated and special transfer line equipment. As a result, manufacturing planned to build 100 preproduction tractors in May 1981.

In December 1980, Youle, Simmons and others took another look at the 2+2s. Farmall Works had produced 7,657, but only 3,790 had sold in the United States, and another 534 went to Canada. Questionable drive trains and rumors of new transmissions kept buyers cool. Export models had gone to 17 foreign countries, ranging from Australia and Argentina to Yugoslavia and Venezuela. Youle outlined future updates, including TR-3A transmissions (hydro and sliding gear types) for August, 1981, the Synchro-Torque and a new 3988 model with 195 PTO horsepower in November 1982, and a revised Control Center cab and optional Vari-Range transmission for 1983. November 1985 would see a shorter version 3388, along with a 100-horsepower 3188 and 90-horsepower 3088 models. He predicted worst year sales in 1982 at 2,654, due to the anticipation of the improved transmissions; the TR-4 tractors would be out in September 1981, but that transmission would not appear in 2+2 models for 14 months.

In February 1981, Youle drove prototype TR-3A and TR-4 tractors at the Phoenix Proving Grounds. He was impressed and made that clear in his memo to Simmons and project manager Roman:

"Without question, the TR-3A was needed 10 years ago. It is unquestionably the easiest shifting tractor that I have ever driven. In the writer's opinion, there is no doubt that the TR-4 is 'TOMORROW'S TRACTOR TODAY,'" he wrote, mimicking the advertising slogan for IHC's 2+2s.

The situation inside IHC was approaching critical mass. In May 1981, to stanch the outward bleeding of cash, McCardell had "sacrificed" IHC's only profitable asset, the Solar Turbine International Group, to Caterpillar for $505 million. The unexpectedly high price helped briefly. By early spring 1982, McCardell proposed yet another restructuring of management and debt. Hayford suggested taking the corporation into Chapter 11 bankruptcy. In March, fed up and without hope, Hayford resigned.

Bud Youle had his own problems. He had to suffer seeing a prediction come true in late April 1982, on the eve of engineering release to manufacturing of the 6788, which would replace the 3788.

"Field inspections by Product Reliability," he wrote in a memo to World Headquarters, "has confirmed original concerns regarding the 3788 power-

train in reliability and hours of usage. It is the writer's opinion the 6788 will not meet or, much less, exceed, the 3788 reliability of the standards now established by the Series 50 [TR-4] powertrain. There should be no misunderstanding with management of the reliability risk with the planned production of the 6788."

The tractors came out, the 30 series in August 1980, the 50 series and revised 2+2s just reaching dealers. The economy that hamstrung IHC hurt farmers as well. Government bans on Soviet grain sales in 1980 gave foreign farmers a windfall market but left their countries hungry. American farmers who no longer fed the communists briefly nourished the others. But President Ronald Reagan's fiscal policies increased the value of the dollar, so that few countries could afford American produce. By 1982, American farmers were becoming an endangered species. So were healthy farm equipment dealers.

Huge stocks of IHC's previous models remained on distributors and dealers' lots. When the 30- and 50 series arrived, churned out by plants running on the theory that large profits came from volume sales, they arrived at dealerships where few people were interested in or capable of buying them. Payment-In-Kind (PIK), a federal program to reduce crop acreage and surpluses, dealt farmers

1984 International 5288
These new tractors were engineering marvels, demonstrating new transmission ideas: a Synchrotorque (TR-4) providing 18 forward speeds with no overlap and full synchromesh shift-on-the-fly capability; and the Vari-Range, a hybrid hydrostatic drive-and-sliding gear transmission. The 5288 used the DT-436B turbo-diesel and was rated at 160 power take-off horsepower. A lower-power series, the 3088 and 3288, provided 80 and 90 power take-off horsepower each.

another severe blow, when the 1983 drought reduced harvests in the fall. Foreign farmers hurried to feed us, accepting strong dollars in payment.

On August 10, 1983, Donald D. Lennox, the new president and chief executive officer, replacing Warren Hayford, signed off on the Super 70s (the 7288, 7488, and 7788 models), with little additional development in response to Youle's memo. Lennox authorized a $16 million engineering completion budget, an August 1984 start and a $46 million working capital commitment through 1987. He and the new AEG president, J. D. Michaels, released the Super 70s as well as experimental models—the TX-194, as a 175-horsepower 7488 model, and TX-195 as the 195-horsepower 7688. Each of these offered full TR-4 features, including the Vari-Range transmission, a "fuel-efficient" engine management program, a 40-gallon-per-minute high-pressure hydraulic pump and the new Control Center cab.

The rear half of the 70 series 2+2s was similar to the rear of the 50 series two-wheel drive tractors, and it was assembled on the same line. The rear then was transferred to a new 78,000-square foot building (completed in 1978, for $18.9 million)

dedicated to assembling and painting 2+2s, and building the front of the 70 series tractors. They were joined and final assembly was completed.

Part of the launch program, running June 1984 to April 1985, included damage control. From October through December 1984, IHC held customer and dealer Weather Vane meetings "to improve the customer image of the 2+2 concept and to provide them with detailed changes as to why the new 2+2 will be more reliable in the future."

AEG couldn't guarantee that reliability.

"The engineering plan includes sufficient examples and test time to achieve 70 percent confidence that the reliability goals will be met on the TX-194 and TX-195 by start of production. However, there are several subsystem improvements for the TX-195 that will be unproved when the reliability tests begin, Hi-Lo Clutch, IPTO and Hitch. Therefore, 70 percent confidence in meeting the reliability goals for the highest power model could cause a delay in production by six months."

To achieve that reliability, engineering budgeted $150,000 for testing two of each, 7488 and 7688 models, for 1,000 hours of field work starting in June 1984 and running through April 1985.

By January 1984, the feeling of doom spread far beyond North Michigan Avenue. Bill Hoeg, in the AEG district office in Bettendorf, Iowa, encountered a salesman at a farm show in Rockford, Illinois, who had just seen a one-door cab prototype while at Hinsdale. Hoeg was dumfounded.

"It concerns me," he wrote to Bud Youle, "that we would even consider a one-door cab after years of having our own people zealously convincing the customer of the benefits of a two-door cab.

"By switching, we would be making liars out of our sales and marketing people. This would add to our deteriorating credibility.

"This action," he continued, "would promote the same type of inconsistency that created the loss of our Number One position in the large four-wheel drive market. We would be telling the world as the leader in safety and convenience, that these are no longer important to us and would turn such leadership over to the competition, who are now changing their models to include two-door cabs in their lines."

1985 International 7488 2+2

Agricultural Equipment Group President J. D. Michaels approved production of these Super 70s as preproduction prototypes, coded the TX-194 and TX-195. (This was a 195-power take-off horsepower version 7688 that was never produced.) Mostly hand assembly took place at the Farmall Works during January 1985.

1981 International 5488
When the sun set on May 14, 1985, Farmall Works had produced its last IHC tractor, an all-wheel drive International 5488 similar to this one. Tenneco-J. I. Case did not want either the aging Farmall Works (in production since 1926), nor did it want any of its tractors, the new 30 or 50 series or the 2+2s.

Youle wrote another memo in late January 1984, addressed to the AEG product marketing manager, A. W. Williams. Youle again pointed out shortcomings of Series 50 tractors and Control Center cabs with door and control lever placements. Due to drastically reduced capital spending and development budgets, corrections and improvements slipped back to 1987 for introduction.

"I'm aware," he wrote, "of the numerous restraints you have concerning budgets, etc. However, today, we cannot wait until the 1987 sales year to correct dealer and customer objection to our Farmall tractors." Again in mid-March he renewed his appeals, and then again in April and May.

It was too late. In late 1981, Tractor Equipment Company, a major parts supplier, heard that Dresser Industries, Inc., a Texas-based oil exploration and development conglomerate, wanted to add construction equipment to its line. Dresser already owned Galion, maker of road grading and surfacing equipment. IHC's Payline Group, with plenty of inventory on hand, fit Dresser's profile. (IHC recently had sold its Paymover products and operations—large aircraft movers and ground power supplies created by Frank G. Hough Company—to Ingersoll Rand.)

Dresser struck a deal, acquiring the Hough operations as well as IHC Payline. The sale left Don Lennox one less group to focus on. Through 1984, he conferred with bankers and courted a potential buyer for AEG. On November 26, 1984, after hundreds of hours of work and negotiation, he announced that the Agricultural Equipment Group had been sold to Tenneco, Inc., of Houston, another large conglomerate with primary interests in oil production but with a wholly owned agricultural subsidiary, J. I. Case. IHC received $301 million in cash and $187 million in Tenneco preferred stock.

Case manufactured about 20 farm tractors. It had quit the harvester business long before, but it wanted IHC's axial-flow combines. Tenneco chose not to acquire IHC's Rock Island or its Memphis plants. Overnight Tenneco and IHC increased Case's market share to 35 percent, making it a contented runner-up to Deere, with 40 percent. IHC brought 33 tractor models to the sale. Case dropped the 2+2 and new 30- and 50 series tractors, because it didn't want Farmall Works and it carefully selected the tooling it wished to own.

1985–2000

CASE
INTERNATIONAL

𝒯n 1983, Case abandoned its yellow and red paint scheme because of too much lead chromate in its paints. It adopted a white and black combination until early in 1985 when sheet metal became Harvester red while chassis remained Case black. Nearly all of IHC's popular Neuss-built and Doncaster-produced tractors remained in production, providing Case much greater European name recognition than before. Case's own 94 series tractors, built at its Racine, Wisconsin, plant, replaced all the domestic-built AEG models.

1990 Case IH 7140 Magnum

The first generation Case IH Magnum tractors adopted IHC's Power-Shift transmission, mating it to a new Case CDC 505-cubic-inch diesel. The Magnum 7140 was rated at 195 power take-off horsepower from its intercooled turbocharged engine, easily pulling this 24-foot disc through this Long Island, New York, potato field.

IHC's engineers had nearly completed work on their Power-shift transmission. They mated this with Case wheels, engines, and hood-work (cabs were IHC) to produce the 7100 series Magnum line of 130- to 195-PTO horse-power two- and four-wheel-drive tractors introduced in 1988 and in production until late 1993. In September, Case IH introduced the 7200 series second-generation Magnums.

Prior to acquiring IHC, Case engineers had begun work on the Maxxum series, Case's World Tractor, offered with adjustable front axle in two-wheel drive or mechanical front wheel drive-assist. These were based on the Case 580 backhoe. Long before prototypes were complete, IHC engineers joined Case. When the prototypes were ready, they went to IHC's former Farm Equipment Research Engineering Center in Hinsdale for testing and customer marketing trials. After engineering was complete, the former IHC Neuss Works did the styling and assembly. The Case IH 5100 series

1991 Case IH 1140 and 9280

Mitsubishi produced small tractors for Case IH, beginning in 1987. Case IH consolidated the line in 1990, resulting in the 1100 series, ranging up to this 27-power take-off horsepower Model 1140. It is dwarfed by the 9280 second generation articulated four-wheel drive. Using a Cummins' 855-cubic-inch intercooled turbo diesel with 344 power take-off horsepower, it pulled a Case IH 800 10-bottom plow.

was introduced in 1989, and the second generation 5200s arrived in late 1992.

In 1987, Tenneco acquired Steiger Tractor Company, of Fargo, North Dakota, which previously produced articulated four-wheel drive models for IHC. Steiger was a victim of the early 1980s farm economy and had gone into Chapter 11 bankruptcy. In 1987, Case IH introduced its quickly rebadged 9100 series, still using Steiger model names—Puma, Cougar, Tiger, and others—for its Steiger dealers, not for Case IH outlets. In August 1990, the second generation Case IH 9200 series of Fargo-built four-wheel drives appeared. Nearly a year earlier in North and South Dakota, Steiger had begun field testing a multitrack prototype based on the 9250. Tests went on for three

years, but few people saw the machine because operators ran it only in the dark where, from a distance, it was indistinguishable from the wheeled model. A shiny version toured Farm Progress and other major shows during 1992, but it was billed more as a "concept tractor" than a work in progress, meant to show Caterpillar that it was not alone in thinking about rubber tracks.

When Case IH introduced the production Quad Trac to dealers in Denver in 1996, those who'd seen the show model were surprised at the growth. It had gone from a 246-horsepower model 9250 to the 360-horsepower 9370 chassis. In mid-1998 Case IH introduced a second version, a 400-horsepower 9380. Model proliferation continues, and the horsepower race never ends.

1998 Case IH MX120 Maxxum Four-Wheel Drive

Case IH's World Tractor, the Maxxum, first appeared in 1990. The latest MX series arrived in 1998 and offered a mechanical front drive system that automatically disengaged at the end of the row. Power came from a Consolidated (merging Case and Cummins) 5.9-liter turbo diesel. The MX120 was rated at 105 power take-off horsepower.

1998 Case IH QuadTrac

It weighed 43,750 pounds as it sat there, but its four 2,055-square-inch tracks spread its weight so effectively that ground pressure was just 5.9 pounds per square inch. Its traction was exceptional. Powered by N14A Cummins intercooled, turbo-diesels, the QuadTracs quoted 360 horsepower at 2,100 rpm. At a highway construction site near Hannibal, Missouri, both of the QuadTracs pulled two Reynolds CEM17 17-cubic-yard scrapers. Each track was 30 inches wide and 10 feet long. The track assembly weighed 3,910 pounds. Overall weight was biased 55 percent to the front.

OWNER INDEX

INDEX